IMAGES
of America

MILLS OF HUMBOLDT COUNTY

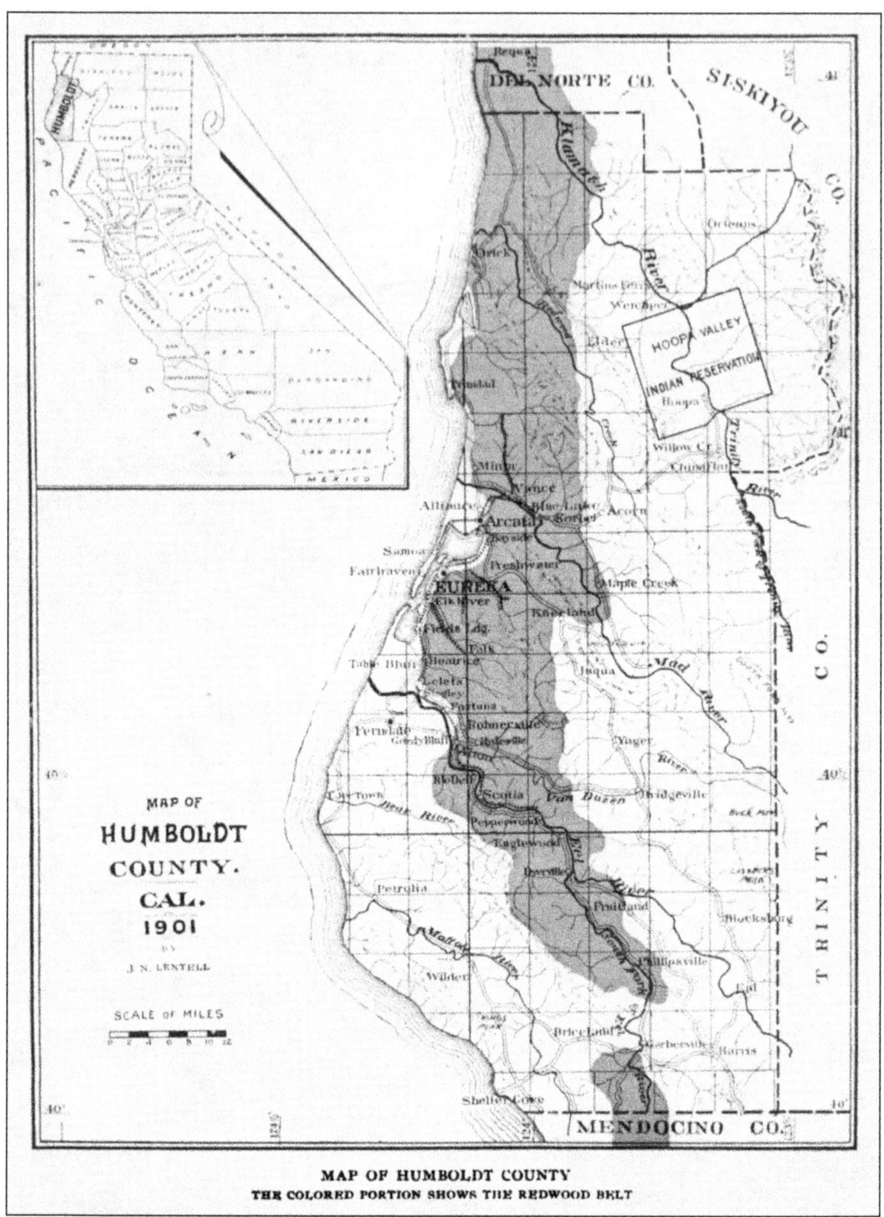

This 1901 Humboldt County map highlights the areas where redwood was found. In this region, it was estimated in 1897 that the average yield was 60 million board feet per acre. One memorable tree yielded 66,500 board feet. Logging the redwood giants produced many millionaires, but the work was hard and dangerous. Technology advanced and adapted to handle the giant trees, which exceeded in size any trees previously encountered. (Fortuna Depot Museum.)

On the Cover: Isaac Minor's Glendale Mill along Mad River opened in 1885, producing both lumber and shingles, as depicted. Minor and his mill are representative of the 13 lumber mills and 26 shingle mills operating in Humboldt County at the turn of the 20th century. Minor operated several mills in the county, building new facilities as nearby forests were depleted. (Fortuna Depot Museum.)

IMAGES
of America

MILLS OF HUMBOLDT COUNTY

Fortuna Depot Museum
Susan J.P. O'Hara and Alex Service

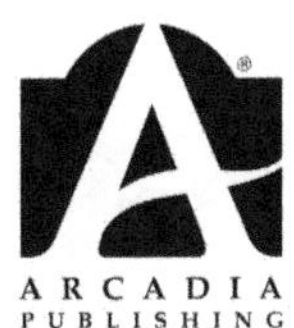

ISBN 978-1-5316-9812-6

Published by Arcadia Publishing
Charleston, South Carolina

Library of Congress Control Number: 2015941988

For all general information, please contact Arcadia Publishing:
Telephone 843-853-2070
Fax 843-853-0044
E-mail sales@arcadiapublishing.com
For customer service and orders:
Toll-Free 1-888-313-2665

Visit us on the Internet at www.arcadiapublishing.com

The authors dedicate this book to their husbands, Mike O'Hara and Michael Gaunt, who have helped make this and other books possible.

Contents

Acknowledgments

The authors thank the Fortuna City Council and Fortuna Historical Commissioners for their ongoing support of the Fortuna Depot Museum. Furthermore, the authors thank the staff at the Humboldt Room, Humboldt State University Library (HSU). Without their support, this book would not have been possible.

Additionally, the authors want to thank those who have donated images to the Fortuna Depot Museum. Photographs in this book are from the Fortuna Depot Museum collection and the collections of the Clarke Historical Museum (Clarke), the Humboldt County Historical Society (HCHS), the Humboldt Redwoods Interpretive Association (HRIA), the San Francisco Maritime National Historical Park, and Greg Rumney, Dave Heinle, Carol Lang, Ross Rowley, and Dave Smeds. These associations and individuals have allowed the authors to illustrate the history of mills in Humboldt County. Unless otherwise noted, all images in this book appear courtesy of the Fortuna Depot Museum.

The authors also acknowledge the work of Lynwood Carranco, whose historical research was invaluable. Additional resources include oral histories, newspaper articles, and publications by the logging industry and the Humboldt County Board of Supervisors. Finally, the authors hope that their work will help to inspire future generations of historians.

INTRODUCTION

Lumber and redwoods have long been associated with Humboldt County in Northern California. The unique qualities and characteristics of *Sequoia sempervirens*, or coast redwood, make it desirable as lumber and as shingles, laths, moldings, railroad ties, doors, and even coffins. Mills were built in Humboldt as soon as Euro-Americans arrived in 1850. However, harvesting redwoods took another five years to begin.

California's coastal redwood is a prehistoric tree, dating to the time of the dinosaurs. At one time, these towering conifers were found across the continent. By the time of settlement, they were found only in a thin band from near the Oregon border to the north, to near Monterey in the south. The dark-reddish wood of the tree earned it its common name. The family name *sempervirens* ("ever living") comes from its ability to grow from its root sprouts, as well as its ability to survive flood, fire, and other disasters that topple less-tenacious trees. Redwood is fine-grained and splits easily, a fact noted and utilized by Native Americans of the region. Additionally, there is little shrinkage in the wood as it dries, making it good building material. For ties and fence posts, and for use in water, tannins in the wood make it resistant to rot and insects. In 1897, the Redwood Lumber Manufacturers Association observed, "it is certainly very difficult to find any constructive wood in the whole realm of building material that for beauty and grandeur of growth, variety of grain, structure or color, or the number of purposes for which it can be used, will surpass the 'Sequoia Sempervirens.' " Finally, redwoods grow to a height of 250–300 feet, with a circumference between 40 and 50 feet. These trees could produce 60 million board feet of lumber per acre in Humboldt. Between 1888 and 1892, Humboldt's sawmills earned a net value of $2,238,853. The men who founded the mills of Humboldt had discovered a different way to harvest gold in California—"red gold," the lumber of the redwoods.

Redwood trees were harvested and milled to a small degree in California by Spanish, Russian, and early American settlers prior to 1849. These early forays into logging met with limited success. The large trees were difficult to manage, splitting easily when felled and damaging the wood. Early mills included an excavated pit, with workers pulling on both ends of a saw. The lumber produced was only for local use, for building homes and barns for farmers, or for creating the outpost of Fort Ross.

In 1849, miners came to California from all corners of the globe in search of gold. In the fall of that year, miners along the Trinity River, near starvation, encouraged a group of men to find a direct route to San Francisco, one hopefully more reliable than that through the Sacramento Valley. These men, led by Josiah Gregg, took several months to find their way to the coast, celebrating Christmas by the bay soon to be known as Humboldt Bay. For these intrepid travelers, the redwoods were both wonders and severe impediments to travel. The explorers either had to hack through the dense bark and wood to walk through where the giants had fallen, or wander in a zigzag fashion through the woodlands. When members of the party reached the settlements at Sonoma, word quickly spread about the almost landlocked bay and rich forestlands surrounding it. In the spring of 1850, the *Laura Virginia*, loaded with eager settlers and speculators, set sail for the bay. An argument arose over what to name the bay, as each of the expedition's leaders wanted to name it after himself. Ultimately, the group settled on the name Humboldt, honoring the German naturalist Alexander von Humboldt.

By the fall of 1850, mills, including the Pioneer Mill, were built to supply building material for the early settlers. The trees logged were the smaller "Oregon pine," as Douglas fir was known at the time. Redwoods were simply too large to manage for these first settlers. The Pioneer Mill operated until 1857, when John Dolbeer acquired it at a sheriff's auction. Early mills often suffered from lack of income, due to the difficulty of getting their product to other markets. Additionally, materials needed for the mills, such as saws and a power source to run them, were expensive and hard to bring to Eureka. Steamships, run aground, powered some of the earliest mills.

Technological advances made during the Civil War for increasing the strength of cannons were transferred to the saws needed to mill large redwoods into lumber. Another outcome of the war was construction of the transcontinental railroad. Ostensibly built to transport California gold to the East Coast, it also provided a way to transport "red gold."

Other advances were made both in mills and woods operations to increase productivity and better handle the large timber. As the trees closest to the mills were harvested, loggers had to cut trees farther away. One way trees were brought to the mill was by oxen or mule teams. The animals hauled timber out of steep river or creek canyons. After 1870, rail lines were built around Humboldt Bay to access the tall trees. In 1882, John Dolbeer patented a portable, upright steam engine used to pull logs to a landing. From there, they were hauled by oxen or train to the mills. Dolbeer modified a "donkey engine" used in steamships, a small subsidiary engine. His first version had only one spool, requiring a horse or mule to move cables after a log was hauled. Later versions included several spools, eliminating the need for cables to be pulled by animals. The larger version became known as a "bull donkey," following the trend in the woods to name large and powerful things "bull." The wood-powered engine greatly increased productivity as the donkey "yarded" (pulled) logs more rapidly than before.

In the mills, similar improvements increased the amount of lumber sawn from each log. In 1869, David Evans, millwright for the Dolbeer & Carson Company, developed the use of a third saw, which allowed cutting large-diameter trees without first splitting the log. Other improvements included moving from circular saws to large up-and-down or band saws. The various mills in Humboldt experimented with many different saw configurations to solve issues of handling large timber.

Other commercial uses were found for redwood. The ease with which it was split led to the split-products industry. In 1896, there were twice as many shingle mills in Humboldt County as lumber mills. Shingles were originally split by hand. Around 1875, Ole Hanson developed a mechanical way to saw shingles. Touted as being fire-safe and less vulnerable to weathering, the shingles were shipped around the world. Between 1888 and 1892, 29,085,321 board feet of shingles were produced in Humboldt County, with a net value of $363,587. While this was significantly less than the net value for lumber, the shingle mills required smaller investment costs to operate. Further, many companies turned the tall stumps left behind by earlier logging into shingle bolts, requiring a smaller outlay to begin operations.

Other redwood mills were devoted to making doors, moldings, and other decorative finished materials. The Swortzell & Williams mill in Fortuna was credited with making more doors than any other Humboldt mill. Other mills were smaller operations focusing on making bowls and other products out of the curly wood from the redwood burl.

Industries developed around Humboldt Bay with close ties to the redwood industry. Shipbuilding relied on Douglas fir. The first shipyards were near Dolbeer & Carson's Bay Mill, and the first ship was launched in 1865. The most successful and prolific shipbuilder was Hans Bendixson, who built more than 100 vessels. He designed his ships with a shallower draft to cross the hazardous Humboldt Bay entrance more safely. To compensate for loss of hull space, he built his ships to have space on the top deck for stacking lumber. Of the ships Bendixson built, the only remaining one is the C.A. *Thayer*, on display at the San Francisco Maritime National Historical Park.

An allied business that lumber companies depended upon was the Eureka Foundry. It made steam donkey engines, boilers for mills, and even locomotives for railroads operated by lumber companies. The foundry was invaluable in repairing heavy equipment.

A lesser-known Humboldt County industry was based on tanoak, *Lithocarpus densiflora*. The tree earned its name because the bark contained tannins (tannic acid), useful in tanning hides. Large lumber companies sent crews to harvest tanoak prior to logging. Otherwise, valuable tanoak bark would have been destroyed when crews burned the woods before removing the logs, a common practice. Other workers specialized in harvesting tanoak in a season ending in August, rather than the September or October end date for redwood loggers. Workers would ring the tree and, after falling it, peel off the bark, allowing it to dry. They left the rest of the wood in the forest to rot, which often caused large forest fires in subsequent years. The bark was shipped to large tanneries near San Francisco, although some was diverted for use at tanneries in Rohnerville, Eureka, and Arcata.

Workers at mills and logging camps were a mixture of local men with families in nearby towns, and transient single men who traveled along the coast seeking employment. Mills farther from Eureka tended to have company towns, where housing, stores, and supplies were provided by the company. Mills such as the Dolbeer & Carson Company's Bay Mill depended on workers finding housing in Eureka. While mills tended to be year-round operations, "logging shows" or camps in the woods were limited by heavy winter rains to the drier months. Temporary houses built on skids were moved from one logging camp to the next. The most important building was the cookhouse. Logging companies advertised in San Francisco newspapers for workers, offering free passage on their ships to Eureka.

The lumber companies' workforce included immigrants from Sweden, Finland, Germany, Italy, Ireland, and England, as well as Americans from the East Coast and Canadians who had earlier emigrated from Scotland. Workers ranged in age from boys in their early teens to men in their fifties and, occasionally, older. Logging was, and remains, a very dangerous profession, and many men were killed or maimed in woods and mills.

In writing *Mills of Humboldt County*, the authors have chosen a thematic approach, examining industries associated with lumbering in 19th-century Humboldt. Attempts have been made to include all of Humboldt's mills from this period, but the authors are limited by the photographic record. The goal is for this book to share knowledge of the lumber industry and of the many ways that logging impacted this region. The authors are donating their royalties from sales of this book to the Fortuna Depot Museum.

One

The Mills

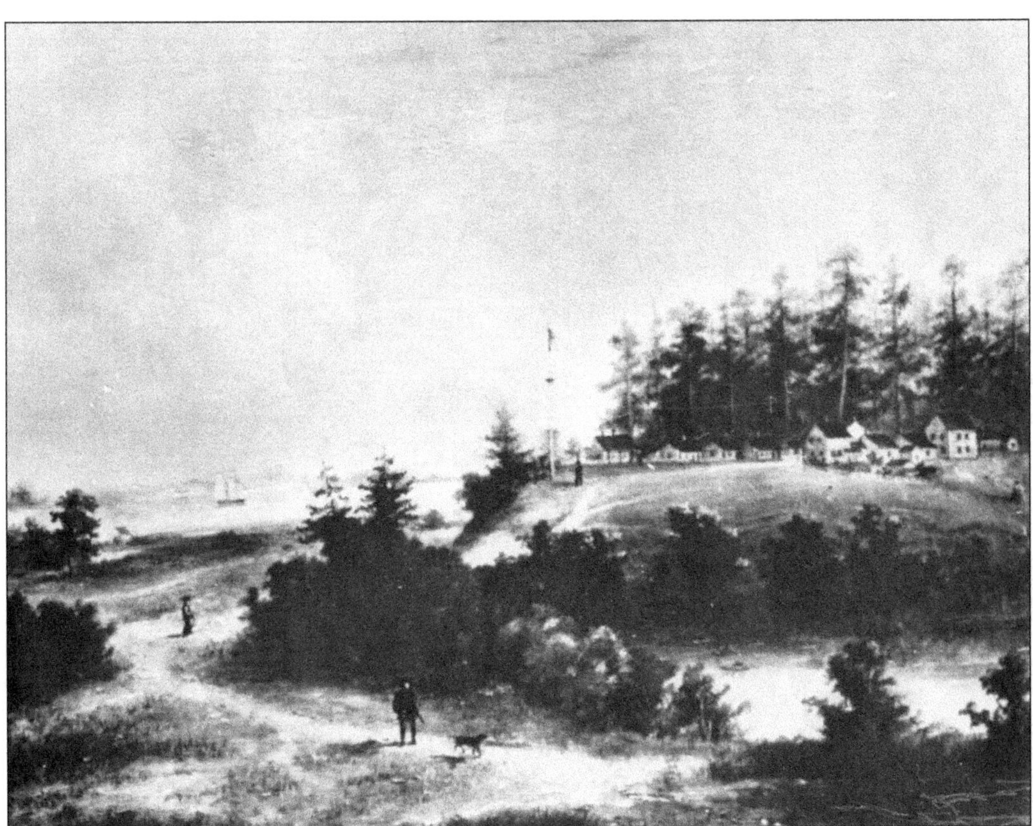

In 1850, American settlers aboard the *Laura Virginia* were impressed by the redwood forest extending as far as they could see, and by the size of the trees. Although several mills began operation shortly after the settlers' arrival, they sawed only fir and pine, mostly for homes and businesses in the new communities. These mills were not capable of managing the redwoods' large girth. (HSU.)

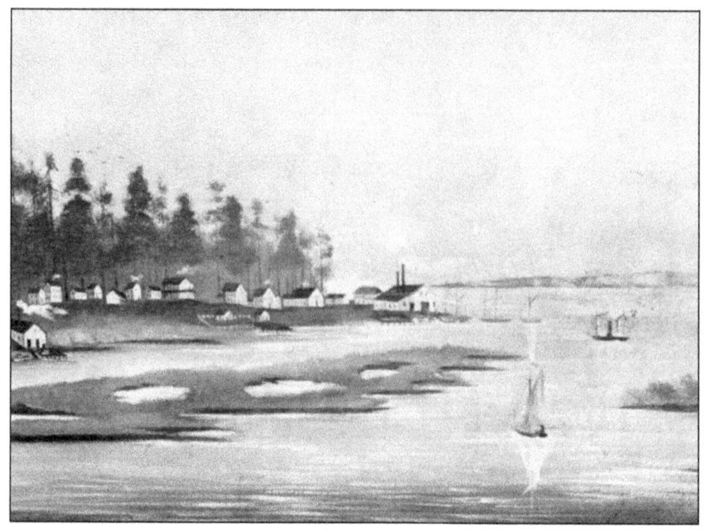

In the fall of 1850, J.M. Eddy and Martin White opened the first mill on Humboldt Bay, the Pioneer Mill. Located at the foot of modern M Street in Eureka, the mill closed in 1855. An unstable market forced its sale in 1857 to John Dolbeer at a sheriff's sale for delinquent taxes. Painted in 1854 by a soldier at Fort Humboldt, this image also shows the Smiley, Muley, and Ryan & Duff Mills. (HSU.)

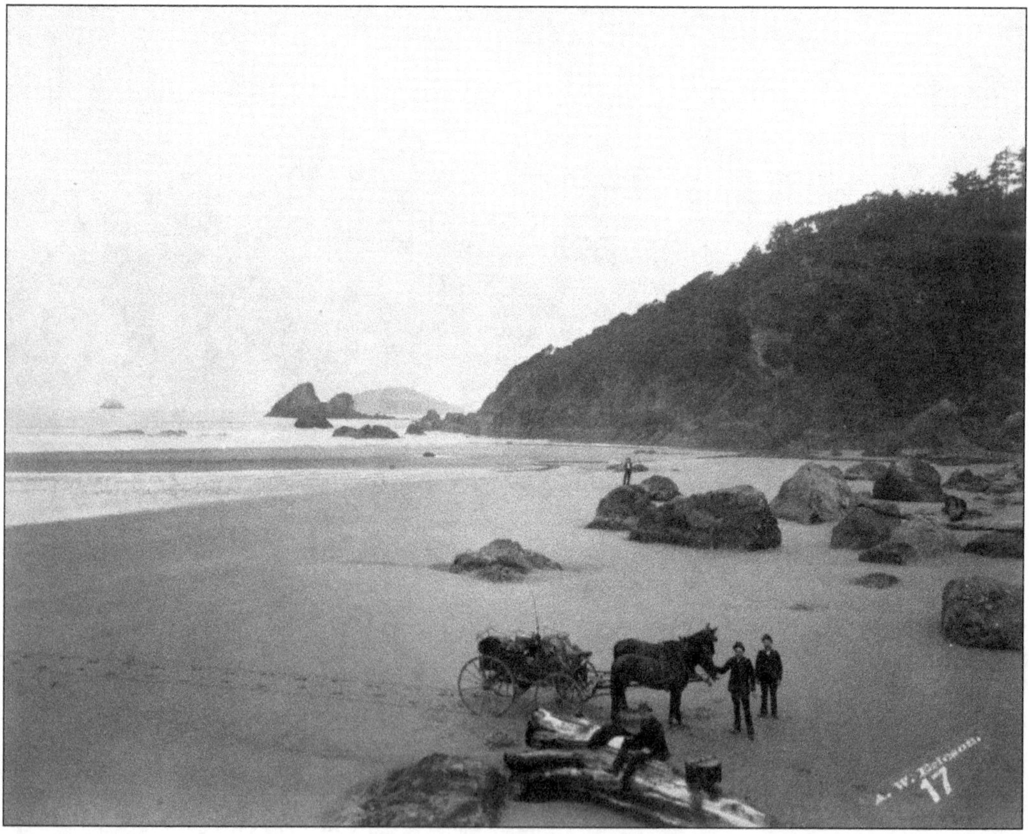

In 1851, German immigrant Baron Karl von Luffelholz started a mill near the mouth of Little River, a small stream 12 miles north of Eureka. Luffelholz's mill prospered for several years, but it was destroyed by floodwaters in 1854. Luffelholz returned to Germany in 1856. A variant of his name, Luffenholtz, still graces an ocean beach and a creek in the region. (HSU.)

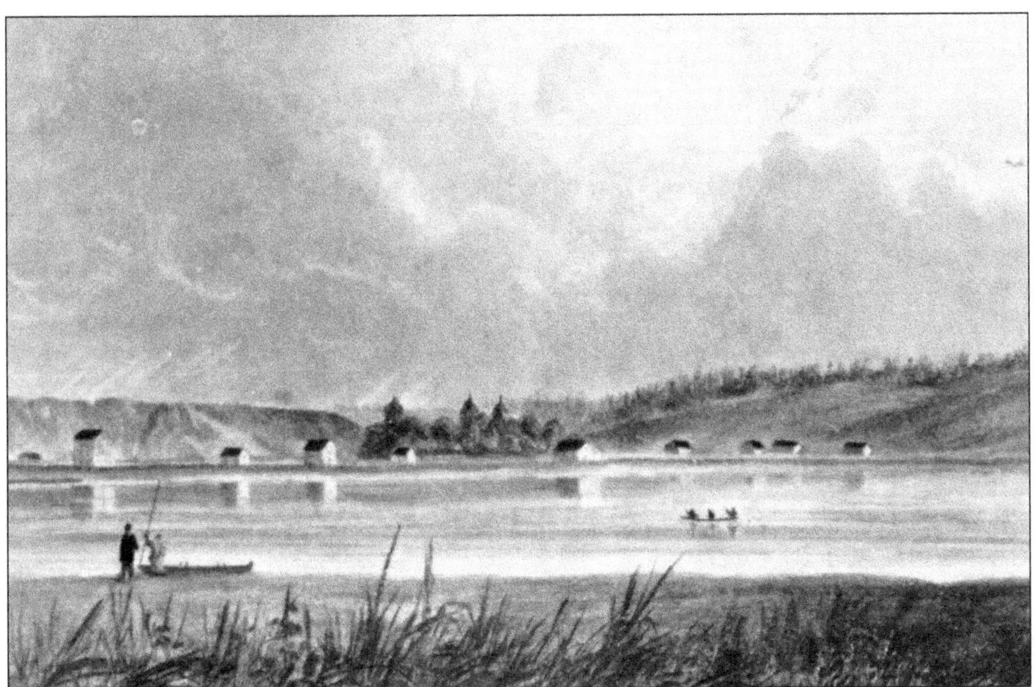

The Modena Mill at Bucksport, a town located near Fort Humboldt and now incorporated into Eureka, began operations in 1852. Powered by the steamship *Chesapeake*, this mill sold for $250 in February 1855 at a sheriff's sale for a mechanic's lien. One cause of the owners' financial failure was the difficulty in sawing redwood into usable lumber with the muley, a type of up-and-down saw. (HSU.)

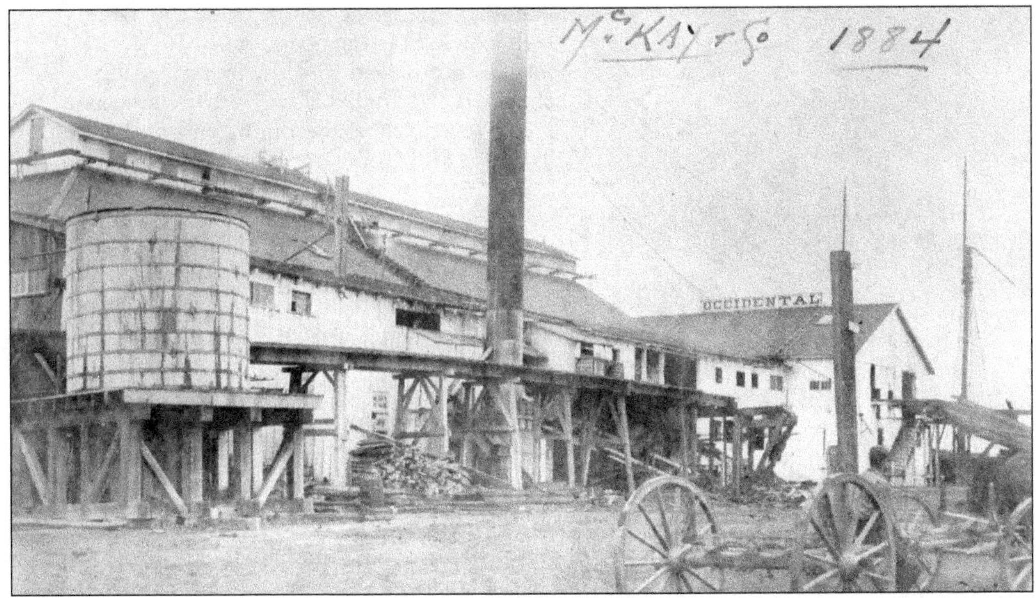

Powered by the steamship *Santa Clara*, the Ryan & Duff Mill opened in 1852 near First and D Streets in Eureka. Irish immigrant James Ryan, who became a state senator, sold his share to William Duff in 1858. A fire in 1862 destroyed the mill. Duff sold the rebuilt mill to David Evans in 1871. Renaming it the Occidental, Evans sold it to Allan McKay in 1875. (HCHS.)

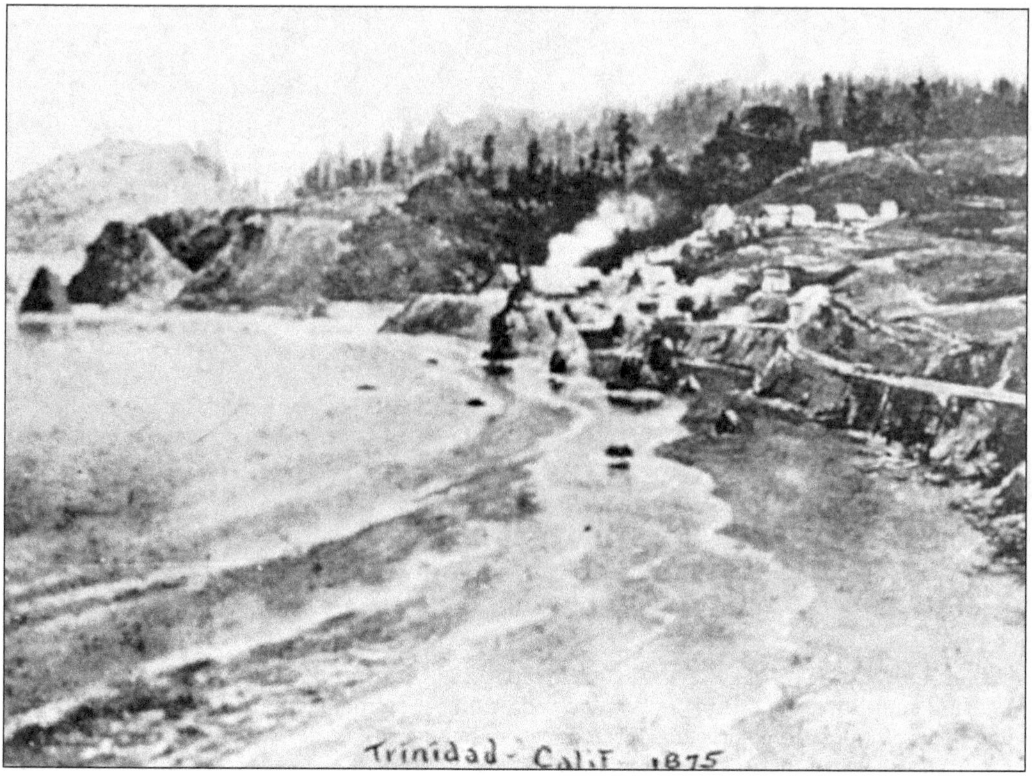

Trinidad - Calif. 1875

Just north of von Luffelholz's mill, Byron Deming and William Marsh opened a mill at Trinidad, giving the nearby creek the name Mill Creek. Starting operations in 1852, the new mill coincided with the incorporation of the town of Trinidad. This facility changed hands several times, becoming part of the Trinidad Mill Company in 1869. (HSU.)

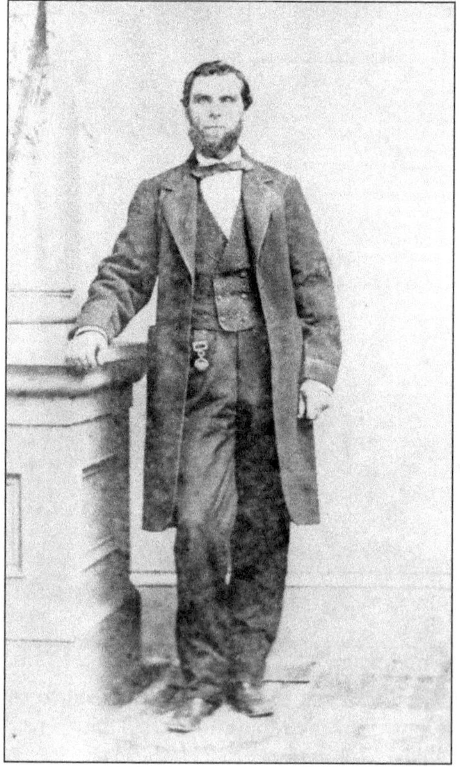

William Carson came to California from New Brunswick, seeking gold, in 1850. En route to the Trinity gold mines, he found work as a timber faller at Ryan's Slough near Eureka. In 1854, he began working at the Muley Mill in Eureka as a sawyer, the person responsible for sawing logs into lumber. He soon leased the mill, beginning his career as a mill owner. (HCHS.)

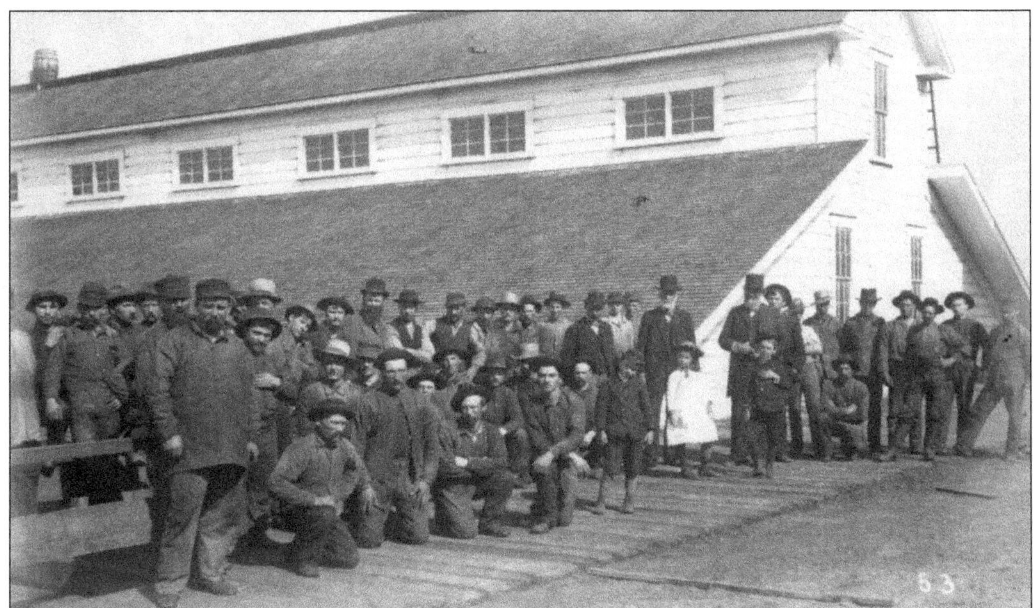

William Carson's partner, John Dolbeer, arrived in Eureka in the early 1850s on his way to Gold Bluffs near Orick in search of gold. Returning to Eureka in 1853, he, along with Martin White, Isaac Upton, Dan Packard, and C.W. Long, started the Bay Mill. The operation was unsuccessful, as a declining lumber market could not meet expenses. Dolbeer managed to keep ownership of the Bay Mill, partnering with Charles McClean in 1856. The mill burned down in 1860. Another tragedy occurred in 1863, when McClean drowned while crossing the Humboldt Bar. Carson became Dolbeer's partner in 1864. Above, the two bearded men standing right of center behind the children are John Dolbeer (left) and William Carson. The Dolbeer & Carson Company mill operated until 1950, when its land and operations were sold to the Pacific Lumber Company. (Both, HSU.)

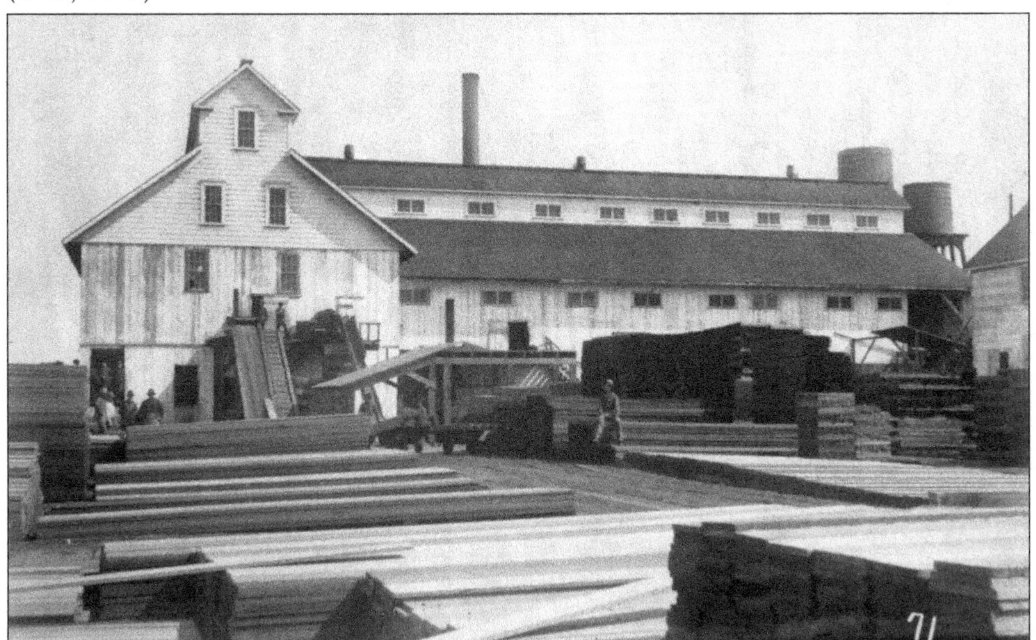

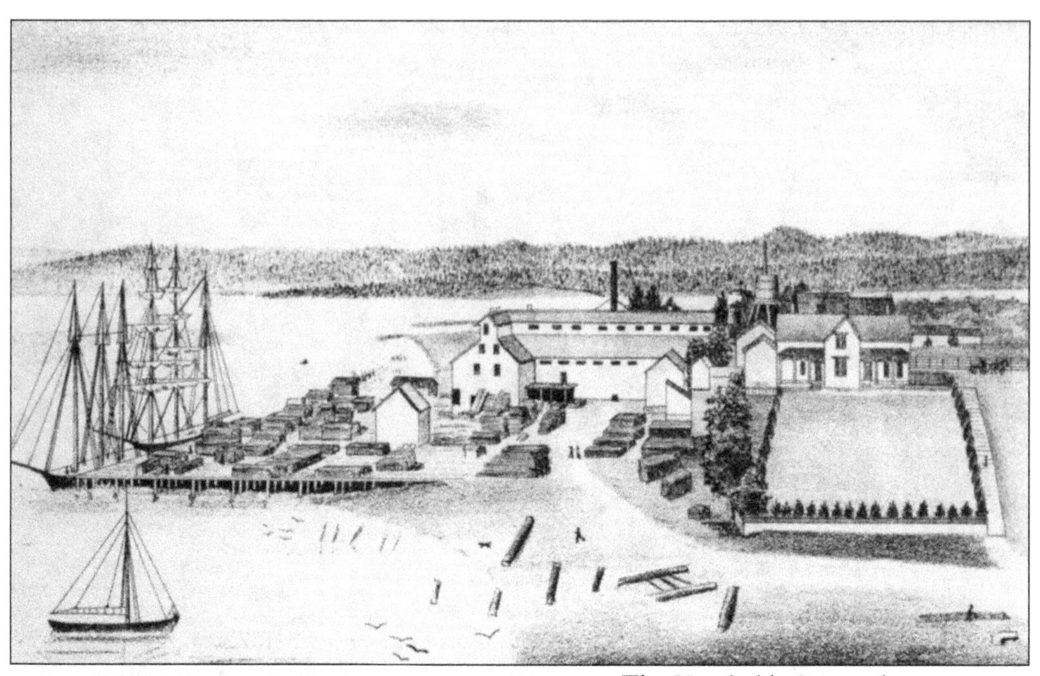

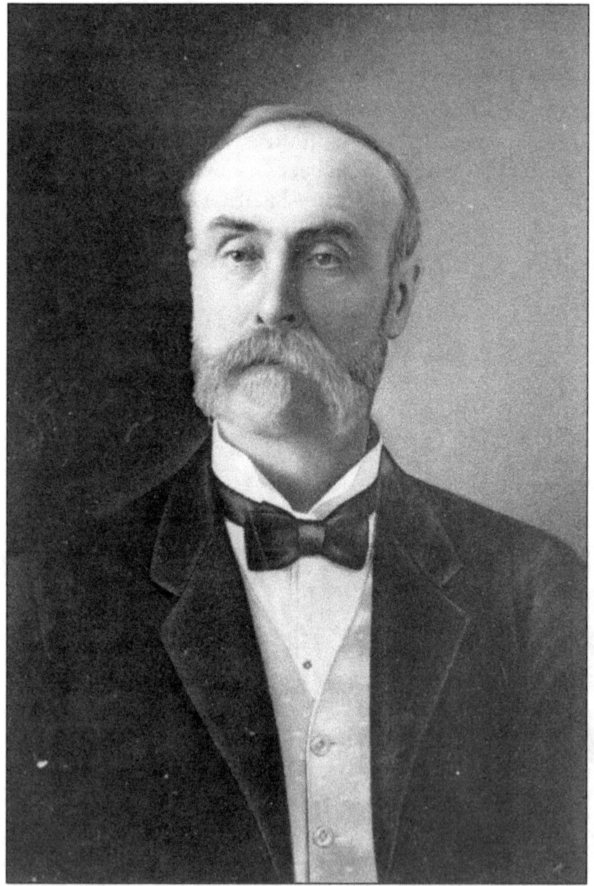

The Humboldt County logging industry began logging redwoods by 1855. In 1853, the Ryan & Duff Mill, the Muley Mill, and the Bay Mill were joined by the Picayune Mill and Vance Mill. The Picayune was operated by William Carson. When it closed in 1860, the machinery was moved from the Picayune to the Bay Mill, pictured here in 1882.

John Vance came to California in 1850 from New Brunswick, arriving in Humboldt County two years later. His first mill was on Humboldt Bay, at the foot of what is now G Street in Eureka. He became well known for his mills along Mad River. In 1854, he employed 31 men and produced 50,000 board feet of lumber a day. (HCHS.)

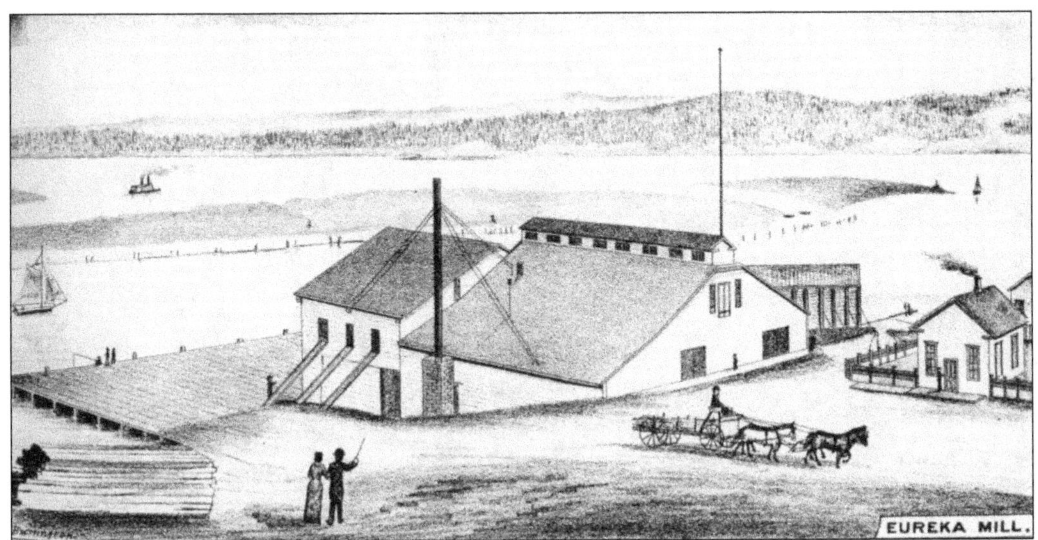

In 1854, partners Hiram Bean and J.C. Smiley opened the Smiley, or Bean Mill, on Humboldt Bay in Eureka. In 1860, D.R. Jones and John Kentfield of San Mateo, California, purchased an interest in the mill and, in 1865, took over operations with Hans Henry Buhne, who also piloted ships across the entrance to Humboldt Bay. The mill, later known as the D.R. Jones Mill, was destroyed by fire in 1898.

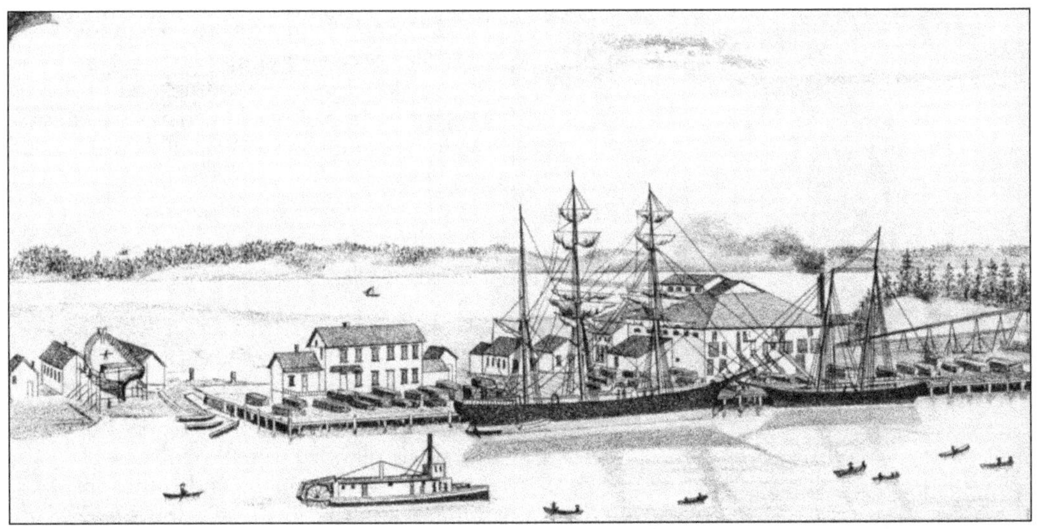

D.R. Jones & Company built a mill on Gunther Island in 1866. The largest mill on the bay at the time, it employed 65 men and had 46 saws operating simultaneously, resulting in a daily output of 70,000 board feet of lumber. The company is credited with having the first steam railroad in Humboldt when it built a line from South Bay along Salmon Creek in 1875 to access its redwood holdings. Rolling stock included a Baldwin locomotive.

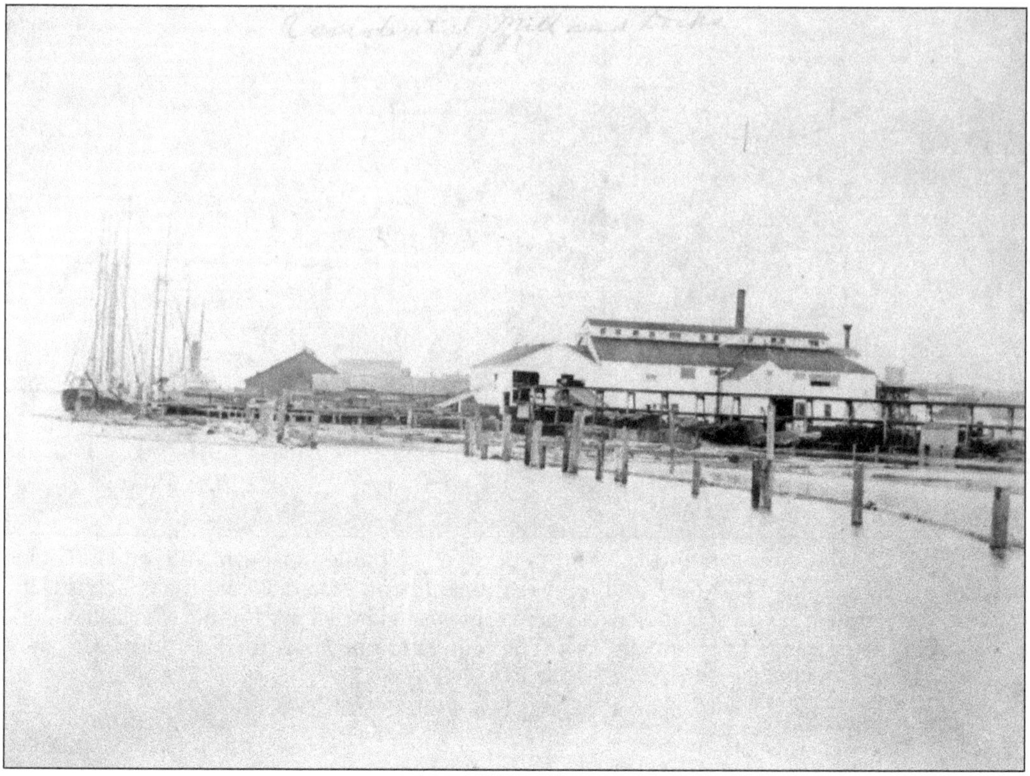

The end of the Civil War brought changes to the Humboldt mills, including technological advances in strengthening steel. The Occidental Mill, based on the 1852 Ryan & Duff Mill, was purchased by Allen McKay and his partners Harris Connick, Alexander Connick, and A.J. Bryant in 1875. Also known as the McKay Mill, it operated until 1932. (Clarke.)

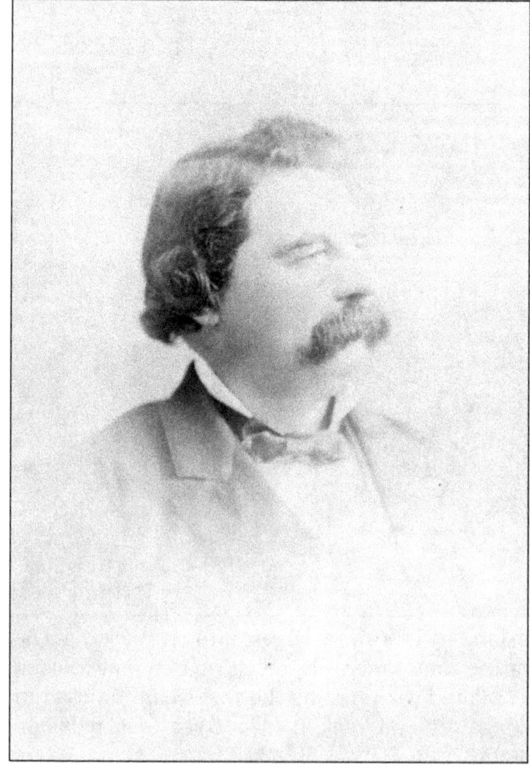

Joseph Russ, another gold seeker, came to Humboldt County in 1852, herding cattle he planned to sell to loggers. He started a ranch and expanded into the lumber industry in the late 1860s with a mill on Price Creek near Ferndale. This mill burned down in 1875. Russ chose not to rebuild since he had built a mill on Gunther Island with Euphronius Cousins in 1869. (HSU.)

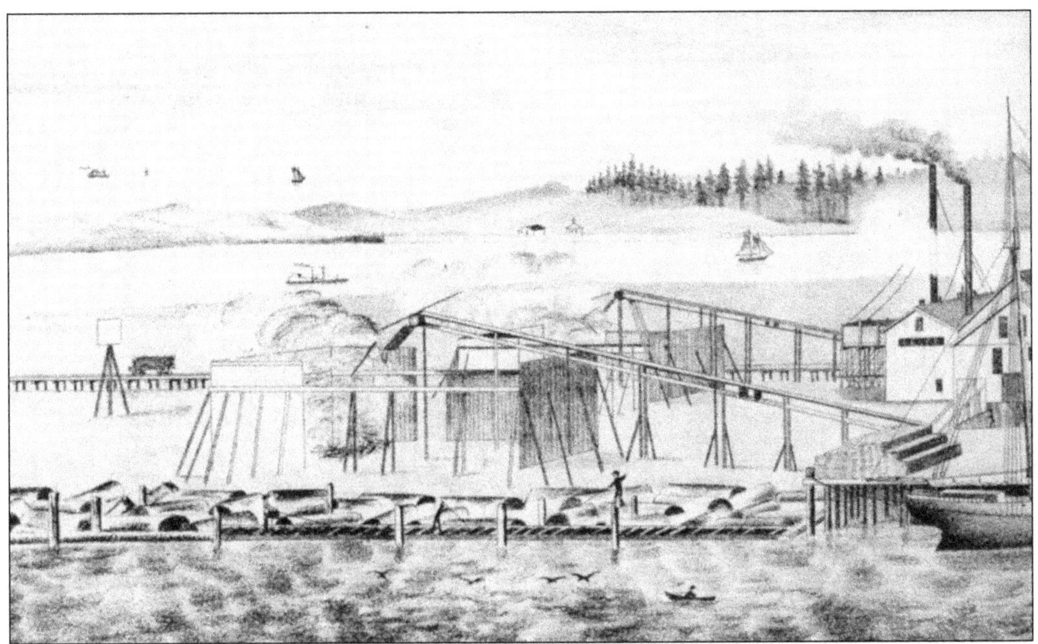

The woods operations of Euphronius Cousins and Joseph Russ were along Elk River. In 1875, their mill produced 45,000 board feet of lumber. This output increased to 19 million board feet in 1888. Most of the company's lumber was shipped to the East Coast and foreign ports, much of it on ships built by Cousins at his nearby shipyard.

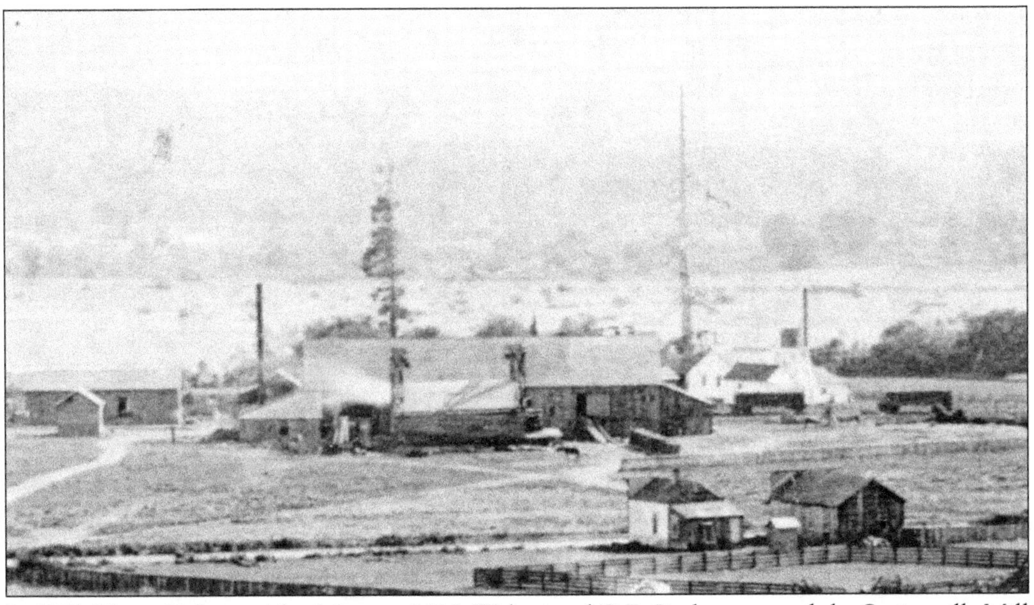

In 1875, Henry Rohner, Alex Masson, M.N. Weber, and G.F. Gushaw started the Springville Mill in Springville (now Fortuna). It was designed as both a sawmill and a gristmill, taking advantage of nearby redwoods and farming in the Eel River Valley. After nine years, the mill was sold to Wyman Murphy of Santa Rosa. Murphy sold it in the late 1880s to W.J. Swortzell and G.W. Williams, who operated it as a shingle mill.

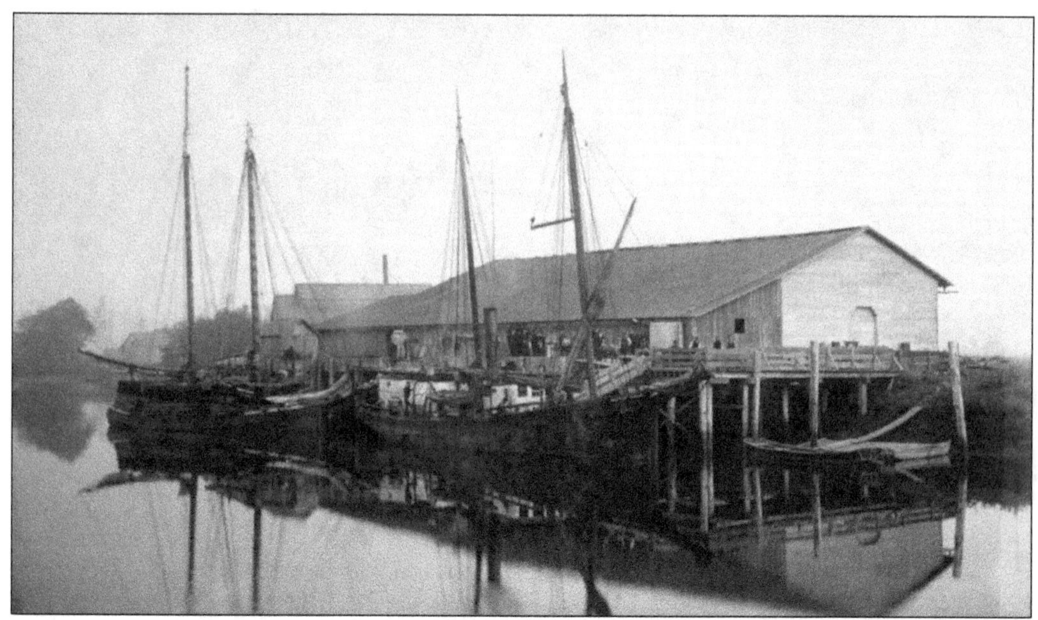

C.C. Dennis, Thomas McDonald, and Albert Bragg built the Enterprise Mill, another gristmill and lumber mill in the Eel River Valley, in 1877. The owners chose to locate at Port Kenyon on the Eel River because this was as far inland as seagoing vessels could navigate. The mill was severely damaged in 1883 when the boiler burst. (HSU.)

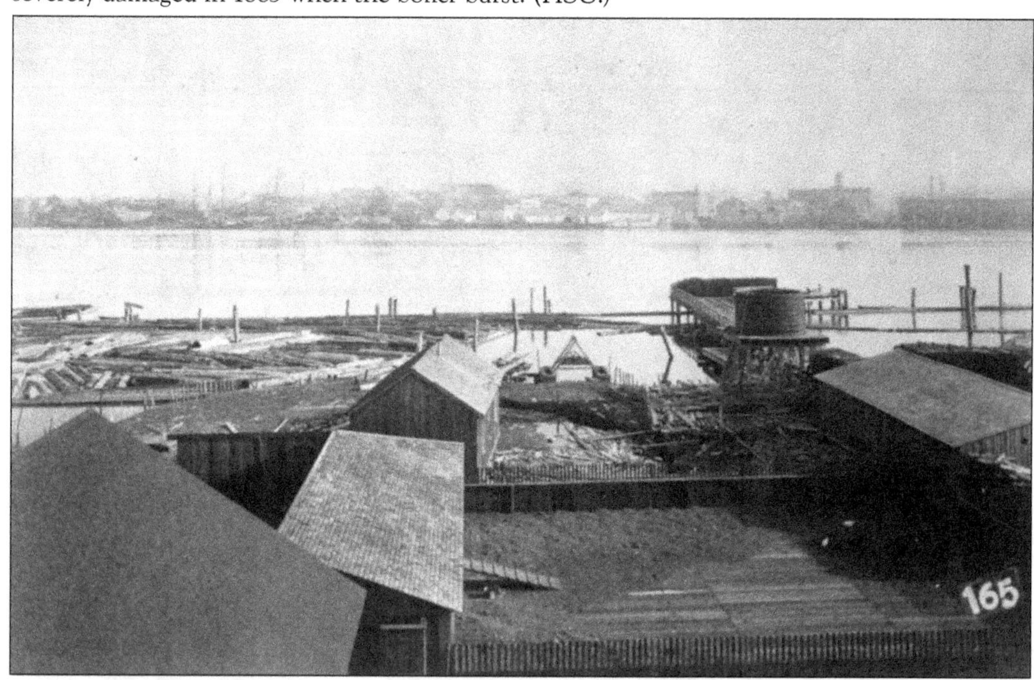

The Cousins & Russ Mill on Gunther Island had several owners and operated under various names. The mill was sold to the California Redwood Company in 1883 and then resold in 1886. Russ remained one of the partners of the facility, renamed Excelsior Mill. In 1891, the Excelsior produced 90,000 board feet of lumber daily. The Excelsior closed in 1893 after depleting its lumber holdings near Freshwater. (HSU.)

The Dougherty & Smith Mill at Trinidad opened in 1869, quickly becoming the largest mill in the area. In 1873, it consolidated with the Hooper Mill. Eureka newspapers noted in 1885 that the Hooper Mill shipped nearly six million board feet of redwood lumber to Liverpool, England, around Cape Horn. (HSU.)

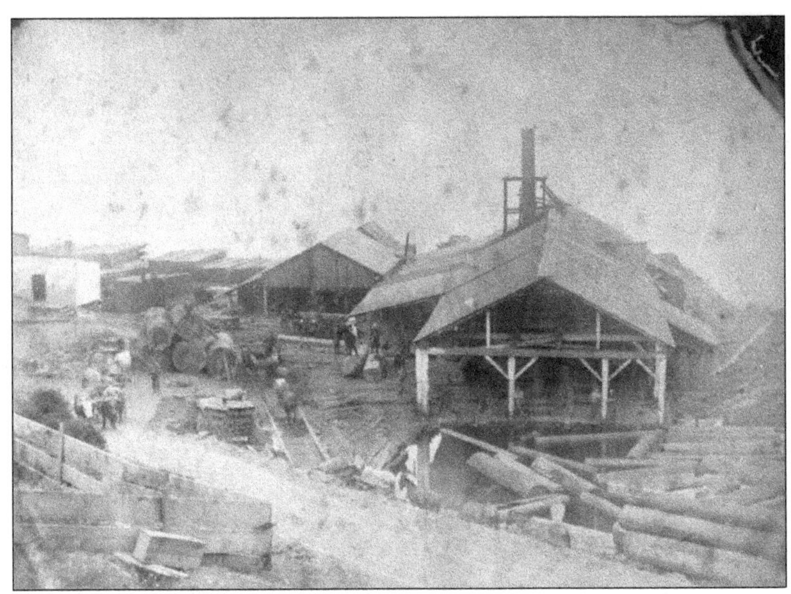

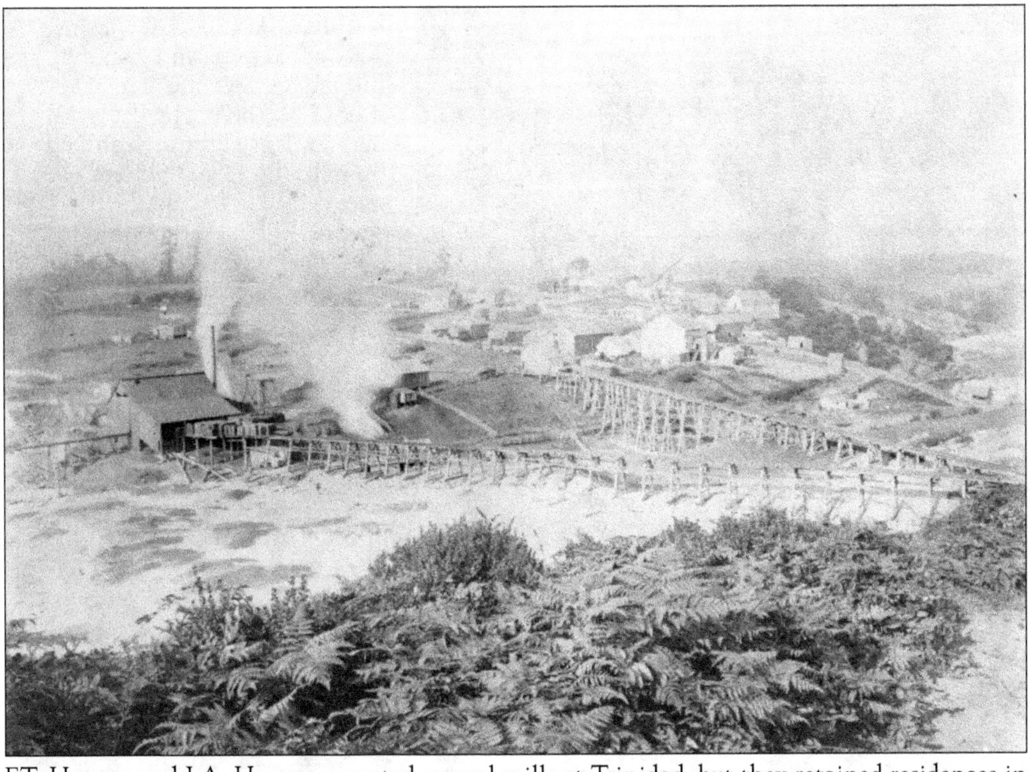

F.T. Hooper and J.A. Hooper operated several mills at Trinidad, but they retained residences in San Francisco. The phenomenon of absentee mill owners was common among the redwood mills. Several larger mills were operated by local men while the owners lived and maintained offices in San Francisco. The Hooper Mill burned down in 1886 and was not rebuilt. (HSU.)

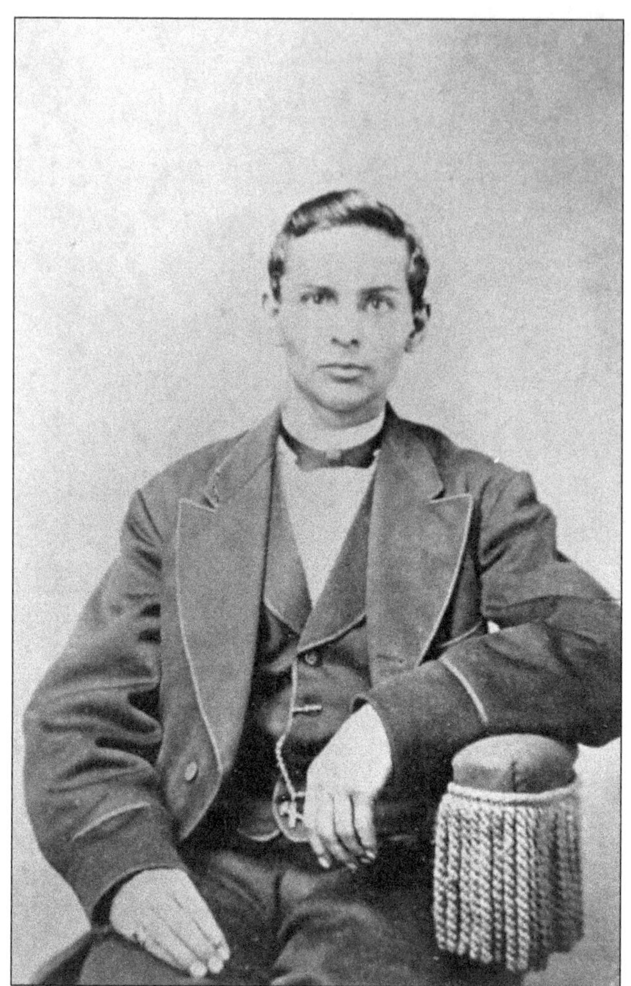

At 18, Noah Falk came to California from Ohio in search of gold. Traveling along the West Coast, he worked as a sawyer in the Puget Sound area and as a baker in Santa Cruz. In 1867 he came to Eureka planning to start a bakery, but soon was working as a sawyer for William Carson. He began operating his own mill, the Janes Creek Mill, in 1869. (HCHS.)

The Janes Creek Mill was run by Falk, Chandler & Company. The logged-over land seen in this photograph of Camp Curtis shows how thoroughly Falk and his crew logged the area around his mills. By 1888, the trees were depleted, forcing the mill's closure. Falk moved his mill to a site near Arcata where timber was more plentiful. (HSU.)

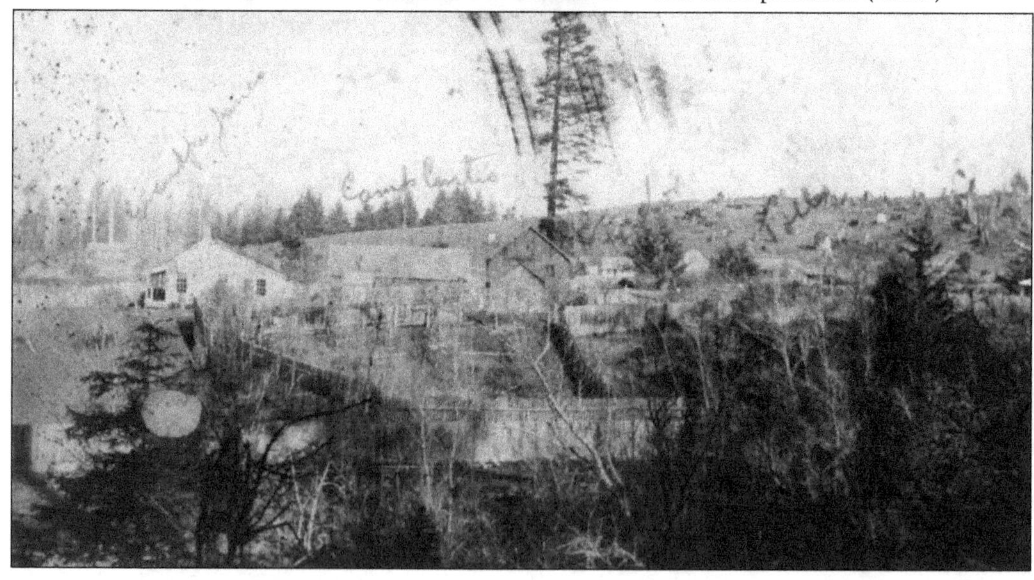

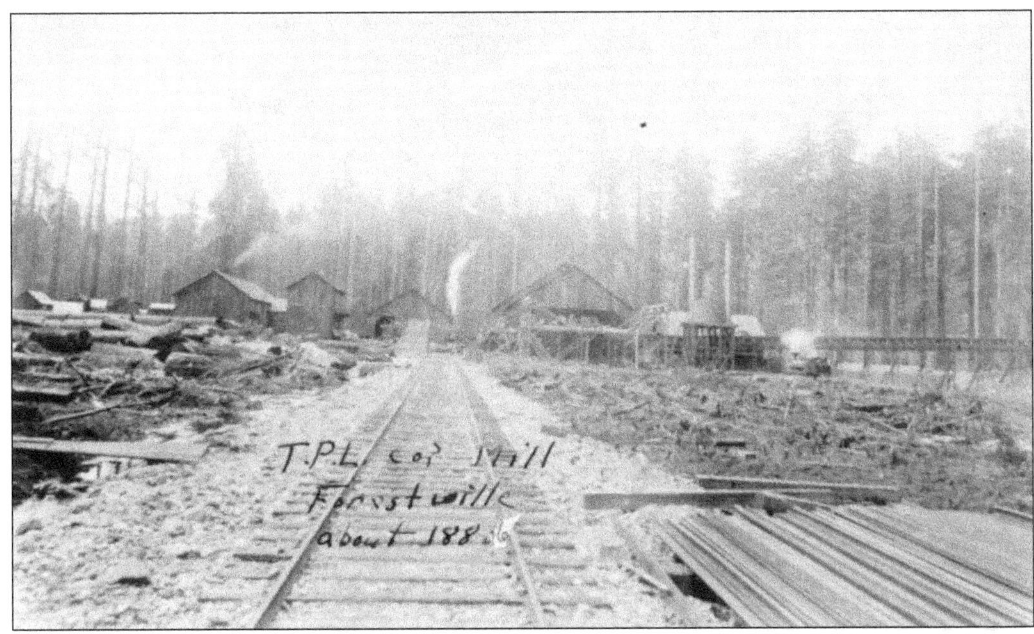

The Pacific Lumber Company (TPL Co.) formed in 1869, but no mill was built or lands logged until 1886. Alexander MacPherson and Henry Wetherbee of Albion, Mendocino County, the original incorporators, were able to gain control of 10,000 acres of timberland, but due to the 1870s depression, never developed their operations. In 1886, MacPherson and Wetherbee sold their interests to Paxton & Curtins of Austin, Nevada, and B.F. Low and James Rigby of San Francisco. Commencing operations in 1886, the company overcame its greatest obstacle, getting its product to market, by building a rail line to connect with the Eel River & Eureka Railroad at Alton. The company acquired waterfront property near Field's Landing for its shipping port. TPL Co. grew to become the largest of the redwood mills.

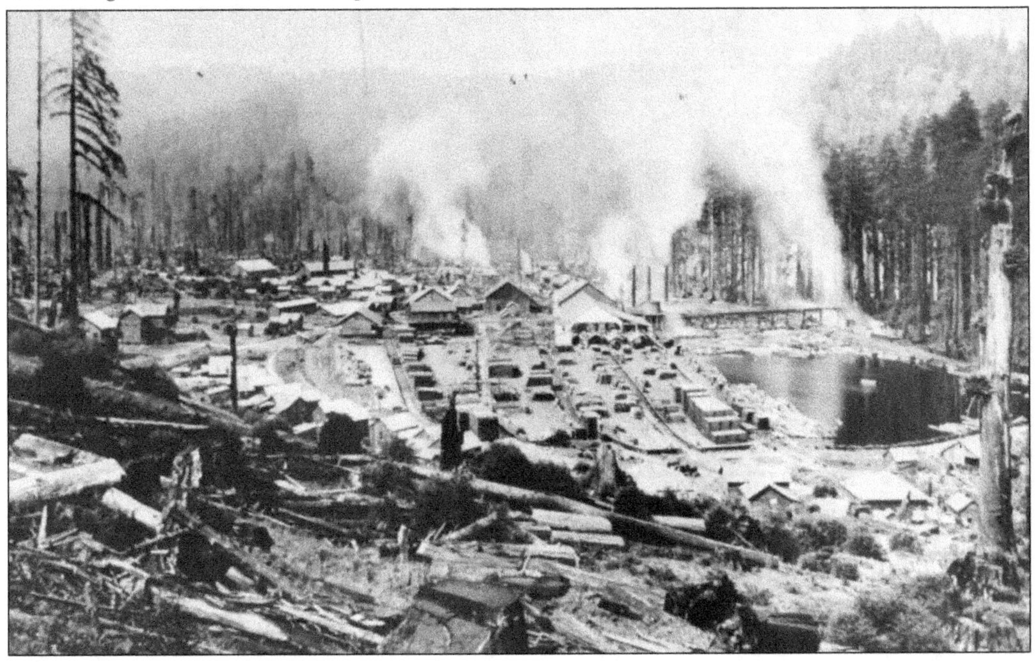

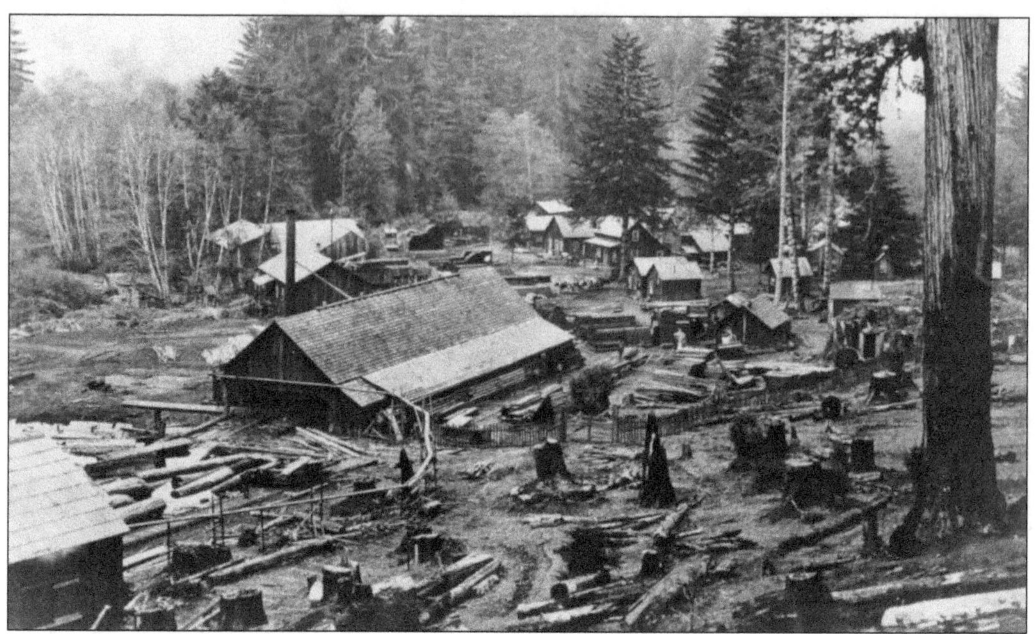

Noah Falk operated two mills in the Arcata area, the Dolly Varden and Jolly Giant. In 1875, the Jolly Giant Mill had a daily output of 25,000 board feet of lumber. As with Falk's Janes Creek Mill, once nearby redwoods were depleted in 1885, the Jolly Giant was closed. The mill was sited along Jolly Giant Creek, near the present-day dormitories of Humboldt State University. The campus housing complex is named after the mill and creek. (HSU.)

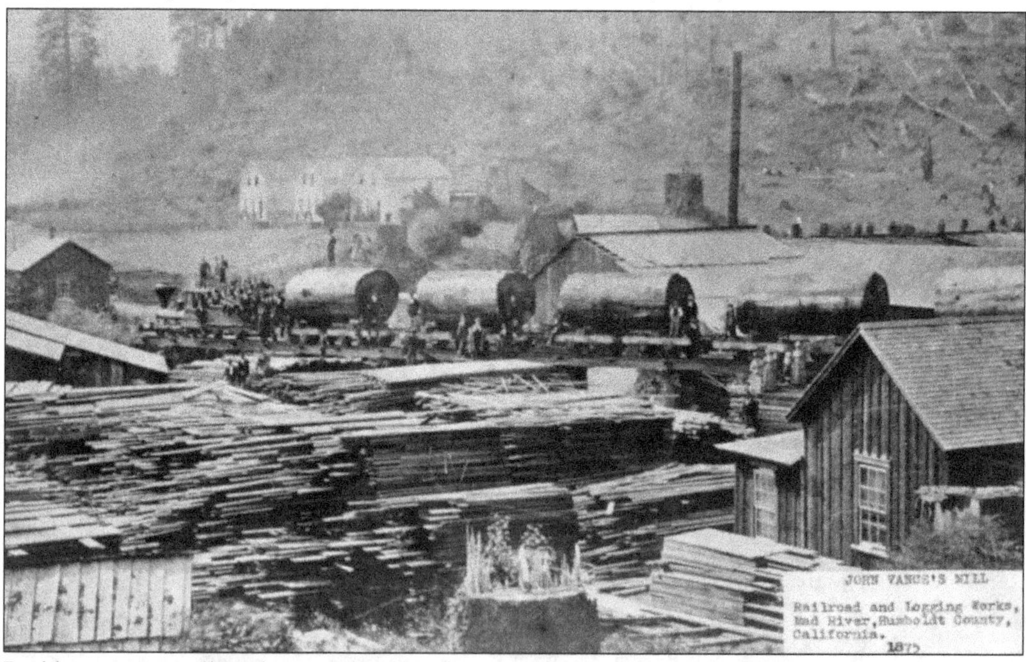

Building a new mill at the mouth of Lindsey Creek along the banks of the Mad River in 1874 allowed John Vance to take advantage of nearby stands of redwoods. Vance's Arcata & Mad River Railroad transported lumber from his mill. This was cheaper and easier than hauling loads of logs to distant mills. (HSU.)

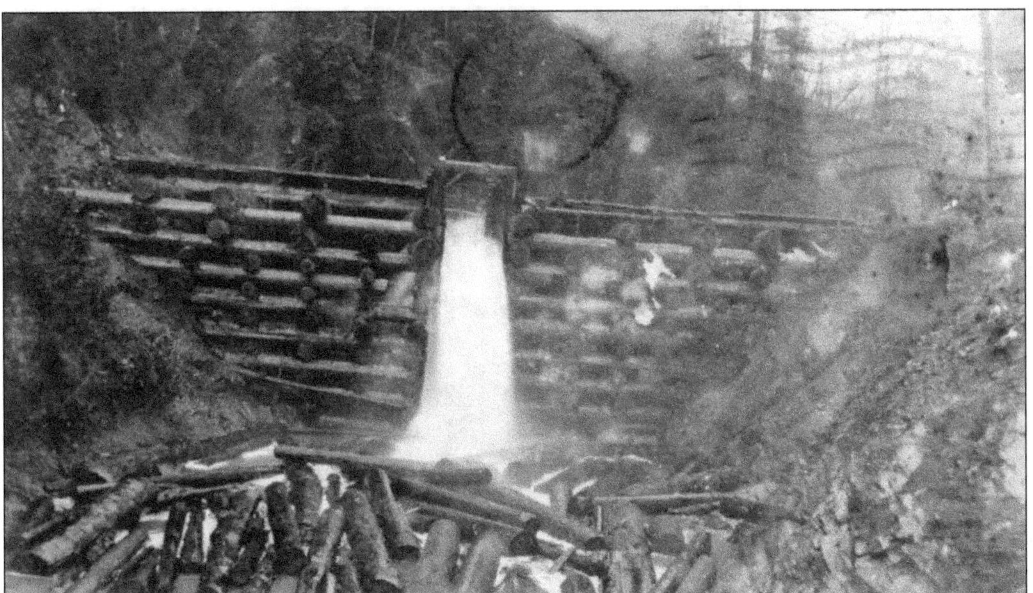

David Evans, John McKay, and H.A. Marks built a mill along Salmon Creek, near South Bay, in 1875. Water for the steam-powered mill came from this dam along Salmon creek. William Carson purchased their operations the next year and continued to log the region. Carson sold the mill in 1902. The lumber produced at the mill was shipped from South Bay.

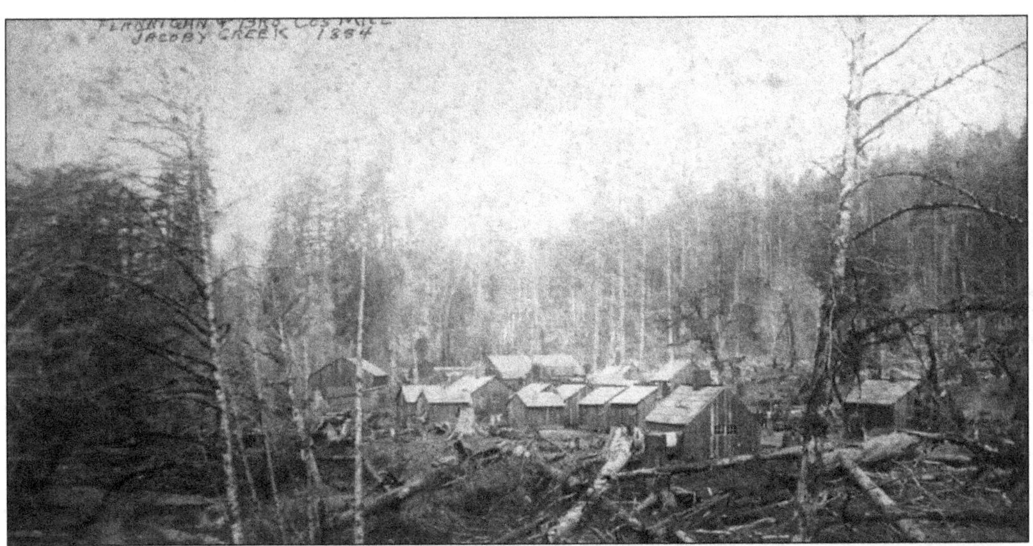

In 1876, Dave Flanigan and Timothy Brosnan, both of Eureka, and John Harpst and James Gannon of Arcata opened their Flanigan, Brosnan & Company mill at the foot of Whipple Street in Eureka. The company had extensive holdings along Jacoby Creek (pictured), where it estimated it could obtain eight million board feet of lumber. As at the Excelsior Mill, logs were brought to the bay, then floated to the mill. (HSU.)

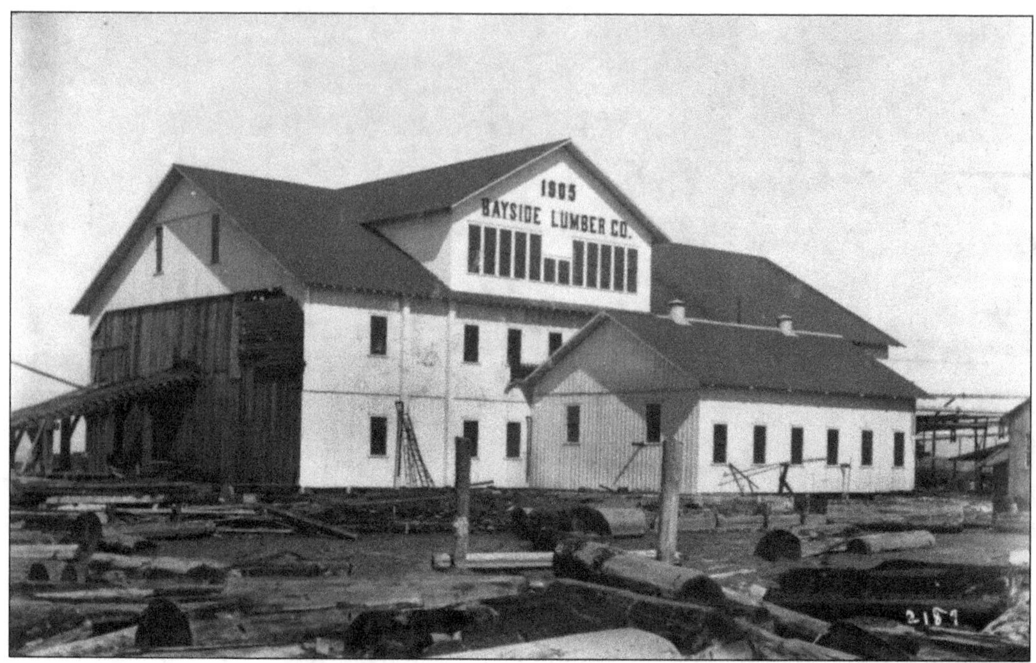

The Redwood Lumber Manufacturers Association noted in 1897 that the Flanigan, Brosnan & Company mill "had a capacity of 50,000 feet per day. For its size it is one of the best equipped mills in the county, and, owing to its position . . . with the main ship channel in front of it, enjoys superior facilities for loading vessels with its output." In 1902, the company was sold and renamed the Bayside Mill & Lumber Company. (HSU.)

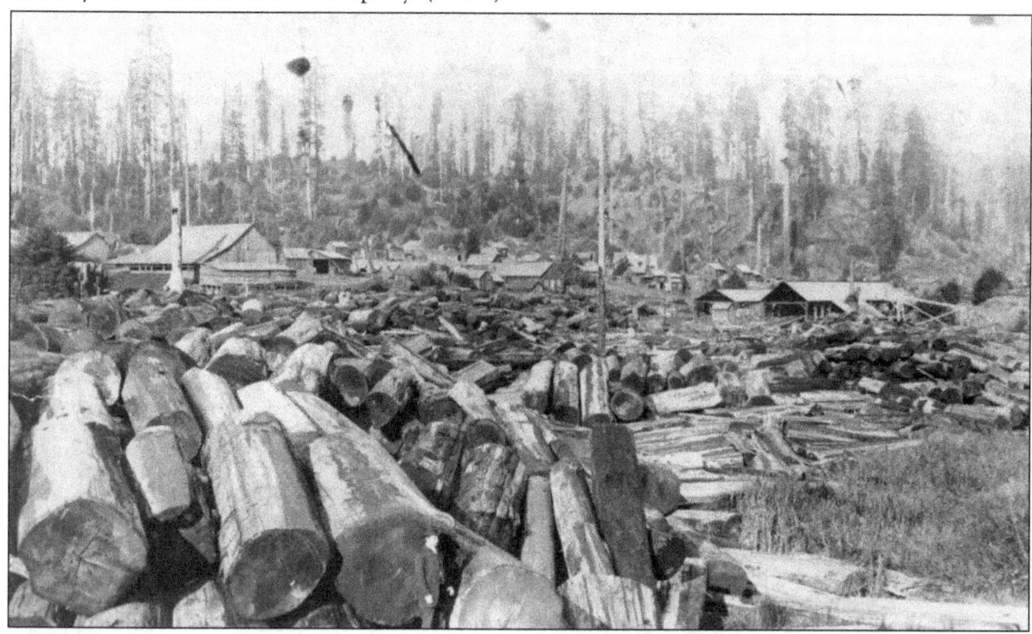

Isaac Minor was another gold seeker who found his fortune in the "red gold." He built a mill in 1881 at Warren Creek, on the south bank of Mad River. The Arcata & Mad River Railroad extended its line to this mill for transporting lumber to the port at Arcata. The mill burned down in 1896 and again in 1902. At that time, it was abandoned. (HCHS.)

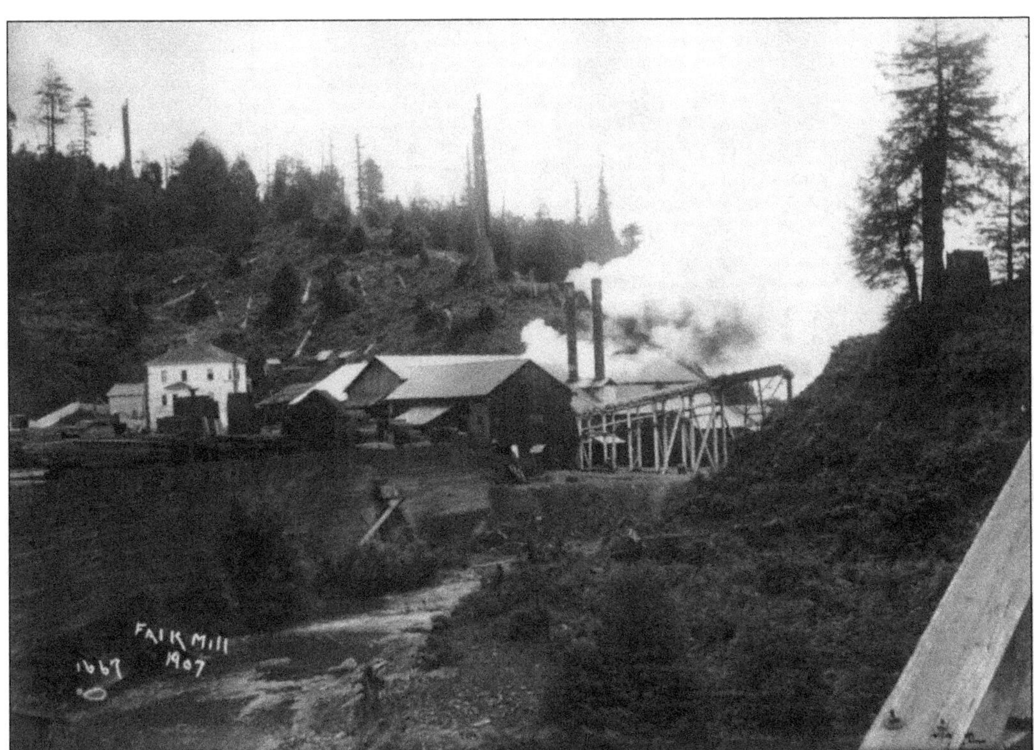

Noah Falk and partners Irwin Harpster, C. Stafford, J. Hawley, and Ben Pendleton opened a new mill along Elk River in 1882, naming their company after the river. The accompanying town became known as Falk. In 1897, the Elk River Lumber Company owned 3,000 acres of timberland along the stream. When the mill burned down in 1896, it was quickly rebuilt. It was the first mill in the county to have a band mill, or band saw. Instead of circular blades, a single, flexible saw blade with teeth on one side went around two pulleys, making a continuous cut. With the new band saw, the facility could produce 38,000 board feet of lumber in a 10-hour day. (Both, HSU.)

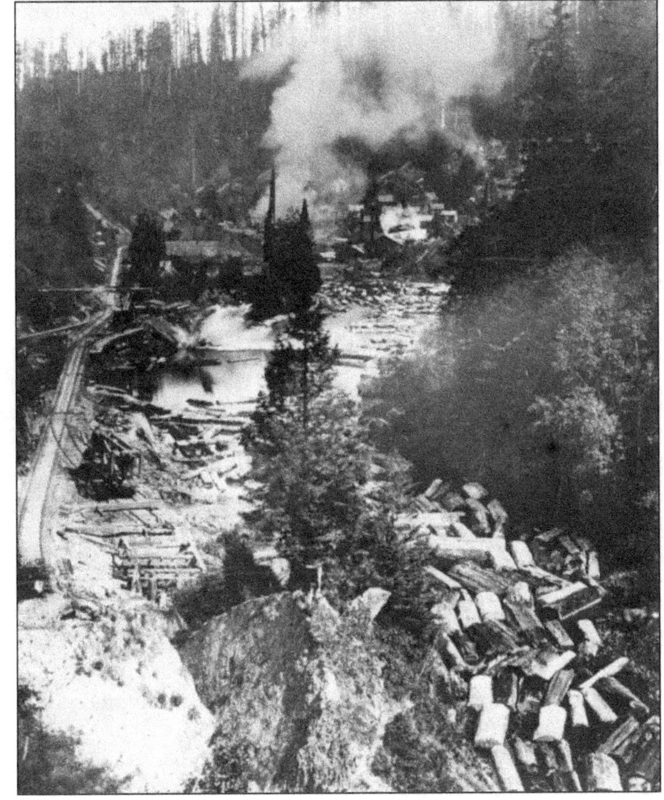

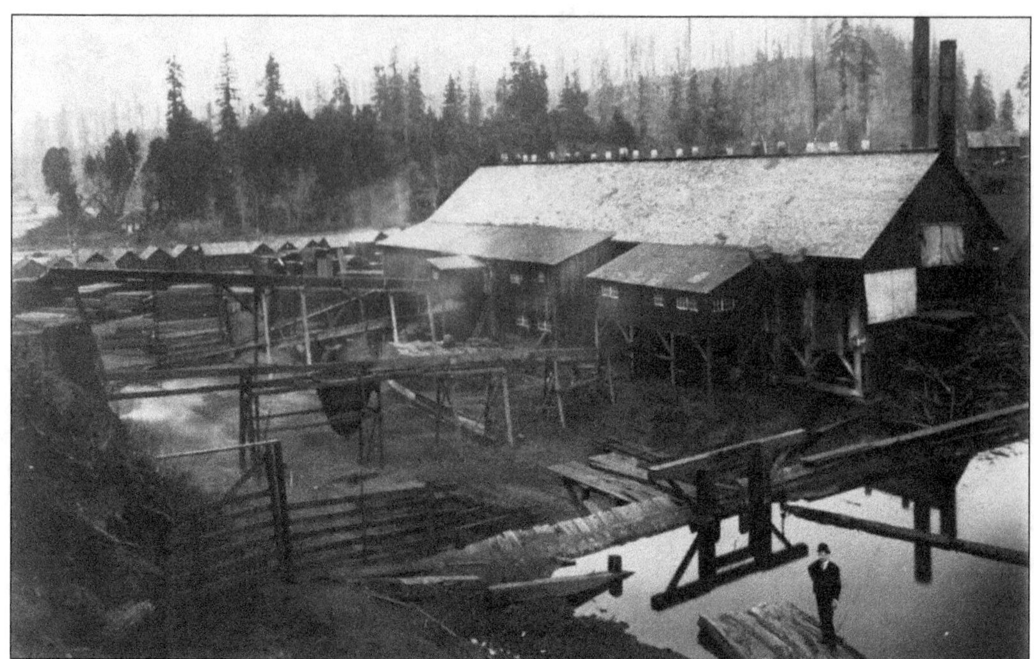

In 1882, C.W. Chandler, M.F. Henderson, A. Kendall, and F. Graham started a mill along Mad River near Blue Lake. In 1886, the mill was moved across the river to Riverside. This company dissolved in 1888, and a new corporation, the Riverside Lumber Company, was established, with Harry Jackson of Arcata as president. The Redwood Lumber Manufacturers Association noted that the "timber owned by the company is the finest in that region." (HSU.)

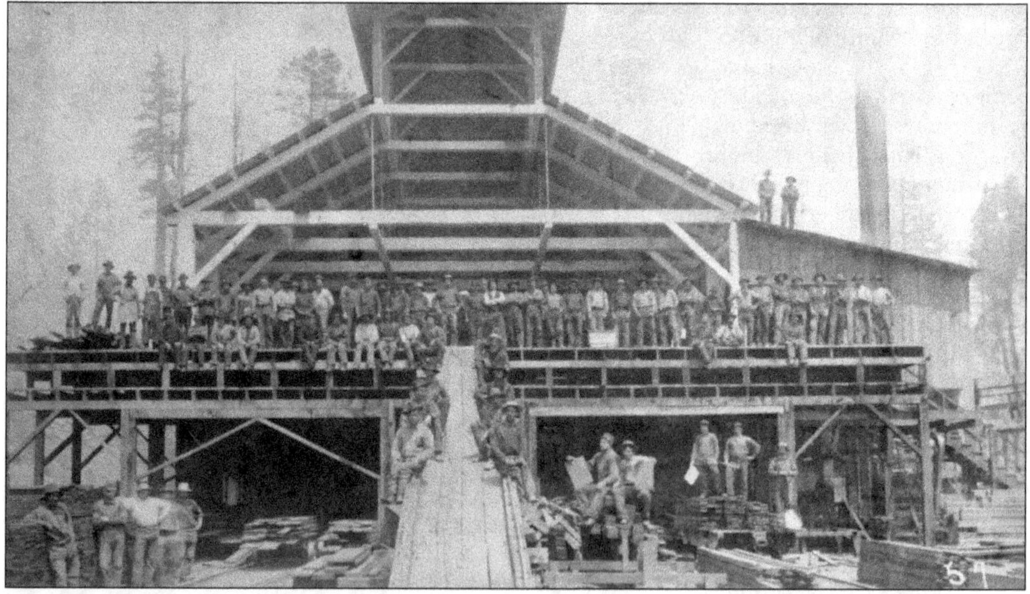

In 1883, a syndicate of wealthy investors from Edinburgh, Scotland, initiated a large landgrab when they formed the California Redwood Company. Purchasing land along Freshwater Creek and Elk River, the company's goal was to control over 60,000 acres of prime timberland. Agents hired sailors and any male adult to claim 160 acres of homestead land and then sell it for $7 an acre to the syndicate. (HSU.)

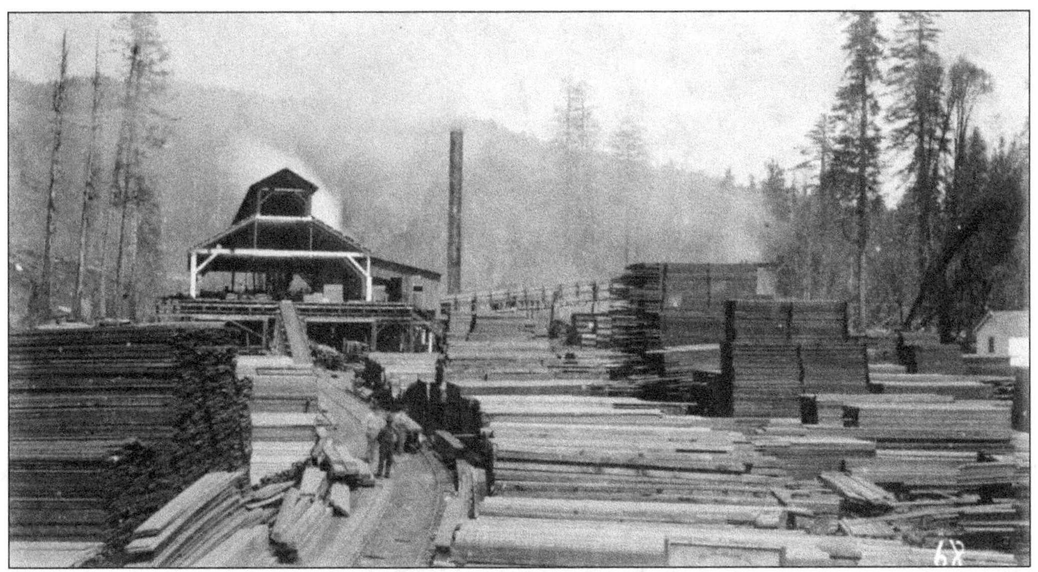

The California Redwood Company owned the Russ & Cousins Mill, the Evans Mill, and the Hooper Mill at Trinidad. It also owned several railroads and owned or controlled over 100,000 acres of redwoods in Humboldt and Del Norte Counties. The fraudulent acquisition of land was contested. A Los Angeles newspaper reported that the land deals were done in saloon back rooms. Following an investigation of foreign investors gaining so much timberland, the company dissolved in 1897. (HSU.)

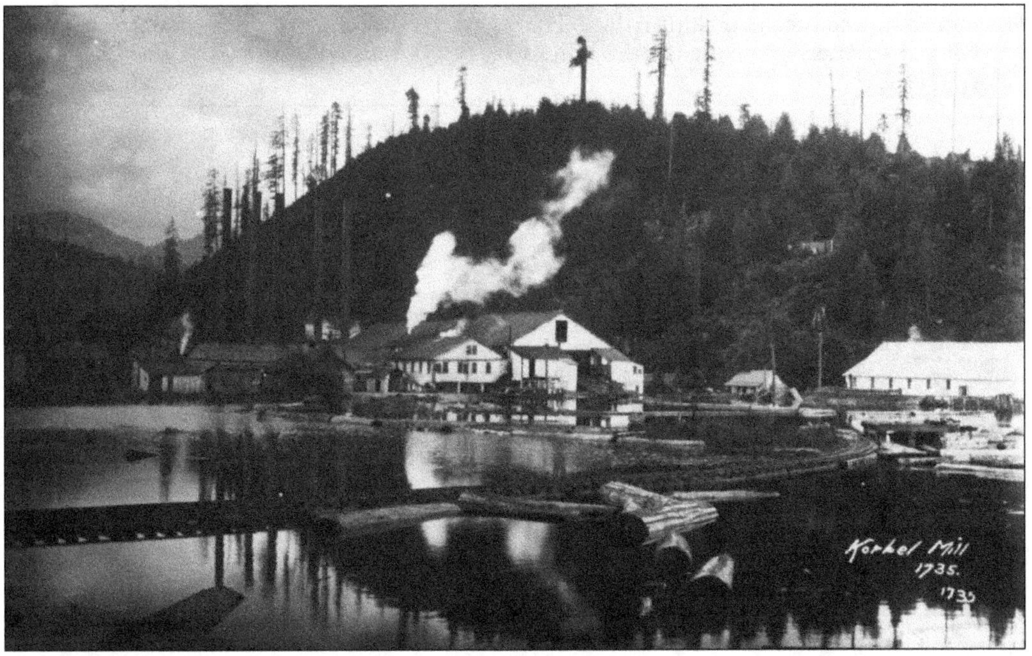

The Humboldt Lumber Mill Company was formed in 1883 by three brothers, Antone, Frank, and Joseph Korbel of Sonoma. They had purchased timberland on the North Fork of the Mad River. To provide housing for their employees, they built a company town, which became known as Korbel. The mill was called the "North Fork Mill" in the 1897 Redwood Lumber Manufacturers Association publication. (HSU.)

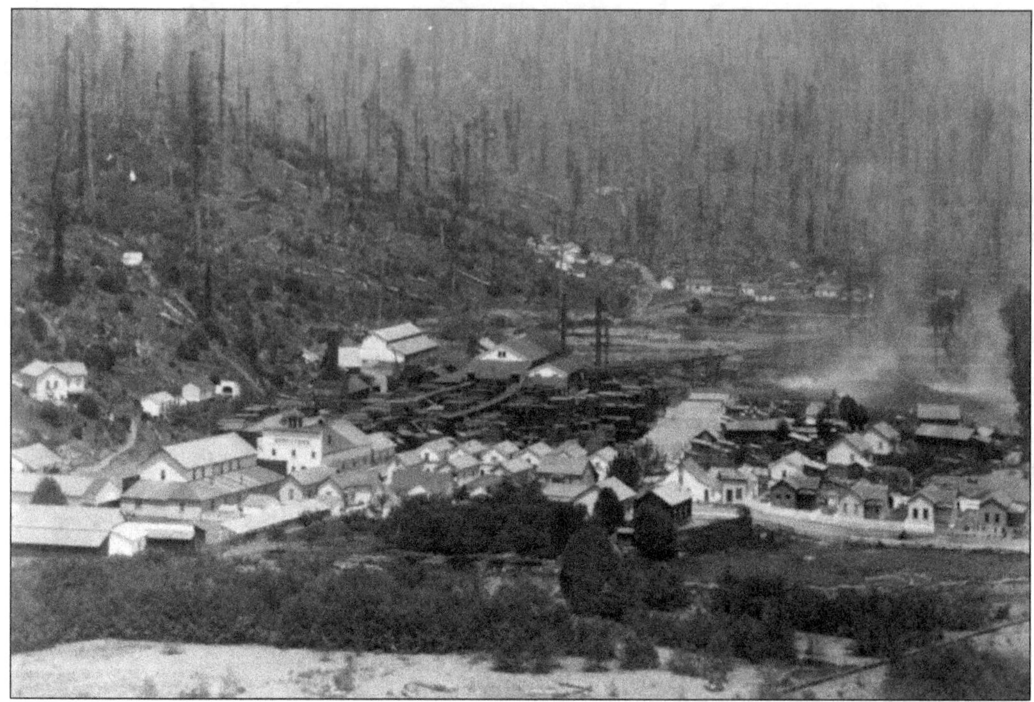

The lumber association observed that the North Fork Mill was "fitted with two bandsaws and other modern equipment and was capable of turning out 70,000 board feet of lumber per day." The mill also specialized in making redwood tanks, which were shipped throughout the country. The company pioneered the use of a dry kiln to dry boards rapidly, allowing the wood to be sold sooner. (HSU.)

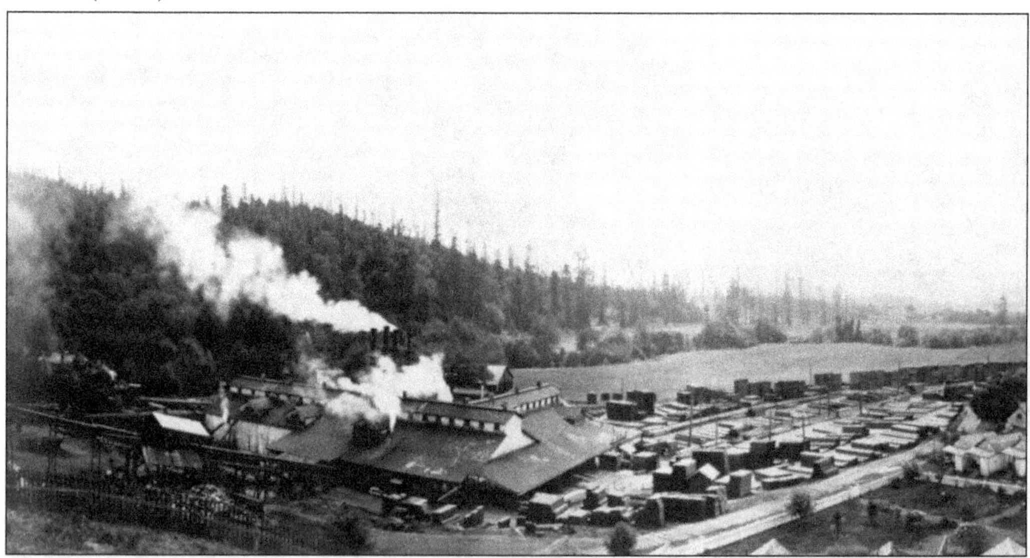

The year 1884 marked the arrival of the Eel River Valley Lumber Company near Fortuna, when E. Dodge, Euphronius Cousins, and H.D. Cousins formed a company. The mill was located along Strongs Creek. After installing a band saw, the facility had an output of nearly 50,000 feet of lumber a day. The company had 4,000 acres of timberland at its disposal and had three miles of railroad by 1897.

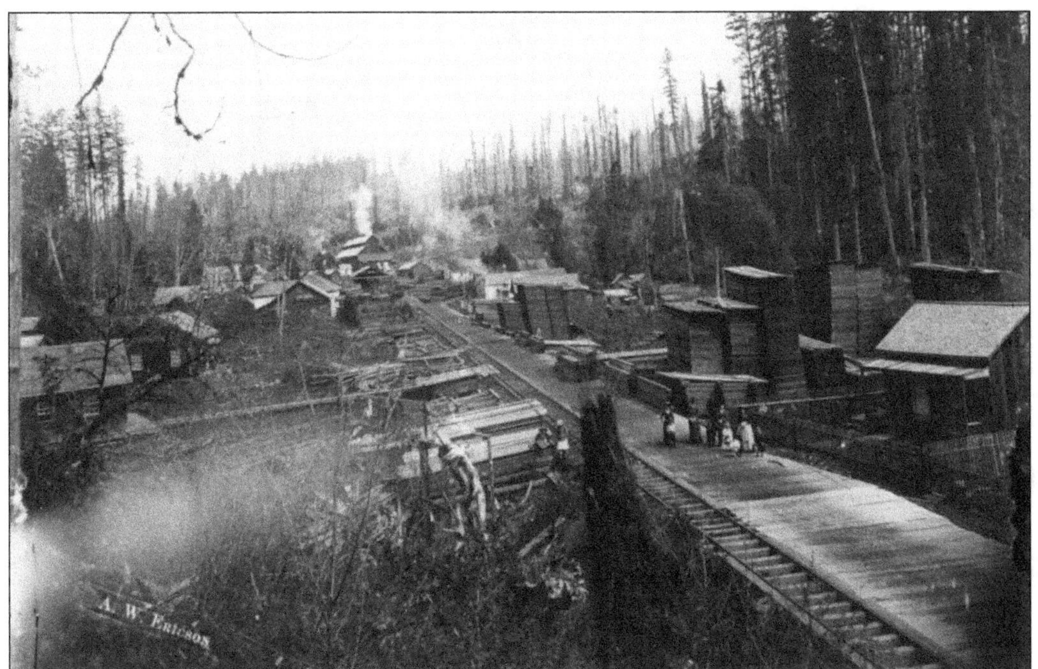

In 1885, Isaac Minor opened the Glendale Mill. In 1897, the Redwood Lumber Manufacturers Association reported: "this is one of the busiest little mills on the coast and is situated on Mad River. The mill derives its supply of logs from some fine timber on Mad River. Minor has developed a large trade with the Hawaiian Islands and is the heaviest shipper of Island cargoes in Humboldt." (HSU.)

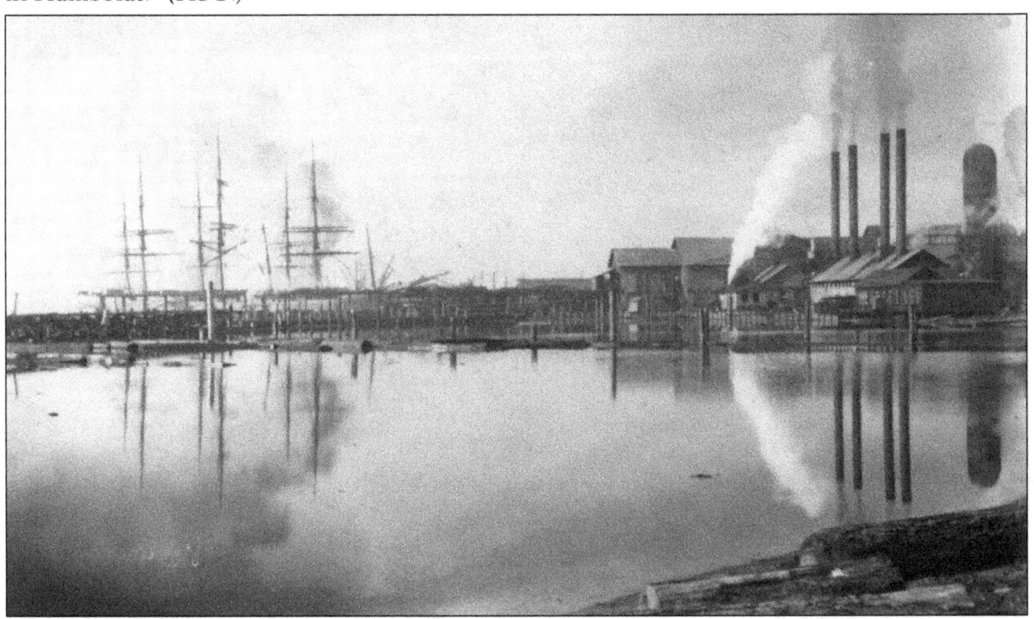

In 1892, John Vance's mill at the foot of G Street in Eureka burned down. He built a new mill across the bay from Eureka at Samoa. The new location allowed him to have his own docks and to utilize the latest technology. The redwood manufacturers noted that the mill had been "in operation only about two years and can therefore be called a modern mill." (HSU.)

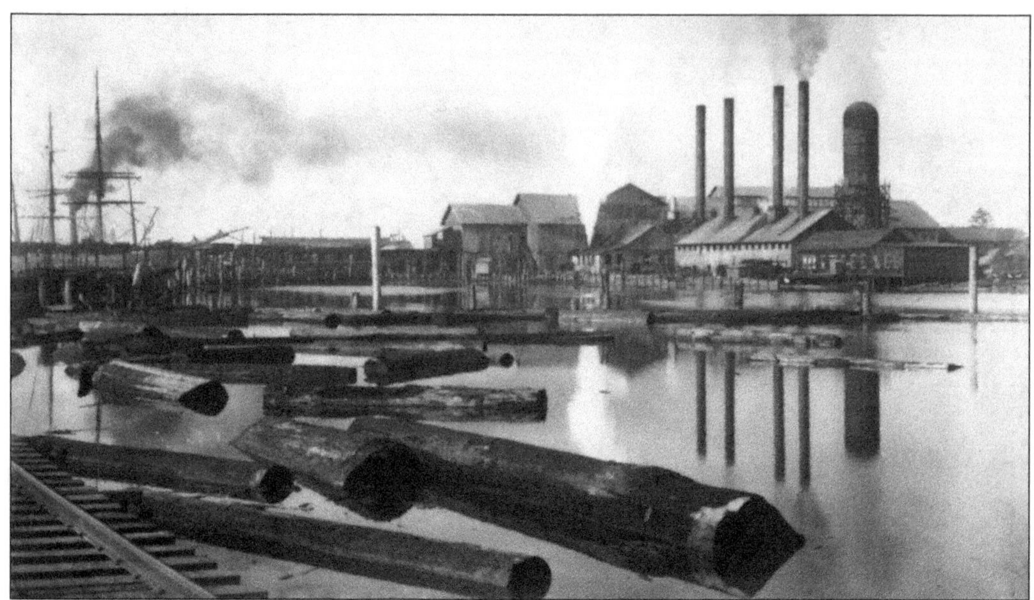

The Redwood Lumber Manufacturers Association credited John Vance's new mill as being "a single band sawmill, using also a band saw 'splitter,' and having besides all the latest improved auxiliary machinery, including a gang [saw] specially suited to redwood timber. In the construction of the mill special attention was given to facilities for economically handling the output." In 1900, Vance's heirs sold the mill to Andrew B. Hammond, who renamed it the Hammond Lumber Company in 1912. (HSU.)

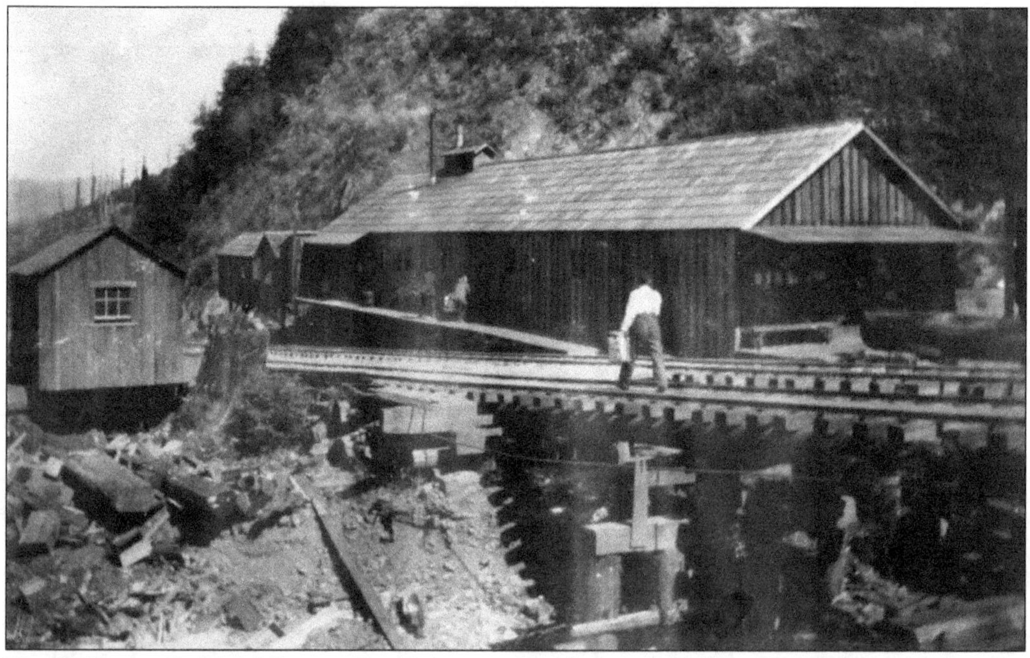

The Williams Creek Mill, near Ferndale, operated between 1892 and 1913. The owners, the Bryant brothers, also had a mill near Price Creek. The mill operated until the timber along the creek had been completely harvested. The Brookings Timber & Lumber Company of Brookings, Oregon, purchased the mill's machinery in 1913. (HSU.)

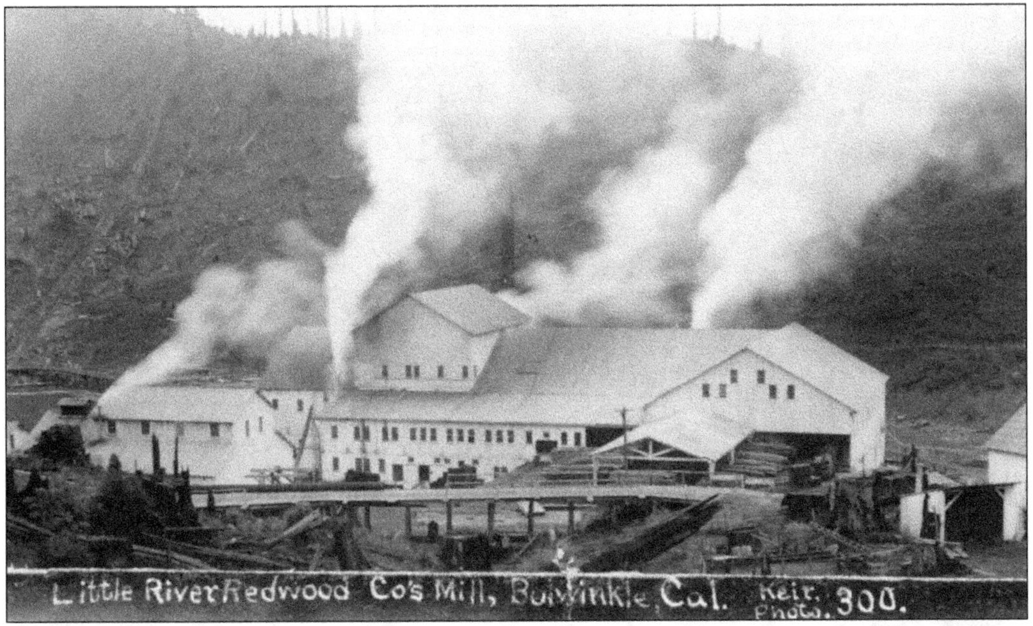

The Little River Lumber Company was created in 1893 by a conglomerate of Canadian and New York investors headquartered in Tonawanda, New York. A mill was built in 1906 along Little River. The company purchased 3,400 acres of lumber from Conrad Bullwinkel for its woods operations. They constructed a company town, Bullwinkle, using a variation of Conrad Bullwinkel's name. Later renamed Crannell, the town was featured in four movie adaptations of Peter Kyne's novel *The Valley of the Giants.*

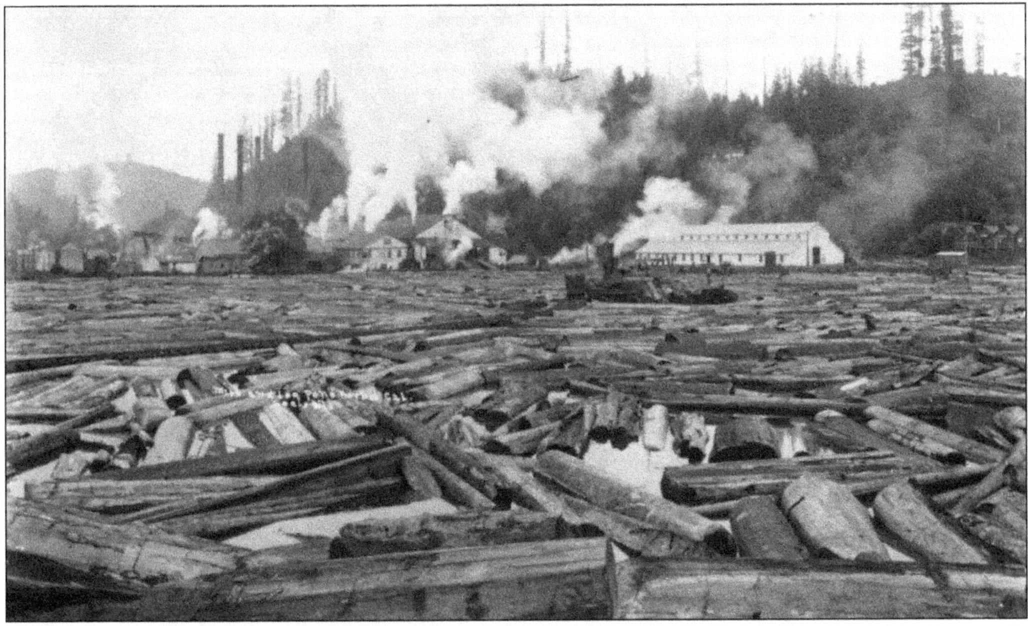

The early 1900s was a period of mergers for the mills of Humboldt County. In 1902, the Riverside Mill of Chandler and the Korbel brothers' Humboldt Lumber Company merged to become the Northern Redwood Lumber Company. Merged mills were more competitive in the marketplace, and these combinations eliminated much of their competition. (HSU.)

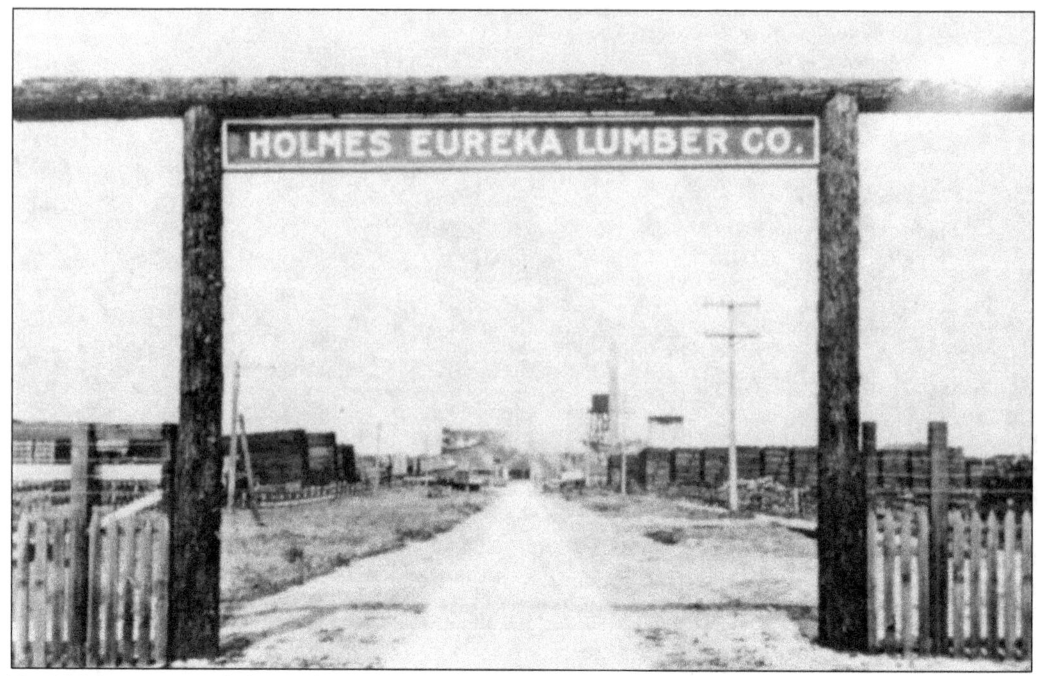

Fred Holmes created the Holmes-Eureka Lumber Company in 1903. Its location is now the site of the Bayshore Mall in Eureka. When opened in 1904, the mill's daily output was 70,000 board feet of lumber. The company owned extensive timber rights along the Eel River. These forestlands were accessed along the Pacific Lumber Company's rail line to Shively and via a trestle across the Eel River to Holmes Flat. (HCHS.)

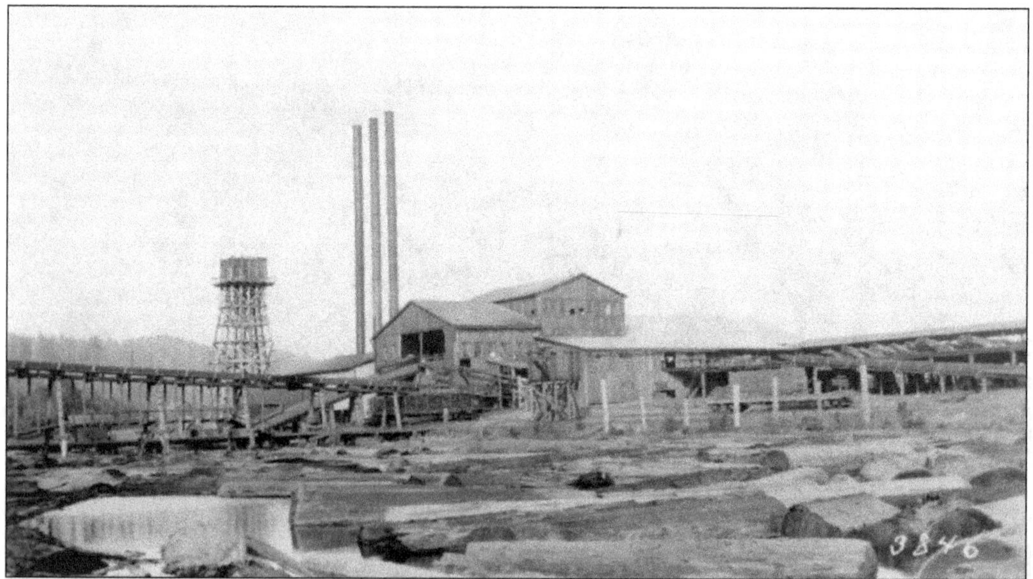

The Metropolitan Mill was built near the mouth of the Van Duzen River, south of Alton. Similar to Holmes-Eureka, the company took advantage of the railroad to Eureka, accessing lands along Slater Creek with a seasonal summer bridge. A coalition of businessmen from Minnesota formed the company, naming it after their hometown, Metropolitan, Minnesota. Once its timber holdings had been harvested, the mill closed in 1925.

Two

Making Lumber

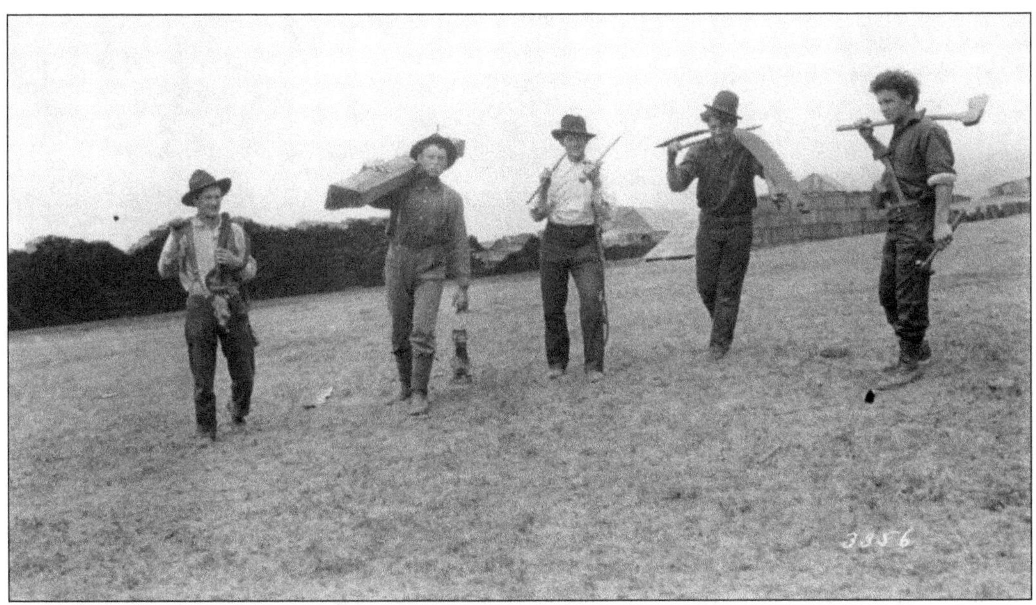

Logging the redwoods required skilled woodsmen. However, woods operations were limited to late spring through early fall, as winter rains made logging difficult. Many workers left the region, spending winters in San Francisco or farther south. When spring arrived, timber companies offered woodsmen free transportation north on the companies' lumber ships. Other workers wintered over in Humboldt, creating farms and ranches. (HSU.)

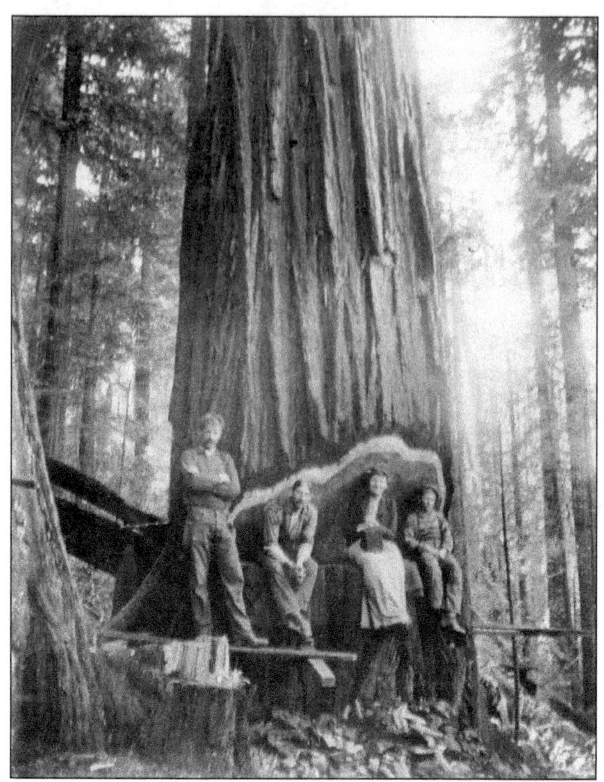

Loggers encountered many challenges. The base of a redwood features a large "butt swell" with dense wood. Prone to sink in millponds, the butt swell was often larger than mills could accommodate. Loggers discovered that, above this dense portion of the tree, the wood was easier to chop. To reach the softer wood, a scaffolding or staging was built above the butt swell. In this photograph, Wylie Gordon stands at left.

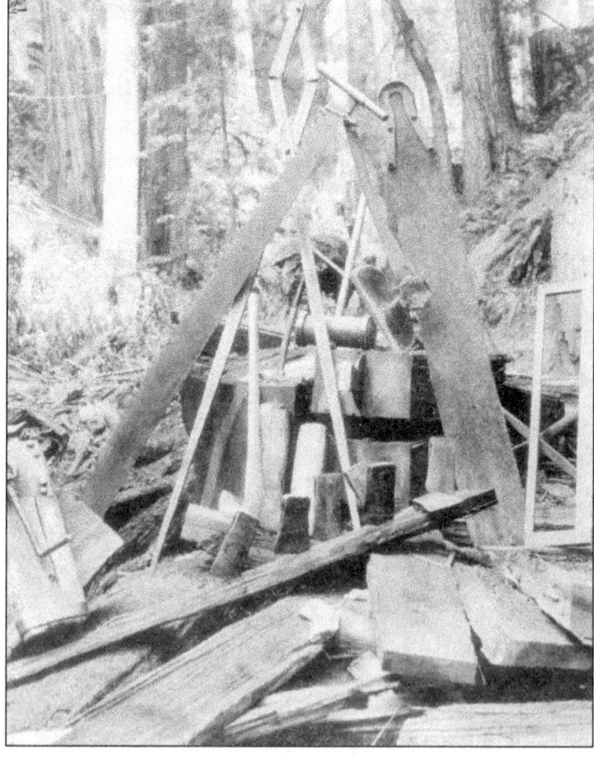

Loggers' tools included axes, mauls, wedges, two-handled saws, and gunning or sighting sticks. Specialized equipment included cork boots with nails in the soles for traction. The long board with a metal tip at right was part of the staging or springboards built up around the tree to get above the butt swell. The metal tip was pushed into the tree, holding the board in place. Springboard notches are still found in stumps from this era. (HRIA.)

The first challenge facing redwood loggers was cutting through the tough, fibrous bark of the redwood tree. Axes were used to hack through bark that could be up to two feet thick. The bark is impervious to insects and protects the tree from burning, as it is fire resistant. In fact, an early use of bark was as insulation for homes and schools.

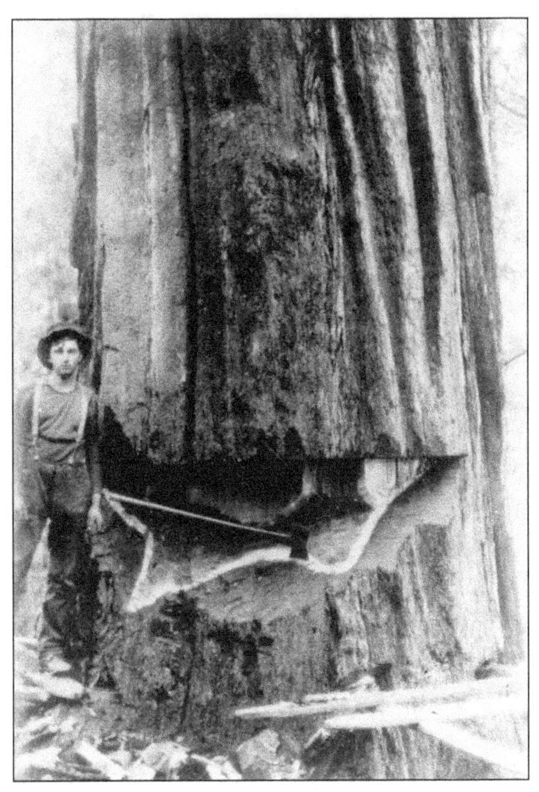

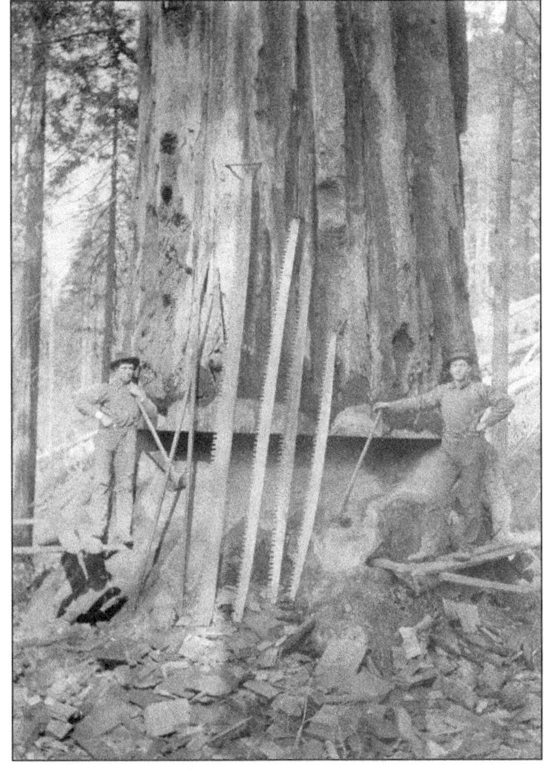

From the 1850s to the 1870s, redwoods were harvested only by ax. The crosscut saw came into use in the late 1870s, when new technology produced blades long enough and sturdy enough to tackle trees with girths of over 20 feet. The saws used on this tree at Pepperwood by fallers Clyde Langles and W.C. Smith in 1905 are 10 feet, 12 feet, 14 feet, and 16 feet in length. (HCHS.)

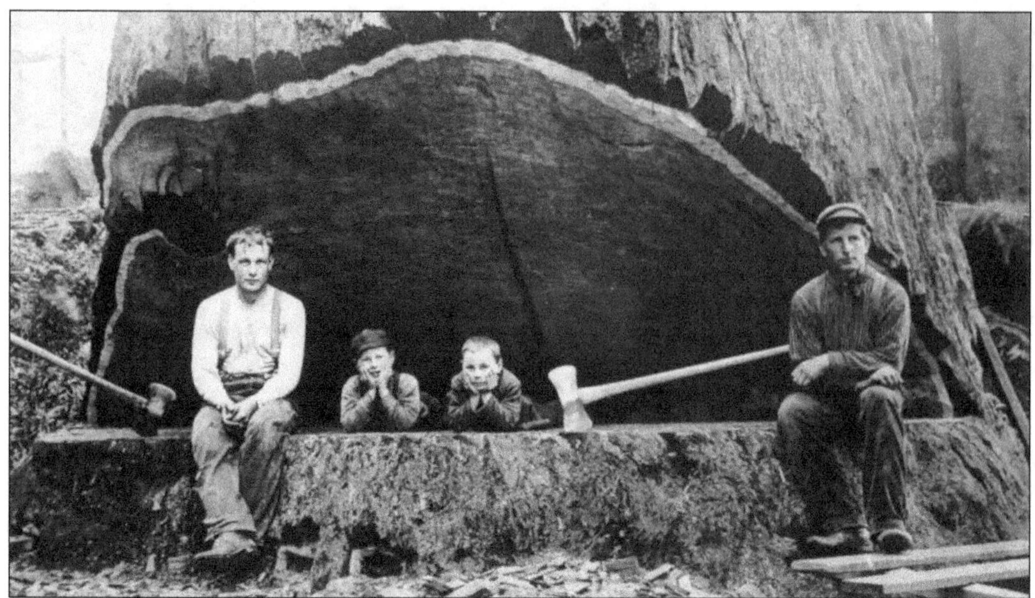

The double-bitted ax seen here was the largest and heaviest ax used in the US lumber industry in the late 1800s, weighing three to four pounds. The 38- to 42-inch-long hickory handles gave redwood choppers greater leverage. Guy Larison (far right), his brother Jim (far left), and Guy's sons Mervin (second from left) and Leonard demonstrate the size of undercuts and axes at Monument Flat near Rio Dell.

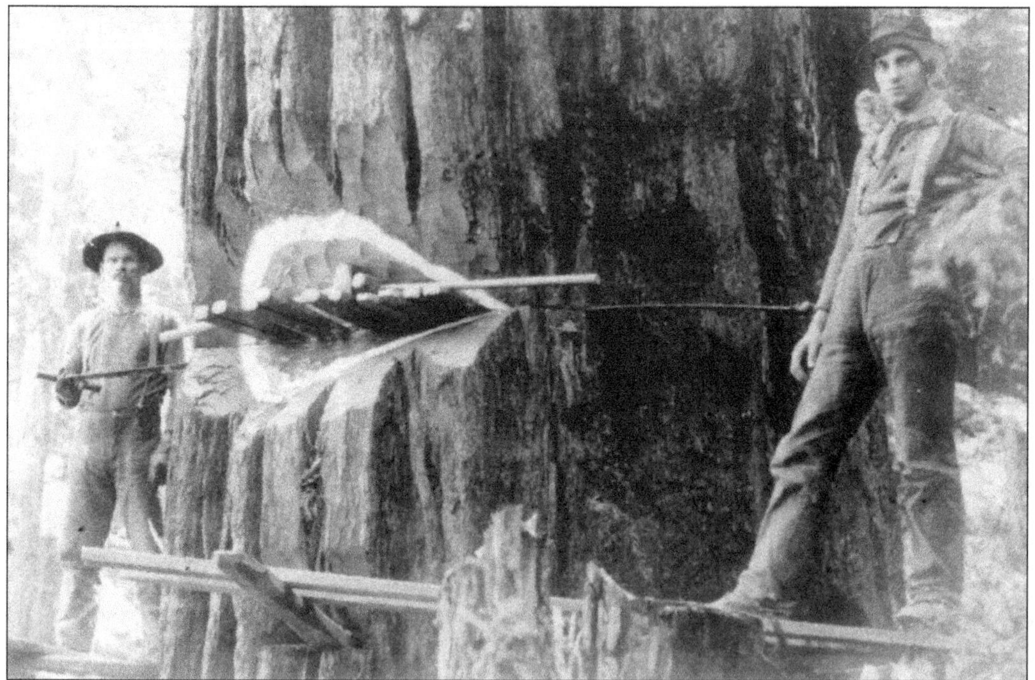

Choppers made the undercut, hewn on the side of the tree where it was to fall. Originally, axes were used to make the back cut on the opposite side of the tree. After 1878, back cuts were made using "misery whip" saws. Steel wedges were driven into the cut to take pressure off the saw blade. The wedges also served to direct the tree's fall in the desired direction.

Redwood is friable, splitting into many pieces if loggers are not careful. Fallers used a gunning stick—the parallelogram the man at center is holding—to determine where the tree would fall. Next, a place for the tree to land was created, using dirt and branches to form a "bed" for the tree, ensuring little or no breakage. (HSU.)

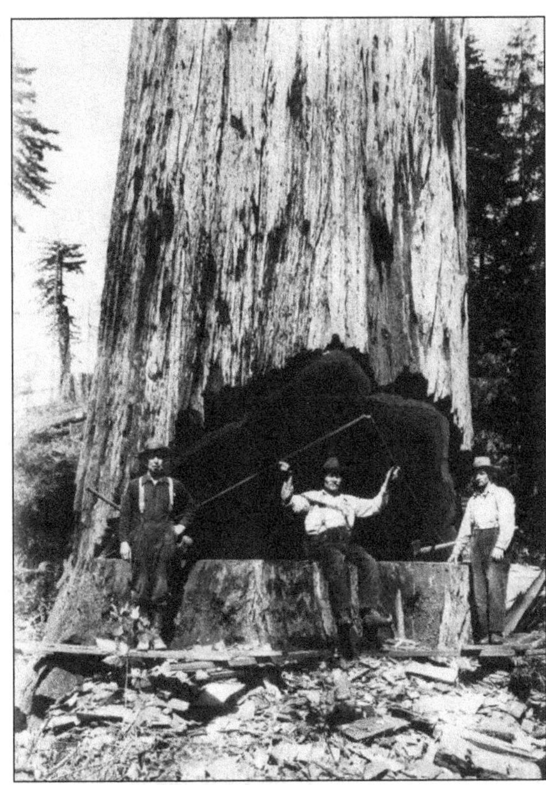

Wastage was a by-product of early logging operations, with 25 percent of the tree, the stump, and the treetop being left in the woods. A common practice according to the 1886 *Business Directory of Humboldt County* was that "a fire [was] run over the ground to burn up the bark and rubbish. Green redwood burns with such difficulty that the good logs are rarely affected by the fire." (HRIA.)

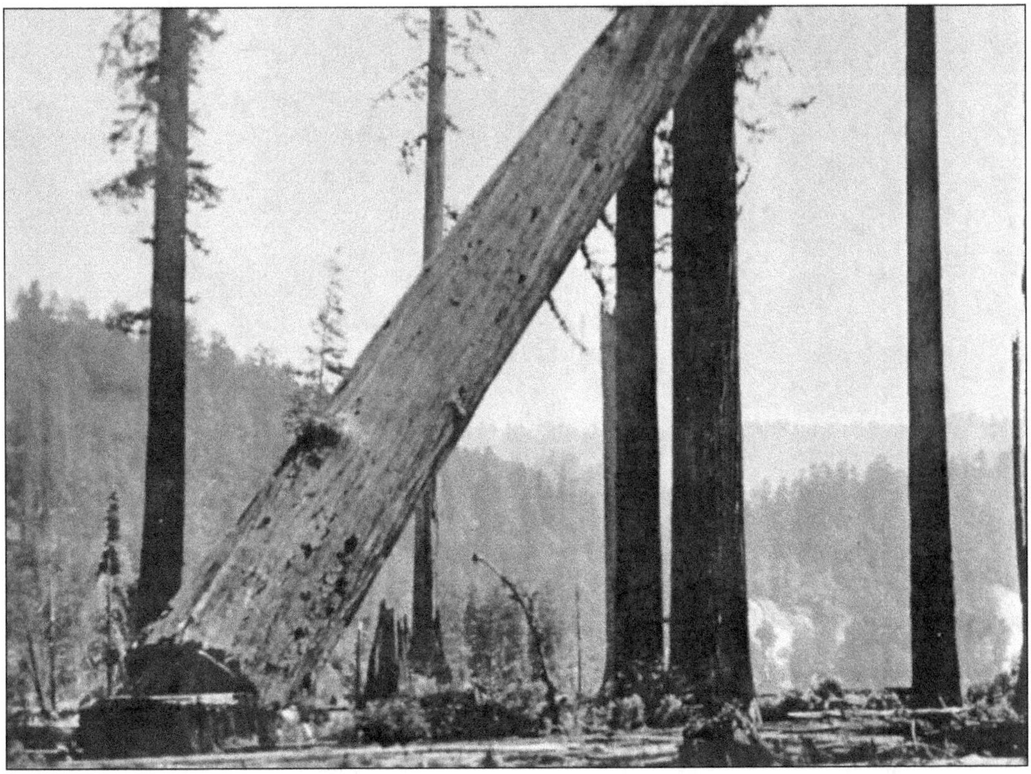

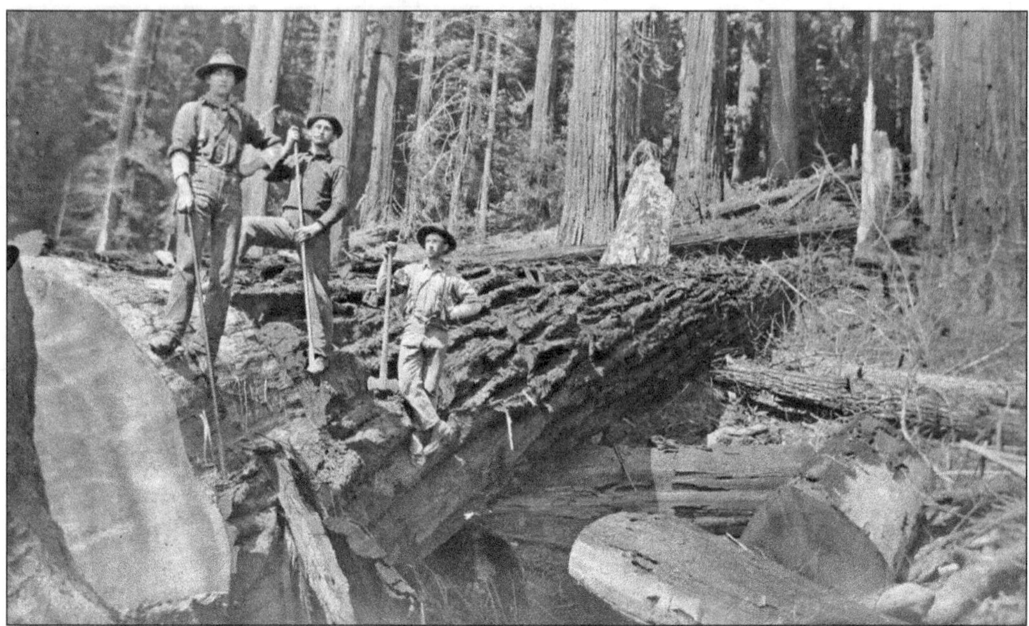

The Redwood Lumber Manufacturers Association described readying logs for transport in 1897: "First there are the ringers who cut circles through the bark around the trees at such distances apart as will enable the peelers who follow, to remove the bark easily." Using six-foot iron bars, peelers like W.C. Smith and his crew, seen here at Pepperwood in 1905, removed the bark, making the log lighter for oxen pulling it and less likely to tangle in debris. (HCHS.)

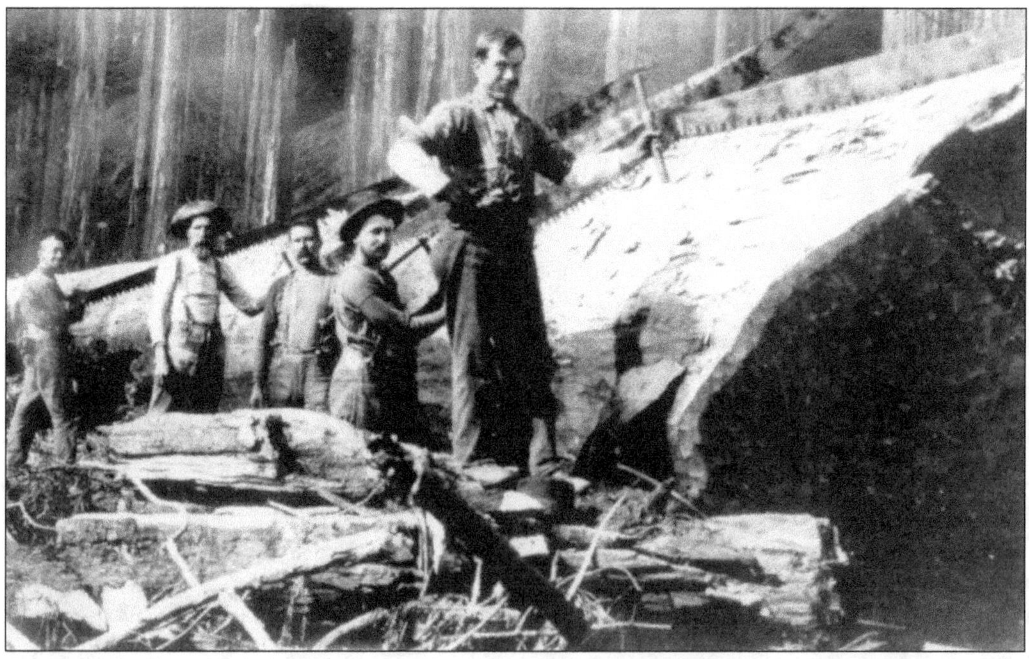

Once the log was peeled, sawyers sawed or "bucked" it into manageable lengths. The lumber association noted that, "on account of the great diameter and consequent difficulty in handling, these logs are rarely cut to exceed 20 to 24 feet long, and few of the redwood mills are built to saw logs over those lengths."

Humboldt loggers experimented with methods of transporting logs. Rafting logs in the bay was successful, but river rafting was not, as high waters caused many of the trees to wash out to sea. Damming creeks and floating trees to a mill was also prone to mishap. Mill owners turned to using oxen, mules, or horses to pull logs to mills. (HSU.)

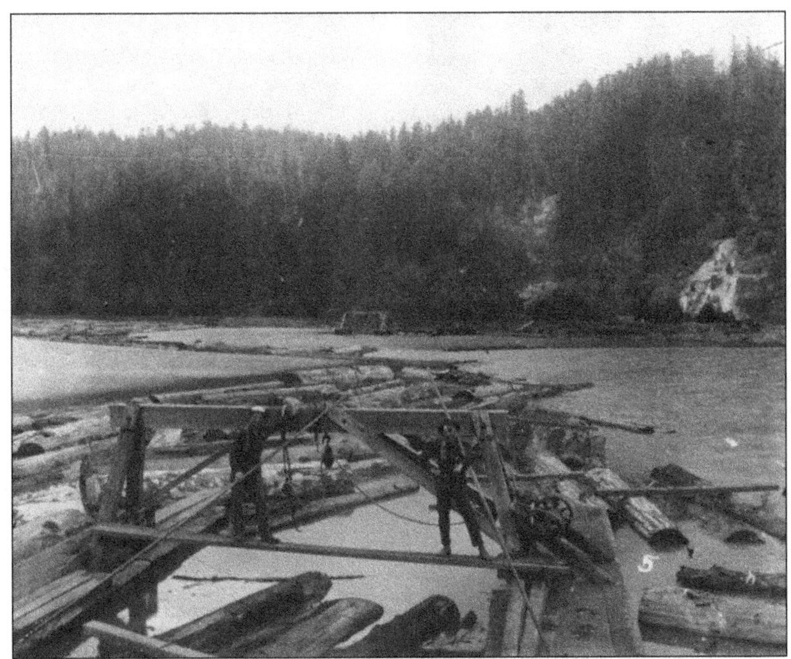

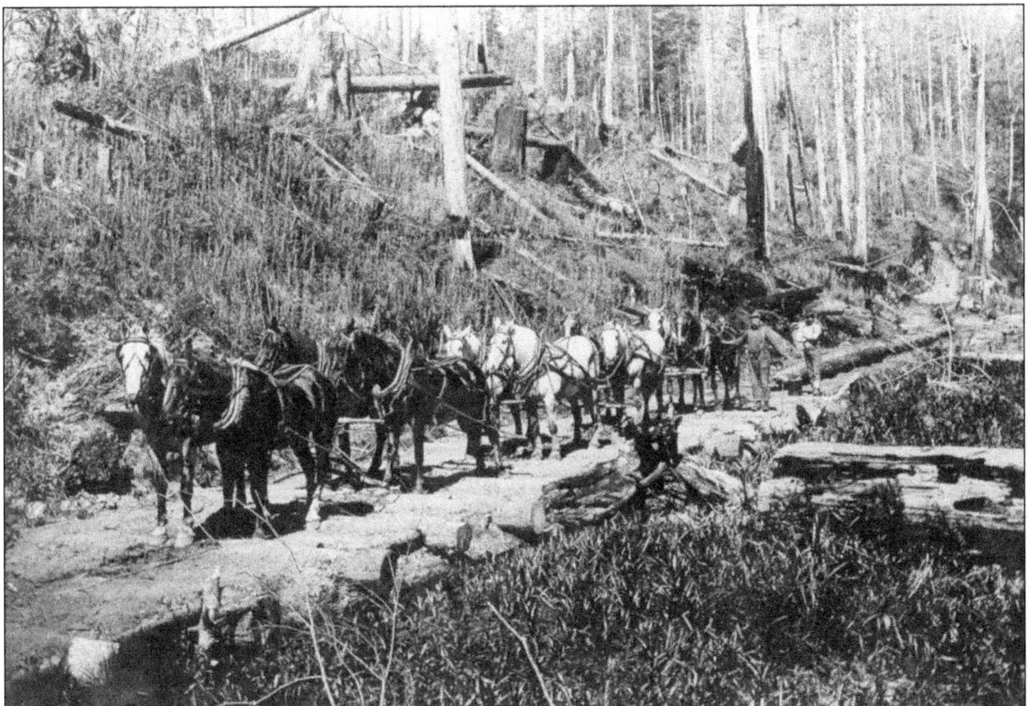

A train of logs was formed, using blocks, tackles, and jackscrews, which draft animals pulled to mills or railroad landings. Skilled teamsters or "bull punchers" were often the highest-paid men in the woods, commanding monthly wages of up to $250. One remarkable load occurred in 1887, when teamster A.A. Marks hauled seven logs to Humboldt Bay with five yoke of oxen, a feat described by the Redwood Lumber Manufacturers Association in 1897. (HCHS.)

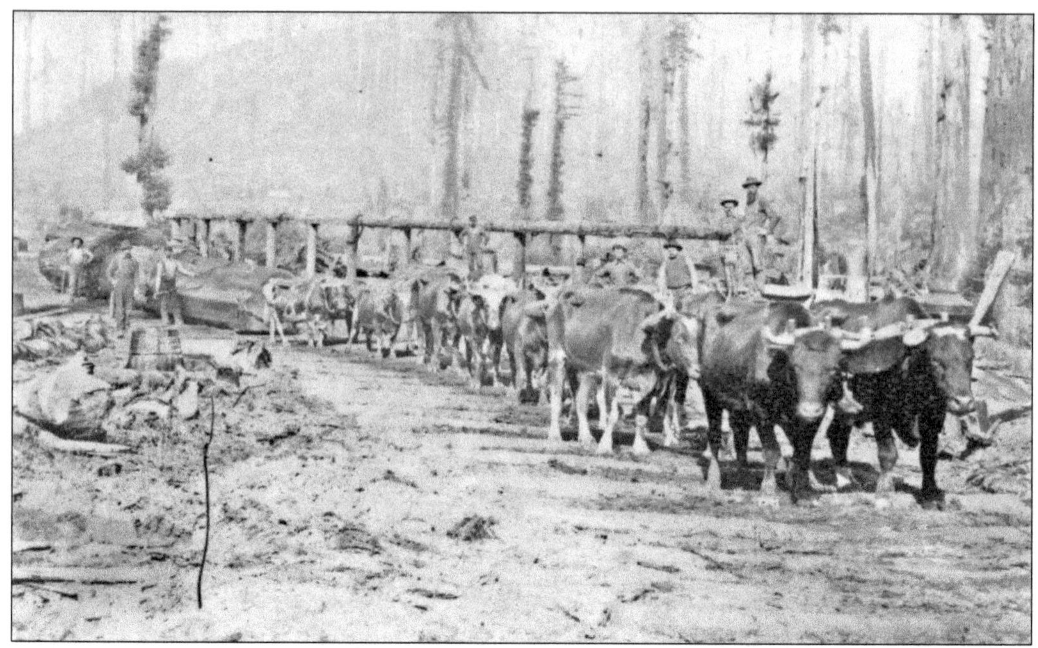

Before logs were hauled, a special "corduroy" road was built. The manufacturers association explained the process: "For handling these monsters, no ordinary road will answer. It must be wide and smooth as a turnpike; all rocks and roots must be carefully removed, all the hollows and gullies filled up." Road preparation was critical, since "no wheeled vehicle of any kind is used in transporting the logs in the woods; they are simply snaked along over the ground."

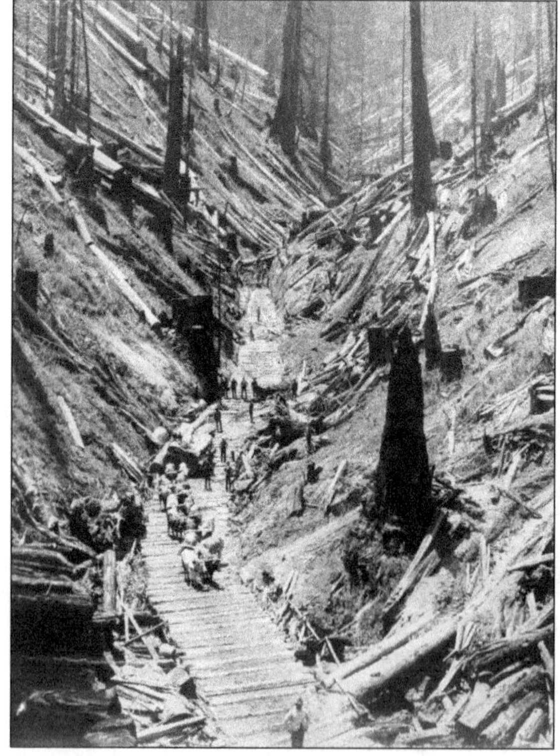

Logs of Douglas fir or oak were placed horizontally about four feet apart to create the road. According to Thomas Moungovan in *Logging with Oxen Teams*, if a skid road was used for a short time, any wood would do; for a more permanent road, redwood saplings were utilized. Greg Gordon, author of *When Money Grew on Trees*, believes that corduroy roads helped protect the environment from damage by the logs' passage.

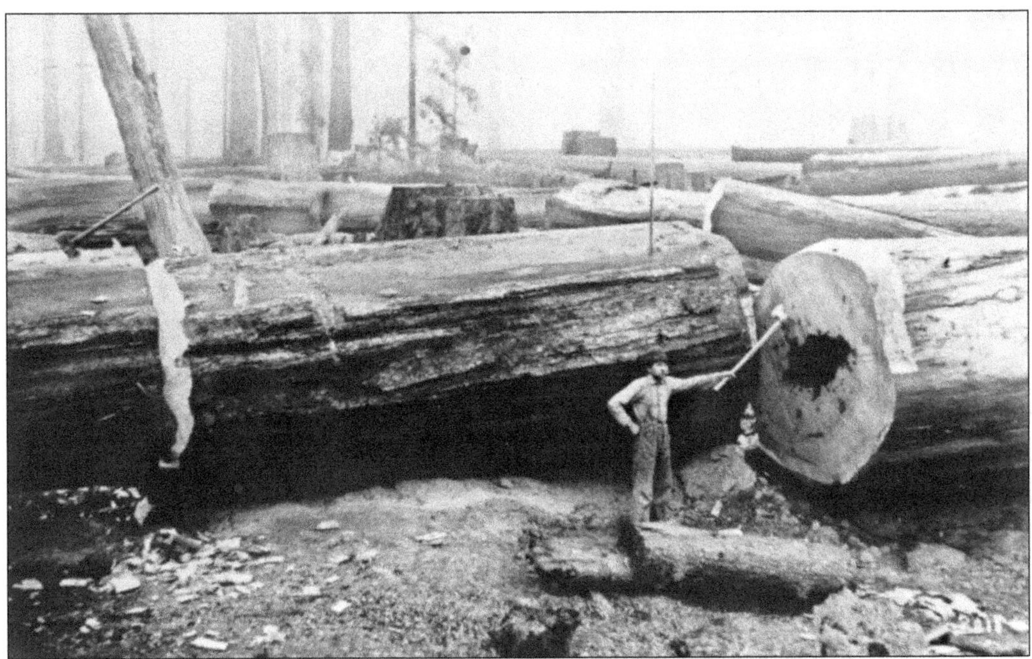

In addition to corduroy road requirements, logs had to be modified to facilitate a smoother pull. In an account of working with bull teams, Fred Pritchard recalled that "the big logs had to be rolled around until they found the ride . . . then with a broad ax, the ride was hewed." The "ride" was the flattest side of the log, which would drag the easiest.

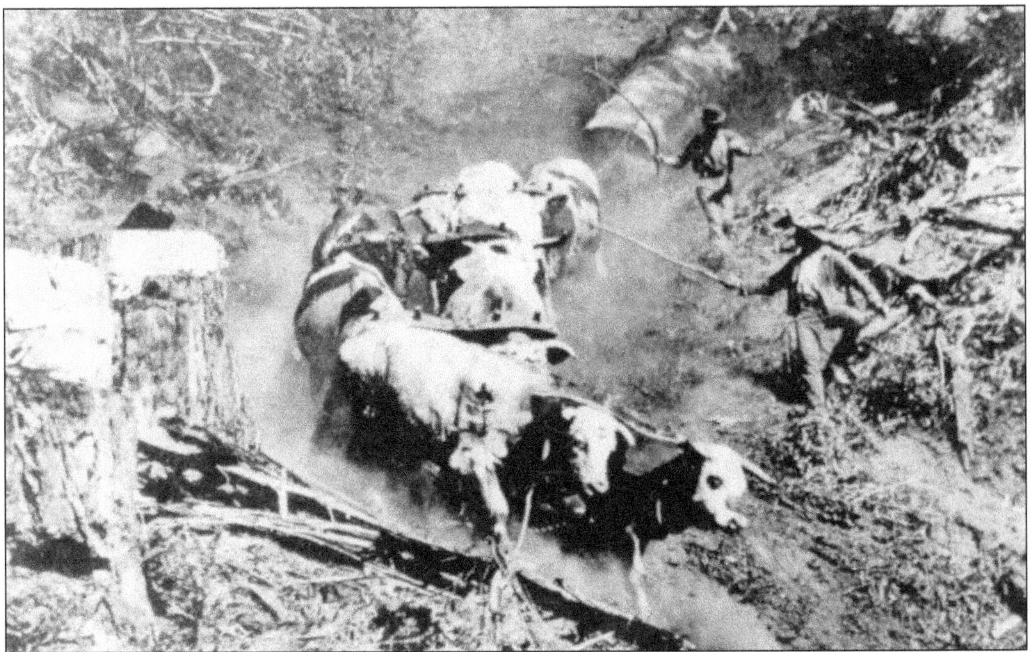

A bull team usually consisted of six to eight yoke, or pair, of oxen. Thomas Moungovan noted that oxen "were generally Brindle Durham, Durham or Durham with Ayrshire bulls and ranged in weight from fourteen to eighteen hundred pounds." William St. Clair's team illustrates the use of oxen. The wheelers, the last yoke next to the load, were used to hold the logs back.

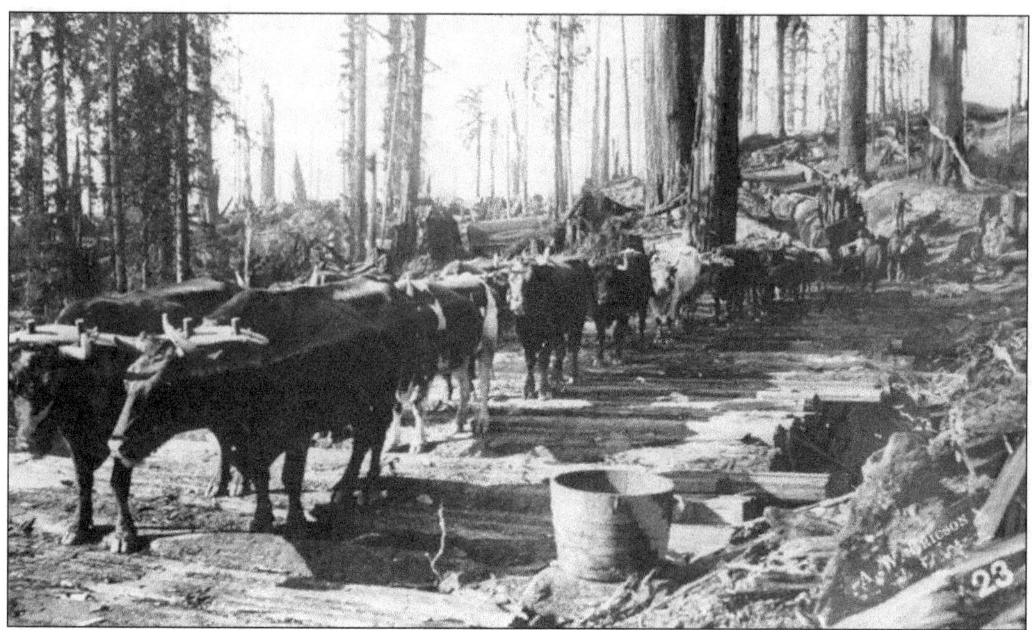

The most important yoke team were the leaders, who responded to the bull puncher's voice commands, such as "haw" for left turns and "gee" for right. The *Humboldt Beacon* noted in a 1915 article that one Korbel bull puncher named Dickey "invented a set of swaying motions by means of which he taught his oxen to obey his will . . . they were as meaningless to observers as they were entirely comprehensible to the brutes." (HSU.)

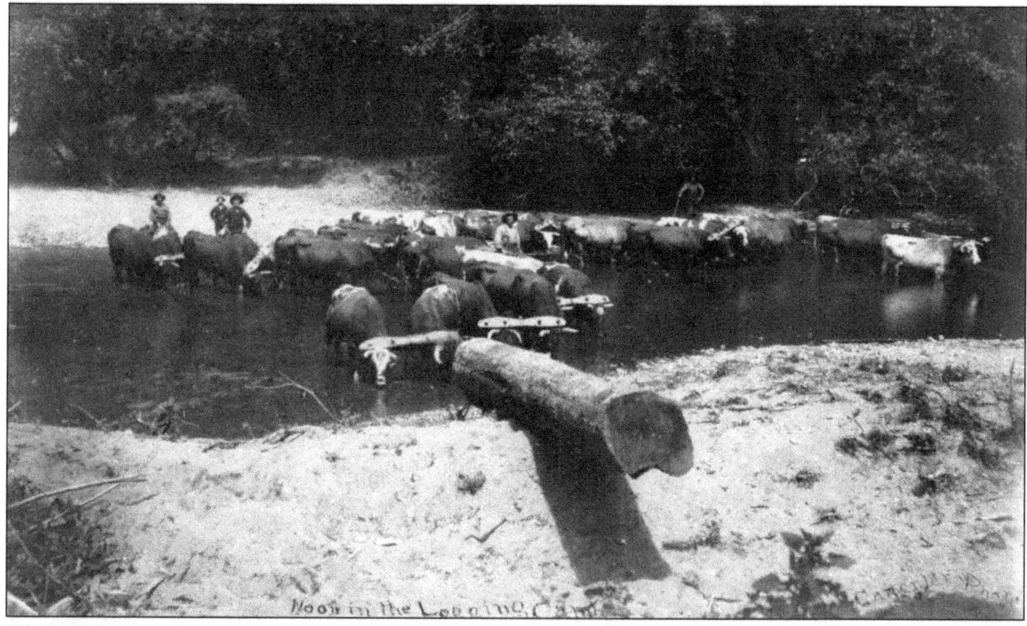

This photograph, captioned "Noon in the Logging Camp," reflects the care given to oxen. According to Fred Pritchard, "a shed [was] built to put the team in at noon." At lunchtime, "the chain tender and water slinger cleaned and brushed up the team." Each morning, the crew checked and cleaned the harness and oiled the bow keys. Additionally, oxen were shod yearly, to help protect their hooves and improve traction. (HSU.)

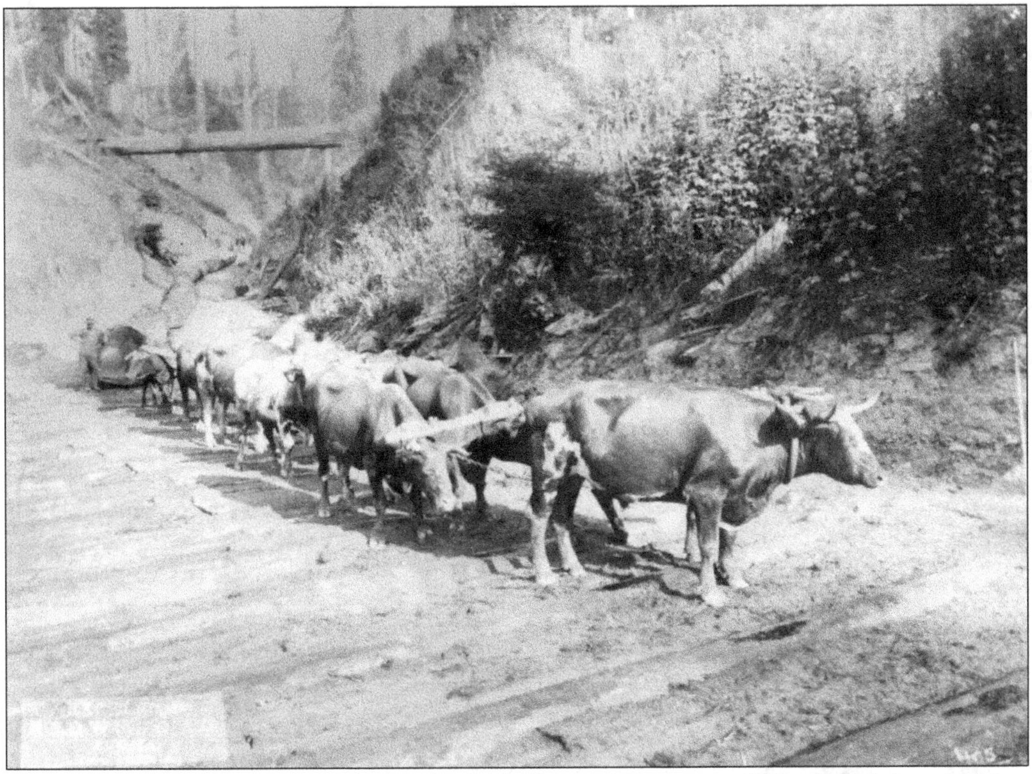

In 1915, the *Humboldt Beacon* observed, "the bull puncher was usually kind and thoughtful to his animals, but sometimes was capable of considerable cruelty when in a tight place." One well-known bull puncher, George Davis, was observed "walking over their backs with his cork shoes, yelling and swearing at them like mad to get them to start a load." (HSU.)

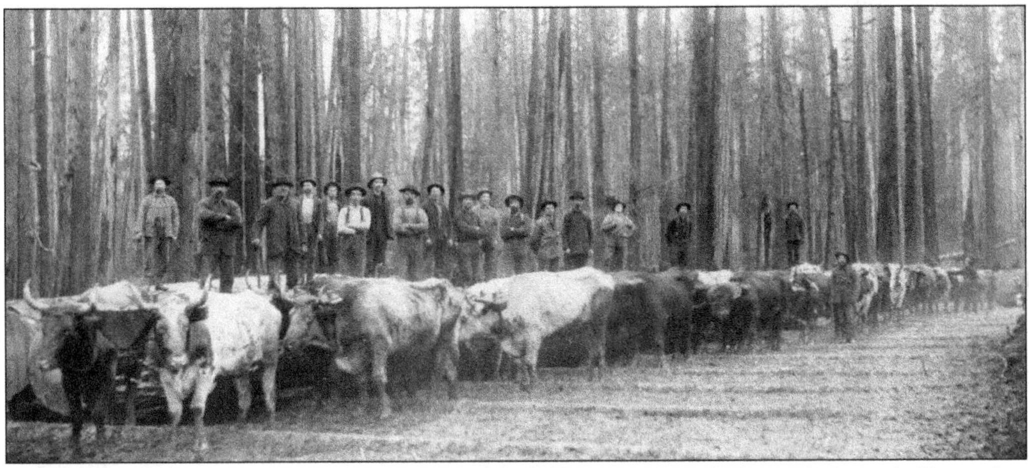

A specialized crew guided bull teams. The *Humboldt Beacon* in 1915 noted that a bull puncher possessed a "high efficiency in his way, requiring the rare talent of an animal trainer, though this talent was generally obscured by a coarse exterior and a volubility of oaths sometimes horrifying." Cursing seems to have been a job necessity; in 1901, the *Overland Monthly* characterized the bull puncher as being "artistically profane." (HSU.)

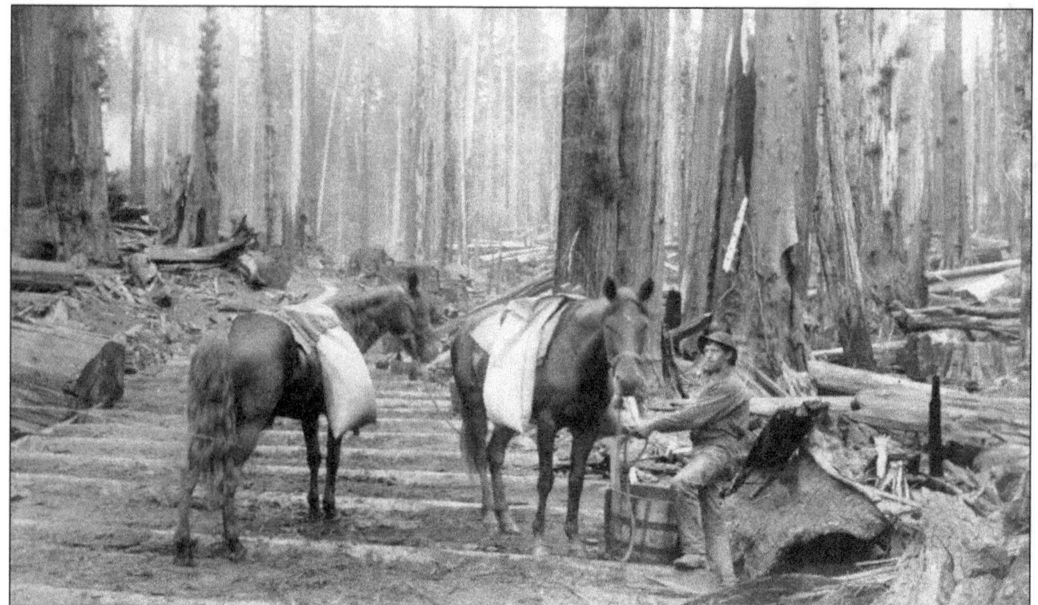

Other crewmen in a bull team included a chain tender, two water slingers, and a waterbuck. The suglar, who chained the load, rode the first log while holding a chain or "rough lock" as a brake. To minimize friction, the roadway was "greased" or watered. Water tubs were placed every 60 feet, and water slingers "greased the skids" and filled the tubs, as seen here. (HSU.)

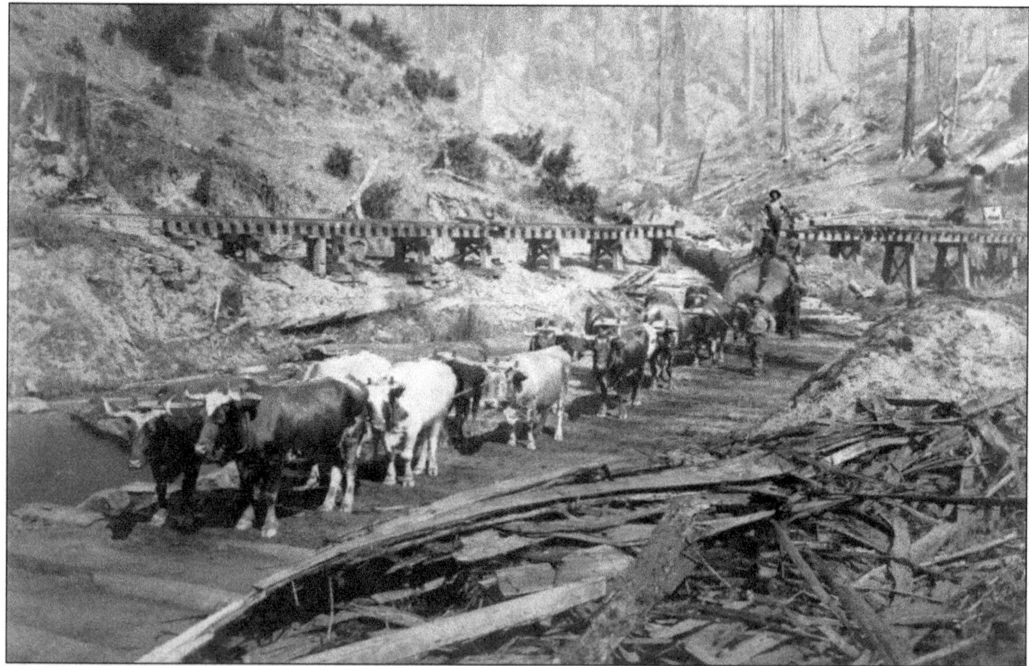

The Redwood Manufacturers Association in 1897 described the action of the oxen pulling the logs: "Here are ten yoke of sturdy oxen, and behind them the trains of ten to fifteen great logs, of all sizes from four to ten feet in diameter, fastened with strong 'dogs' and chains, one behind the other." The "dogs" were iron hooks hammered into logs for the chains to connect the "train" together. (HSU.)

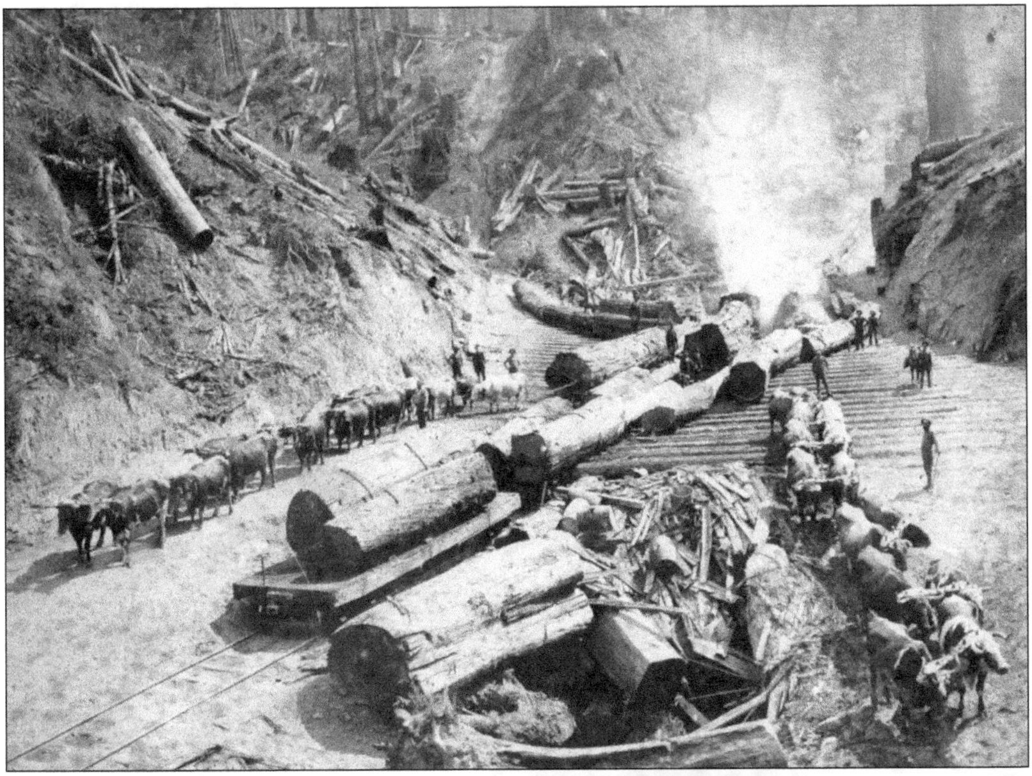

The manufacturers association explained the team driver's task: "The driver walks up and down the length of his team, speaking softly to this or that one by name, until he sees that every animal is bearing equally on the yoke. Now for it! He shouts and yells, curses and swears . . . while amid the din and uproar every beast strains himself to the utmost." Bull teams averaged about two miles per hour. (HSU.)

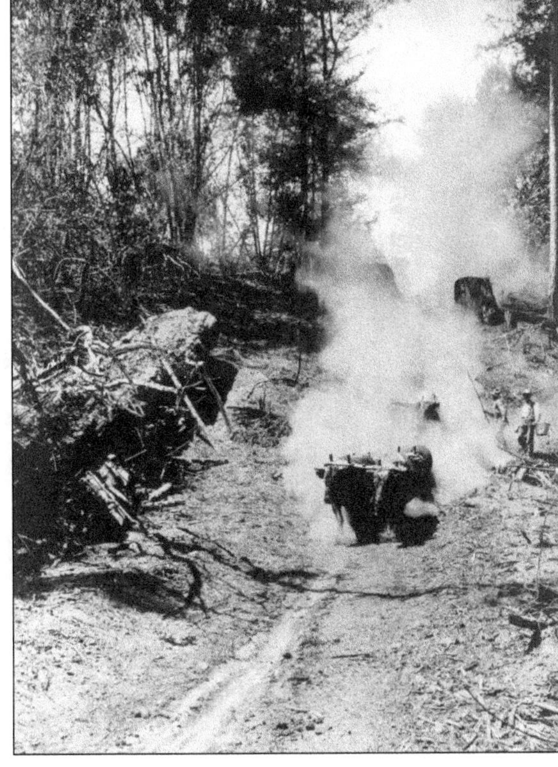

Hauling logs with oxen was dangerous, as described in a 1915 article in the *Humboldt Beacon*: "Sometimes the string of logs would start on its own accord and, gaining momentum, would compel the oxen to break into a run to avoid being crushed by the oncoming load." Usually, the oxen outran disaster, "but occasionally the logs would catch them, and, plowing through, would break horns and hides and leave masses of quivering flesh in their wake."

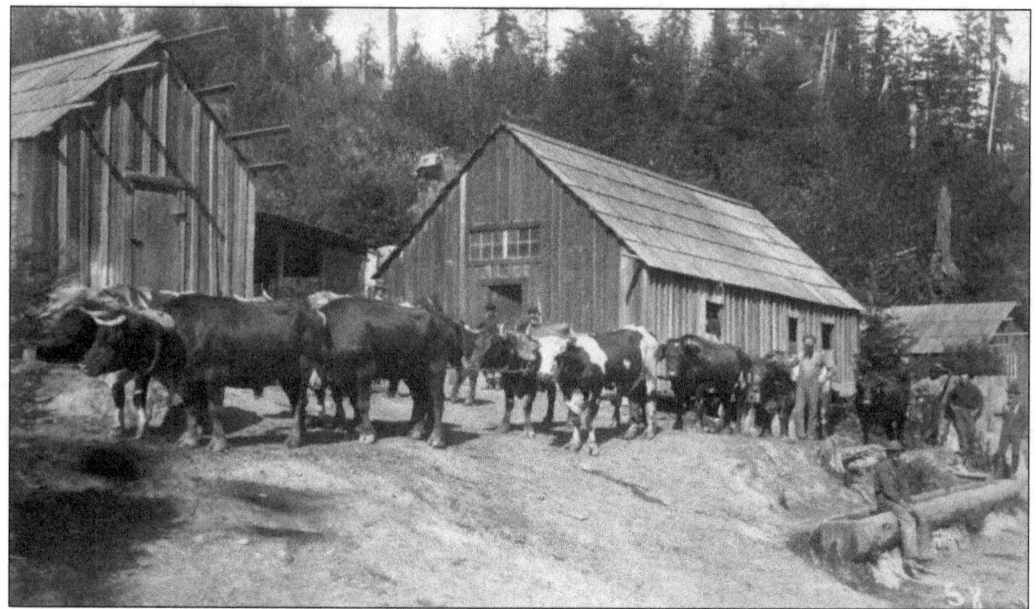

Oxen were used to haul logs for nearly 50 years. Gradually eliminated as Dolbeer's upright steam engine became more popular, the bull teams' importance remains in loggers' lexicons. "Bull" is an adjective used to describe anything strong or important. The boss was known as the "bull of the woods," the largest upright steam engine was a "bull donkey," and, when tractor crawlers replaced steam engines, they became "bulldozers." (HSU.)

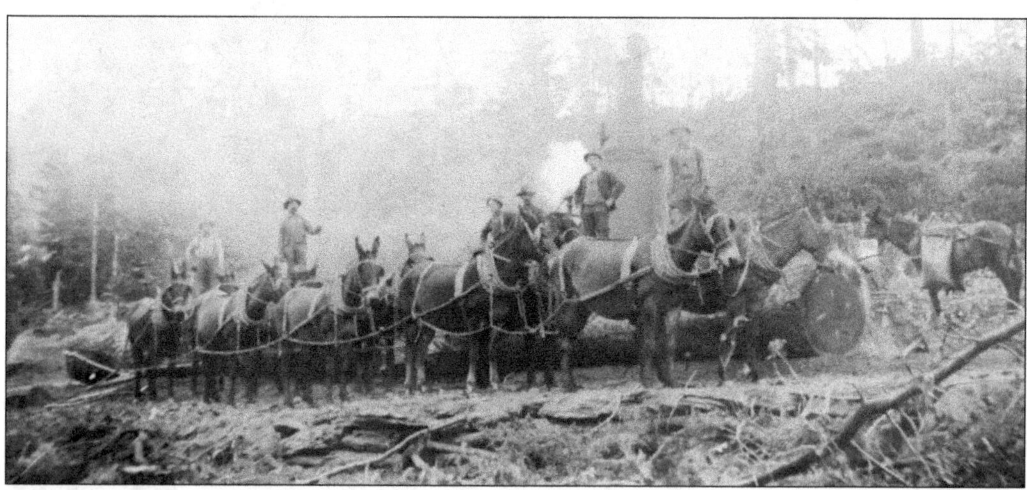

In the late 1870s, redwoods were being felled farther away from mills, resulting in logs being hauled over longer distances. In 1881, John Dolbeer invented and patented the upright steam, or donkey, engine to speed up log transportation. Dolbeer modified a donkey engine, a subsidiary engine from a steamship, to pull and load logs. On ships, the term "donkey" arose since it produced less power than a horse.

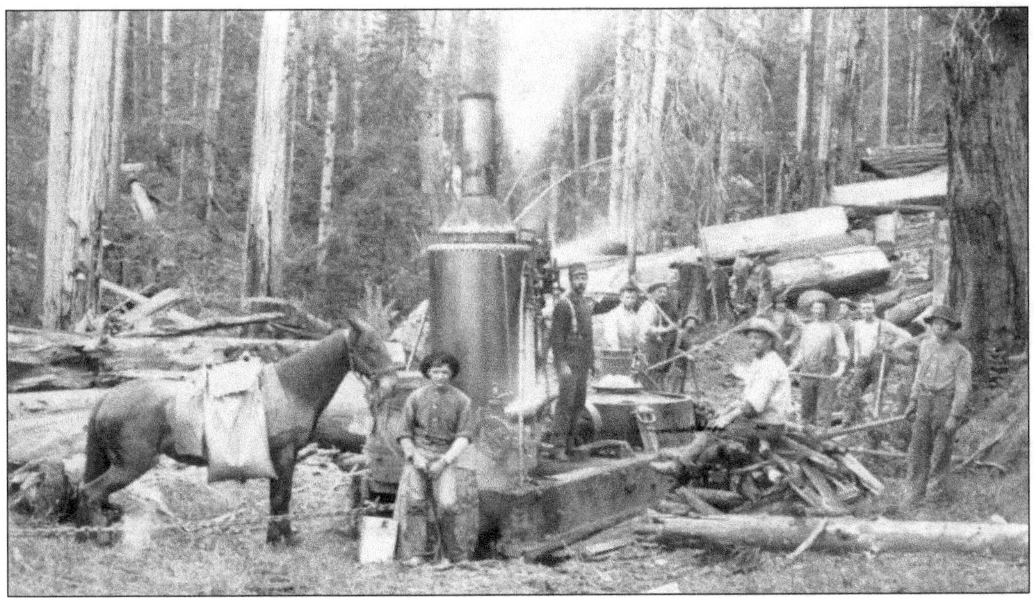

Although welcomed in woods operations with great acclaim, Dolbeer's invention had limitations. The engine had a single spool, requiring a mule or horse to bring back the chains or rope used to pull the logs, as illustrated by this woods crew for Isaac Minor's Glendale Mill. Donkey engines were first built in San Francisco by the firm Marshalz & Cantrell. Later versions were built at the Eureka Foundry. (HSU.)

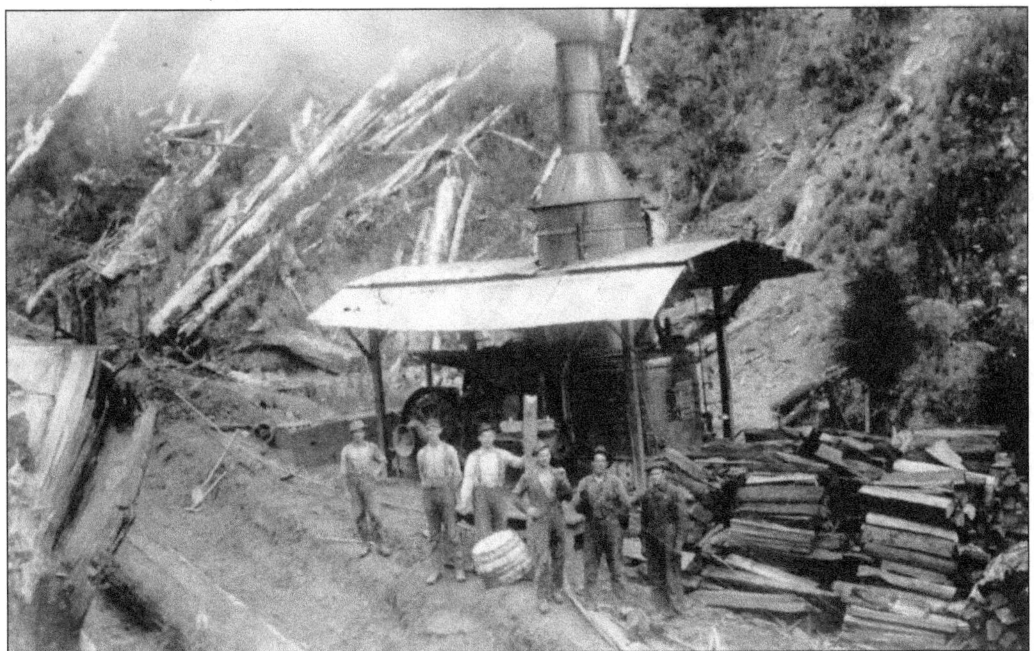

The engineer, or "donkey puncher," worked with a choker setter, who attached chains to logs being hauled. The spool tender guided ropes or cables with a stick. A boy kept the fire lit and supplied water to the boiler. The whistle punk communicated to the engineer that a log was ready to be yarded in. Communication ranged from toots on the donkey's whistle to an elaborate cable system. Shown here is a donkey crew at Laribee in the early 1900s.

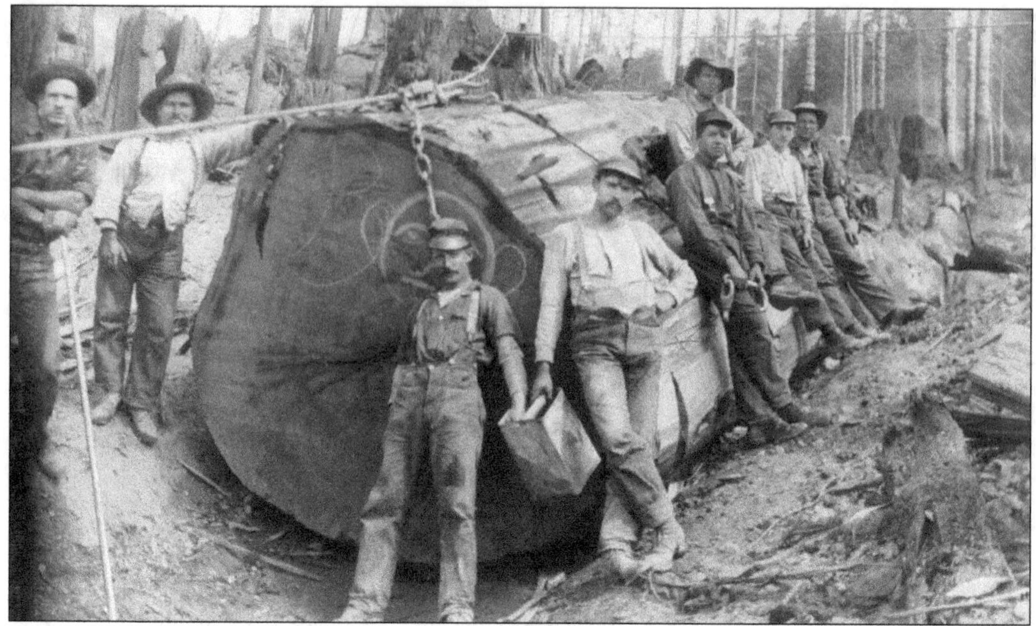

The 1891 *Humboldt Business Directory* described the donkey in use. Tethered to a stump, a line is run from the machine "to the log to be removed, and by means of snatch blocks the log is hauled in any direction desired." Here, a log is chained for a donkey to pull. The men in front are carrying part of the dog to latch the logs. Vilhelm Smeds is fourth from right. (Dave Smeds.)

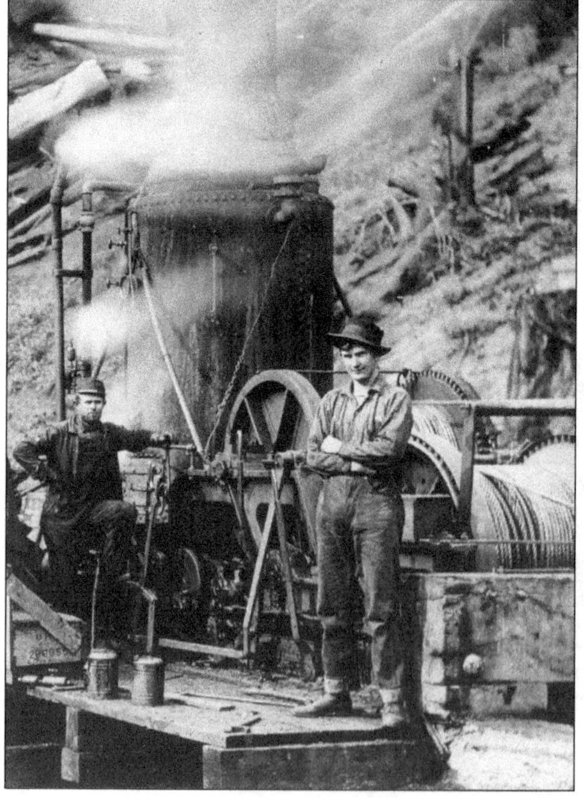

In 1883, John Dolbeer, in association with David Evans, developed a larger machine, which became known as a "bull donkey." Featuring an upright spool and two cylinders or gypsy heads mounted on skids, the machine retrieved cables and pulled larger loads. The 1891 business directory noted that the donkey allowed "heavy logs to be brought out of ravines and bad places where it would be impossible to get them with oxen and horses." (Clarke.)

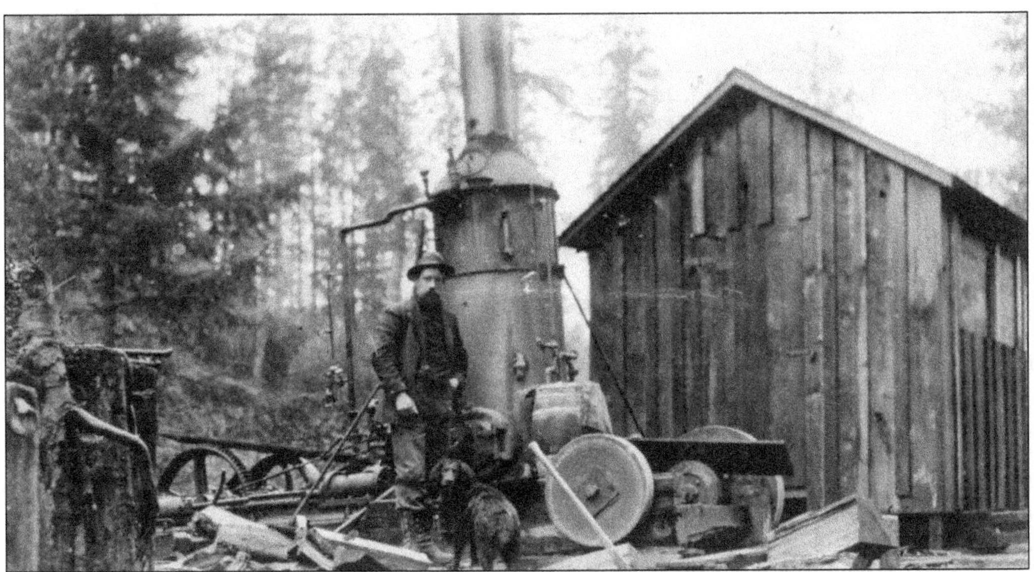

The donkey engine was soon ubiquitous in Pacific Coast woods operations. Often, several operated in the same logging show. In 1897, the Redwood Lumber Manufacturers observed that the engine was capable of "dragging to it a dozen or more logs at a greater speed than ever cattle hauled them." The manufacturers also noted that in "nearly all of the logging woods of the redwood belt the ox and horse have disappeared, and in their places are puffing and snorting steam engines."

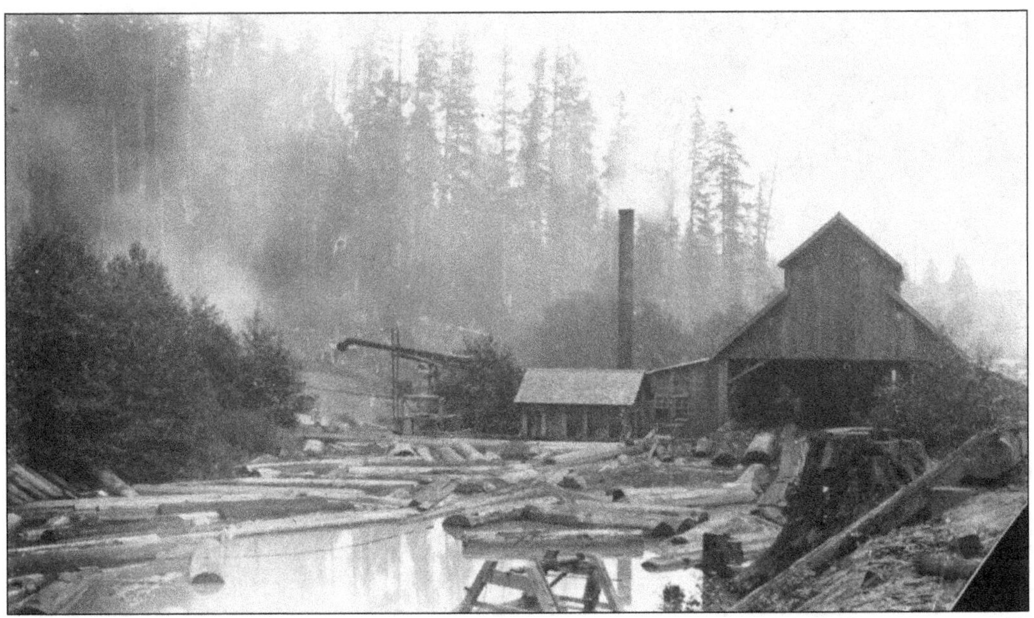

In the early decades of logging in Humboldt County, oxen hauled logs short distances to mills or to the bay, where logs could be floated to bayside mills. With logging limited to late spring through early fall, logs were stored in millponds, such as this one at the Glendale Mill, or, in the case of the bay mills, in roped-off sections of the bay. (HSU.)

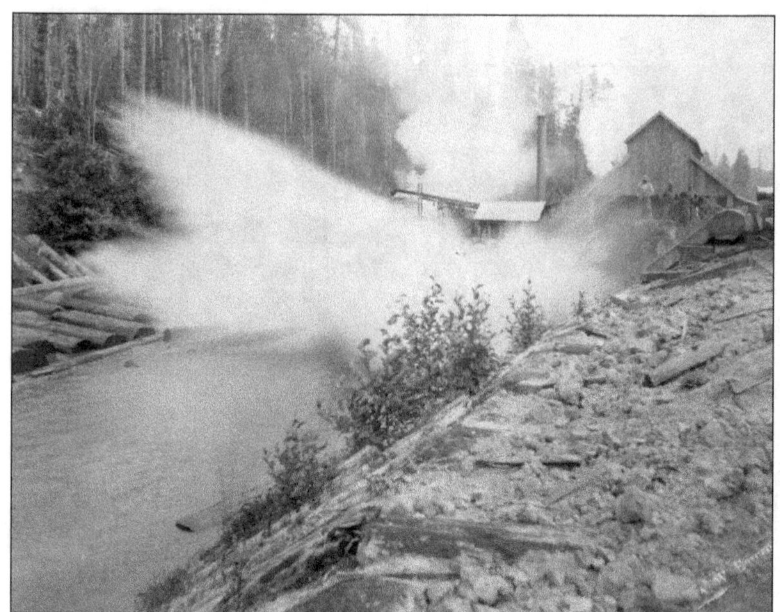

When logs were dumped into the millpond, whether from the oxen train or the railroad, there was always a dramatic splash, as seen here at the Glendale Mill and pond. Log ponds required yearly maintenance to ensure that sunken logs were removed. By the end of the logging season, the pond would be filled to capacity. (HSU.)

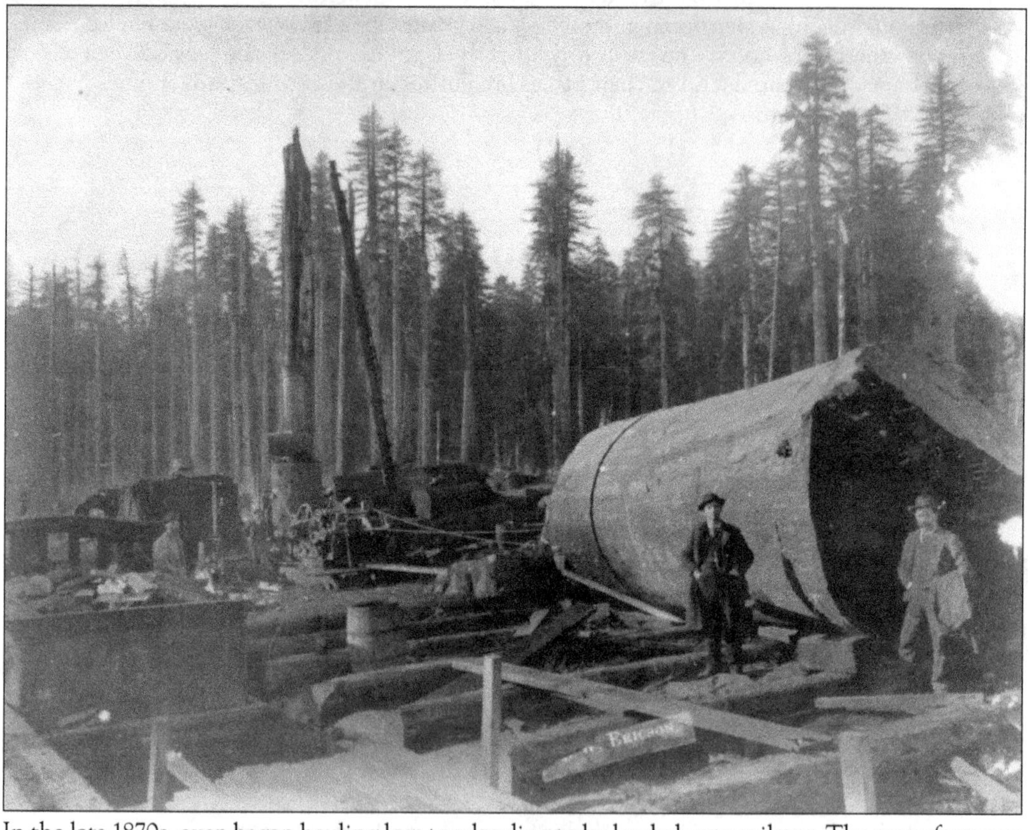

In the late 1870s, oxen began hauling logs to a landing to be loaded onto railcars. The manufacturers association described the process: "handling requires considerable skill as well as power. The loading is usually done by means of jack screws or lifting jacks; the log being rolled over and over and on to the car, where it is secured with chains and wedges or chocks."

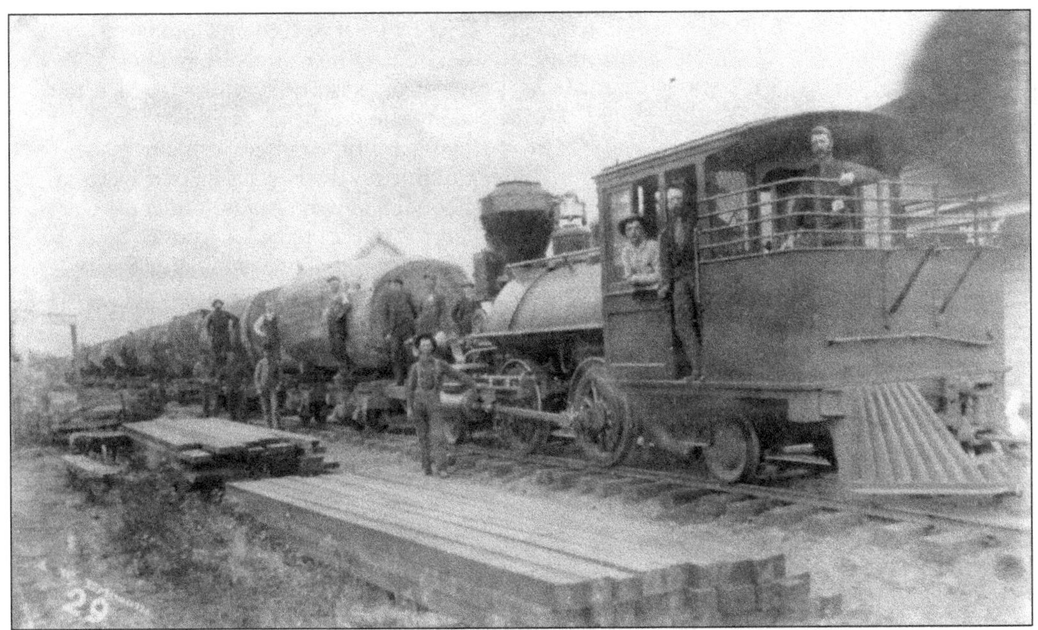

Railroads were used around Humboldt Bay since the 1850s. The power source for the first local railroad in Arcata, a track connecting the deepwater port to the town nearly two miles away, was a horse. Completion of the transcontinental railroad in 1869 made it possible to import railroad equipment to redwood country. Lumber companies utilized railroads extensively to transport logs. (HSU.)

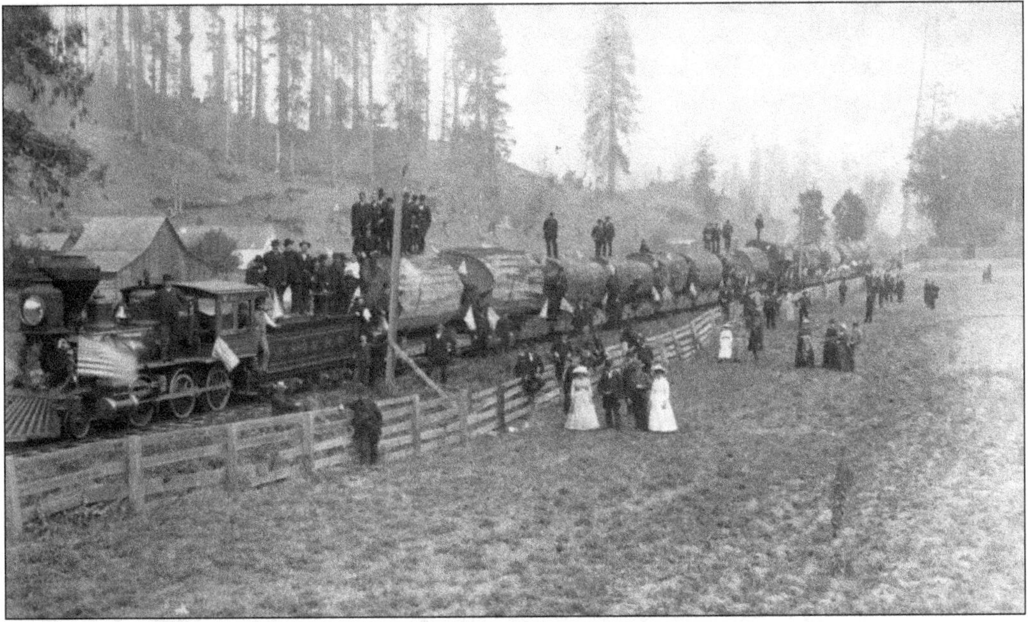

In 1874, John Vance erected his Big Bonanza Mill on Mad River and, at the same time, built a railroad connecting the mill with the wharf at Arcata. The following year, a line extended north from Arcata to mills operated by Isaac Minor and Noah Falk, the Jolly Giant, and the Dolly Varden. Soon, other companies began connecting to this line, the Arcata & Mad River Railroad. (HSU.)

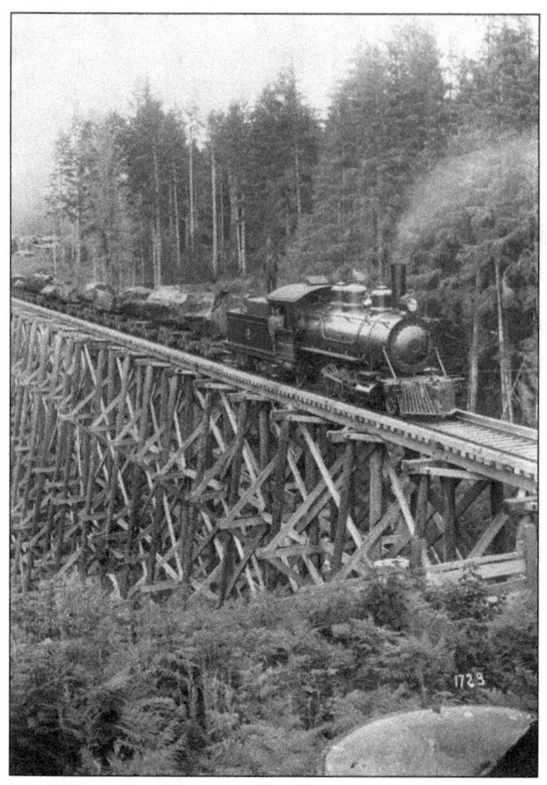

The Dolbeer & Carson Company, whose logging train is shown here, constructed its own railroad, which ran along the south side of Jacoby Creek. Flanigan, Brosnan & Company had a rail line on the north side of the creek. Soon, logging railroads connected the large stands of redwoods along the creeks that fed into Humboldt Bay with the mills on the bay. (HSU.)

Another of John Dolbeer's inventions, according to the patent he filed, was "a combined locomotive and logging engine, consisting of an engine and boiler and a gipsy mounted upon a frame, which is supported upon driving and bearing wheels." His combination steam donkey and locomotive is shown in operation at Ryan's Slough in 1903.

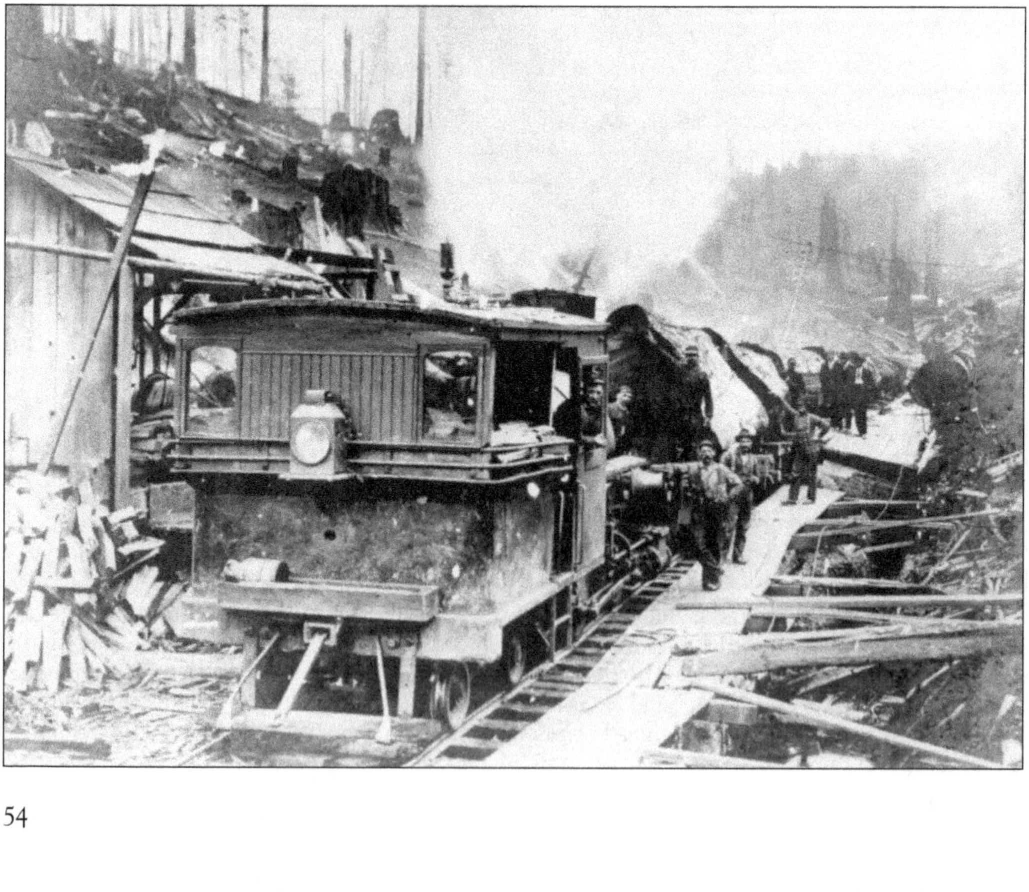

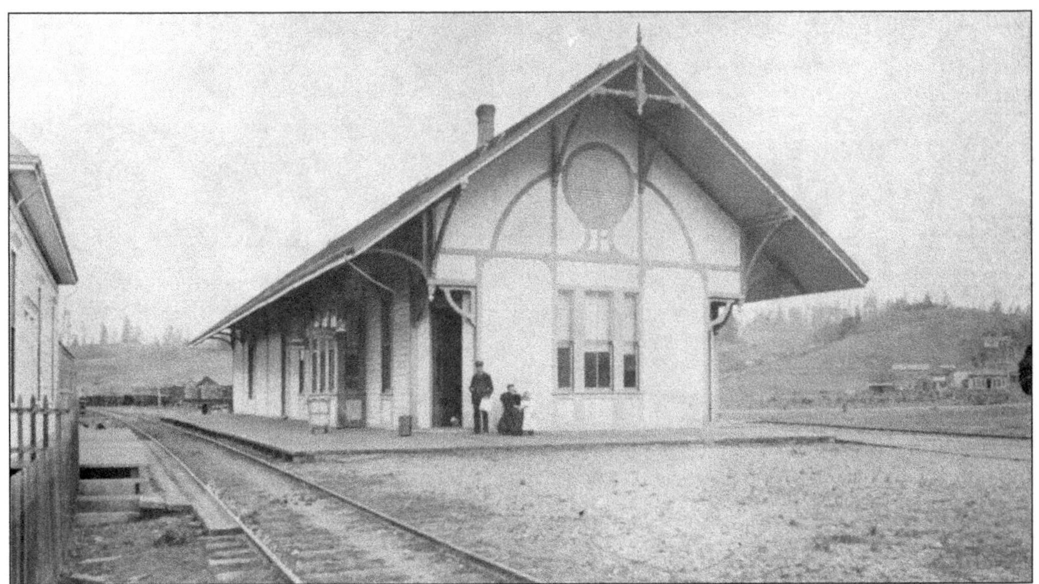

In 1884, William Carson and John Vance formed a partnership to build a railroad from Field's Landing to Fortuna. Providing transportation for lumber, logs, people, and agricultural produce of the Eel River Valley, the Eel River & Eureka Railroad was a successful enterprise. In 1885, the Pacific Lumber Company extended a line north from its mill at Scotia. Stationmaster A.W. Pratt and his family are shown at the Fortuna depot in 1892. (Clarke.)

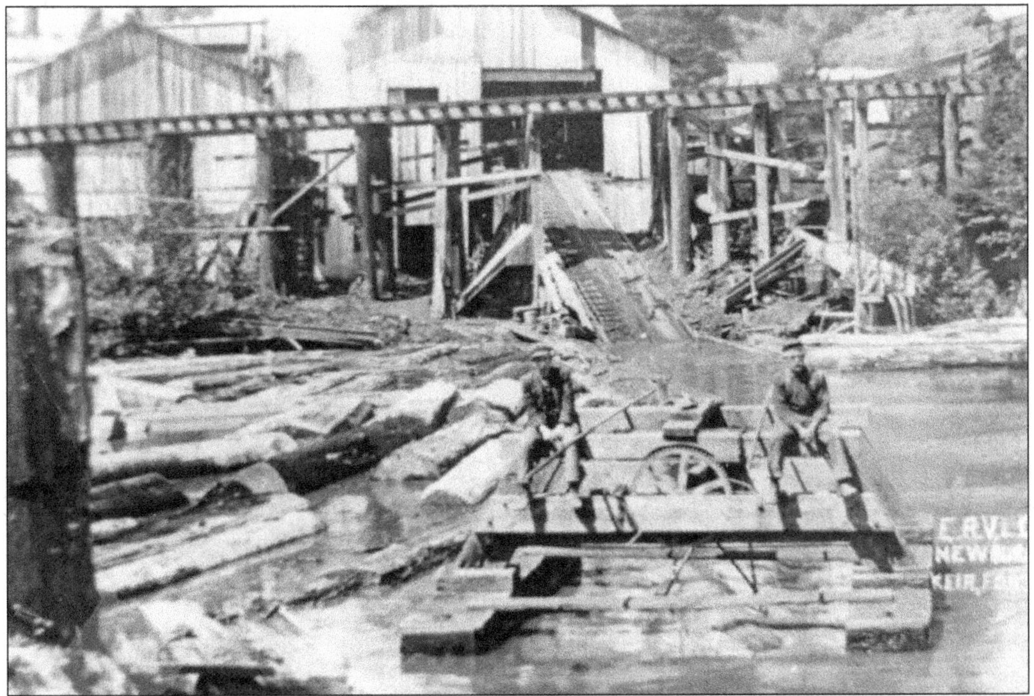

Once at the mill, the work of turning logs into lumber began. Sawmills were the location of many technological innovations in the 1800s, most notably in the types of saws used. During the Civil War, advances were made in steel manufacturing and durability. Stronger saws led to more lumber being sawn, keeping mills such as this one at Newburg operating all year.

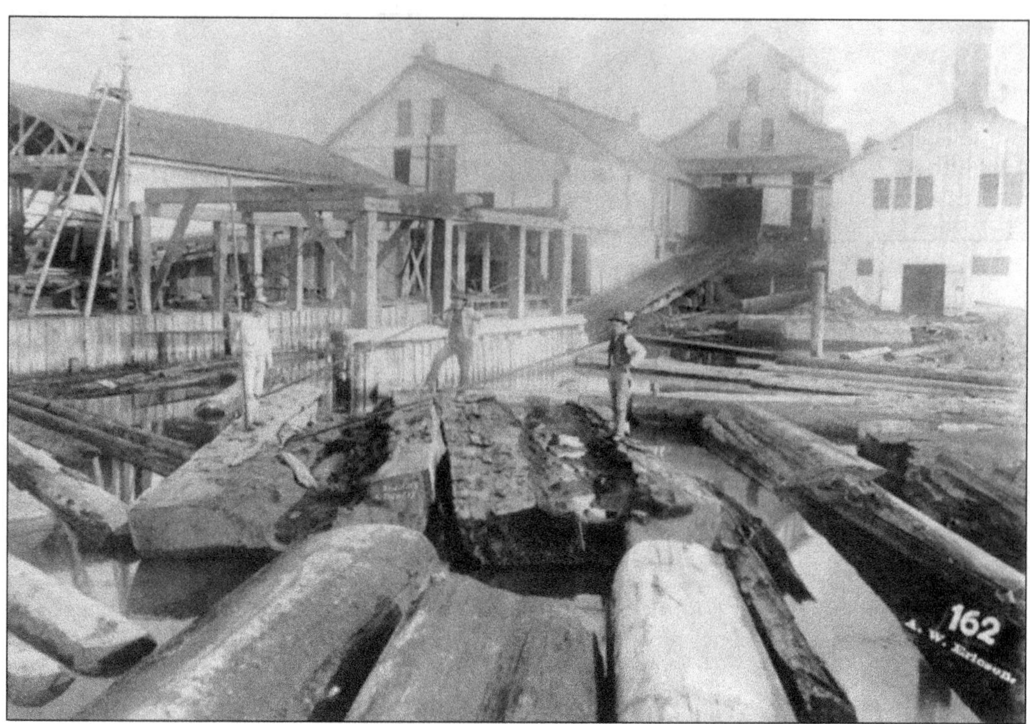

The log-pond crew, under direction of the "captain of the pond," guided logs onto the log haul and thence into the mill. Called "pond monkeys" because of their agility, these men used poles to push logs onto the carriage. Powered by steam, the log carriage was similar to a conveyor belt, as seen here at the Excelsior Mill on Gunther Island in Humboldt Bay. (HSU.)

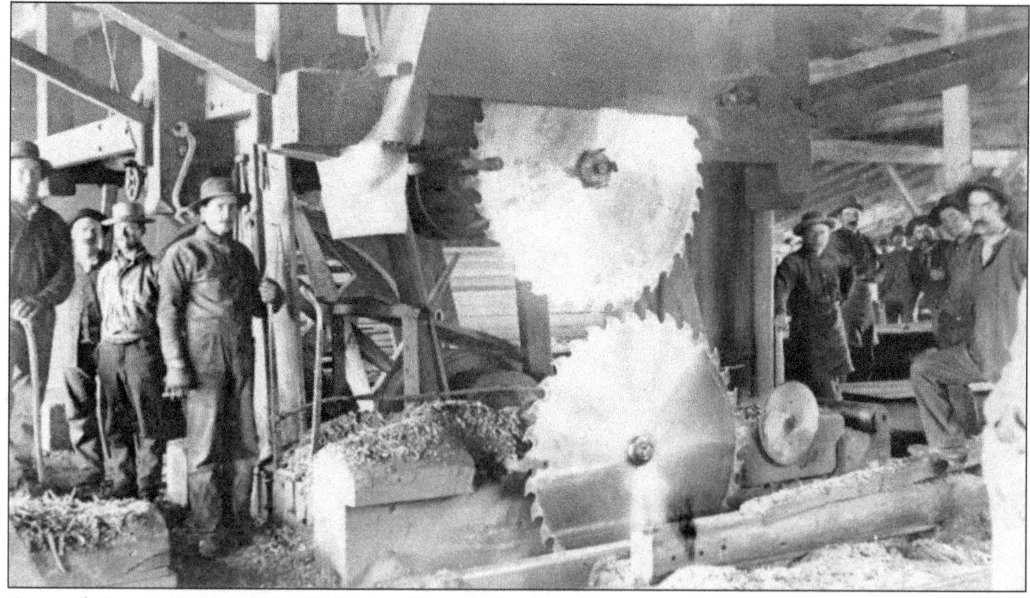

An early innovation in Humboldt's mills was the use of two circular saws. The distance between the two shafts on the saw determined the maximum depth of a cut. The man holding the lever at left is the head sawyer. Responsible for controlling the movement of the carriage, the sawyer decided where to cut to make the most lumber from a log. (HSU.)

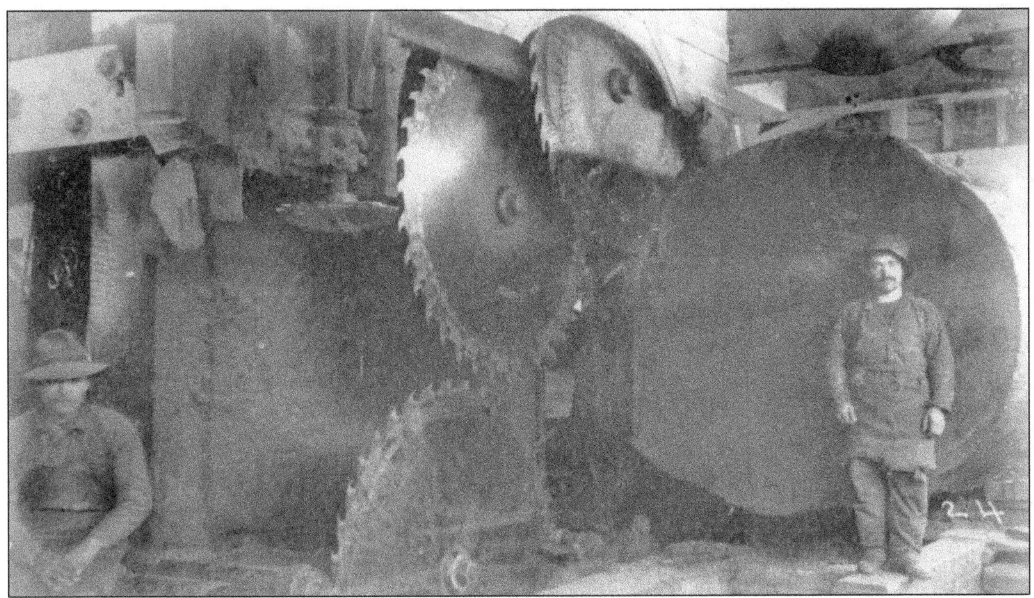

Another invention was installed at the Dolbeer & Carson mill in 1879. The facility had burned down in 1878. In rebuilding, the company hired millwright David Evans. In 1869, Evans had invented a process using a third saw. William Carson and John Dolbeer had utilized this technique. Evans's third saw allowed the sawyer to make lumber out of logs eight feet in diameter. Each saw had a diameter of up to 64 inches. (HSU.)

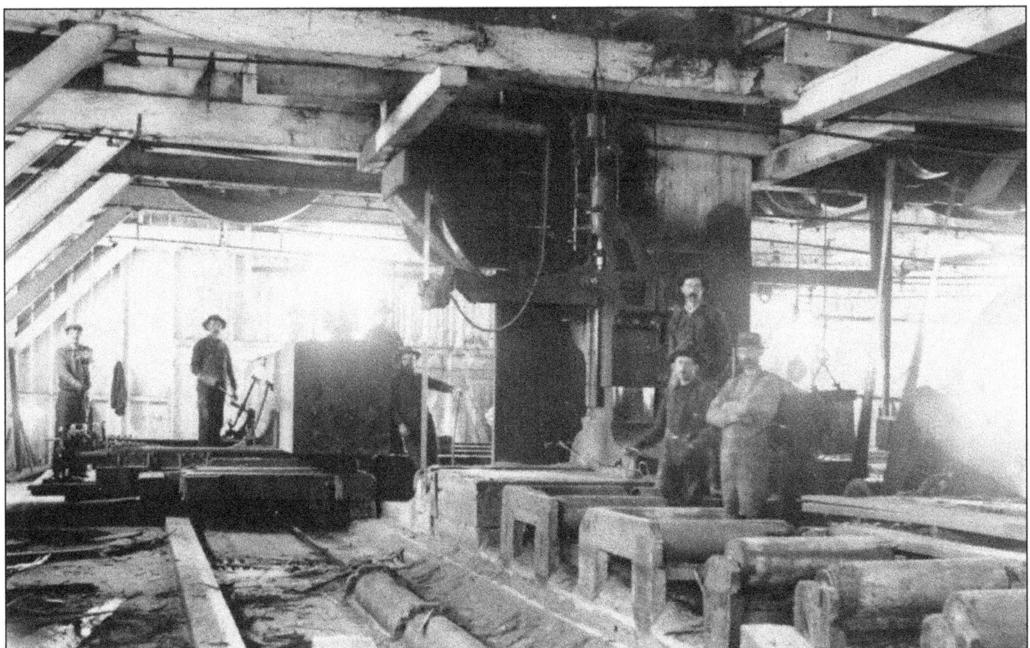

Implemented in the 1890s, the band saw cut in a continuous motion. Its advantages included being thinner, making a more accurate cut, not producing as much sawdust, and not damaging the lumber. The Redwood Lumber Manufacturers in 1897 noted that the band saw, such as this one at the Milford Company Mill, "cuts its way through the mighty giants and lands at the tail of the mill the lumber in perfect condition." (HSU.)

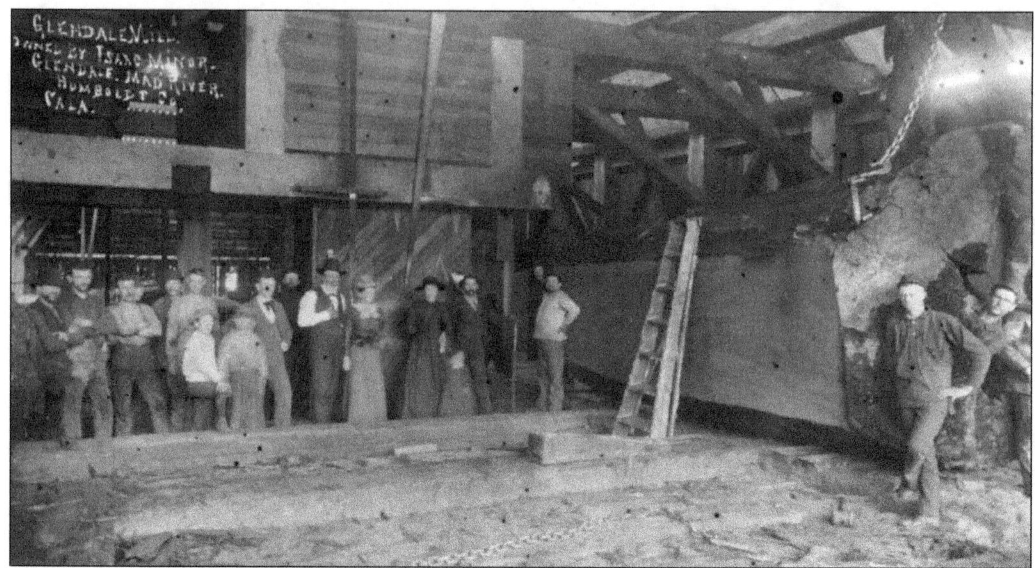

In addition to pond monkeys and sawyers, the mill crew consisted of saw filers, who kept saw blades sharp; ratchet setters, who determined the width of the cut; offbearers, who pulled newly sawn lumber away from the saw; turndown men, who rolled logs on the carriage; edgermen, who made dimensional lumber; and millwrights, responsible for repairs. Shown here is the Glendale Mill in the late 1800s. (HSU.)

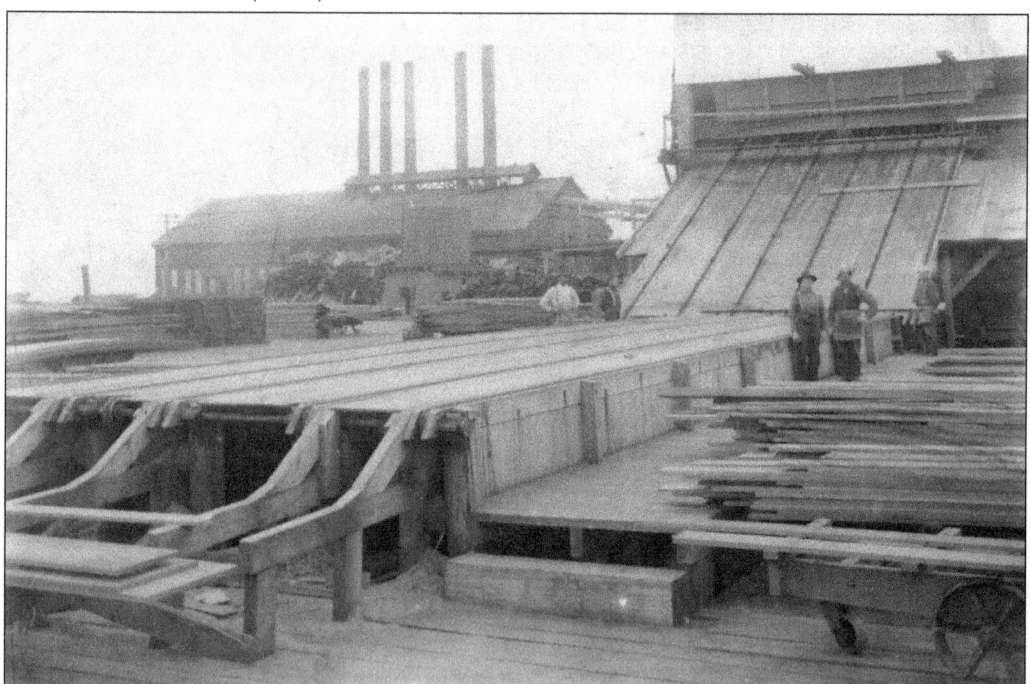

The Dolbeer & Carson Company's "green chain" is pictured in the 1880s. The green chain was where finished boards and rough cants were sorted by dimension. Mills were laid out in an L shape, with the green chain positioned perpendicular to the saws. Boards came down a slide and onto a series of chains that carried the lumber sideways, from whence they were pulled by hand. Typically, working on a green chain was an entry-level position in mills. (Clarke.)

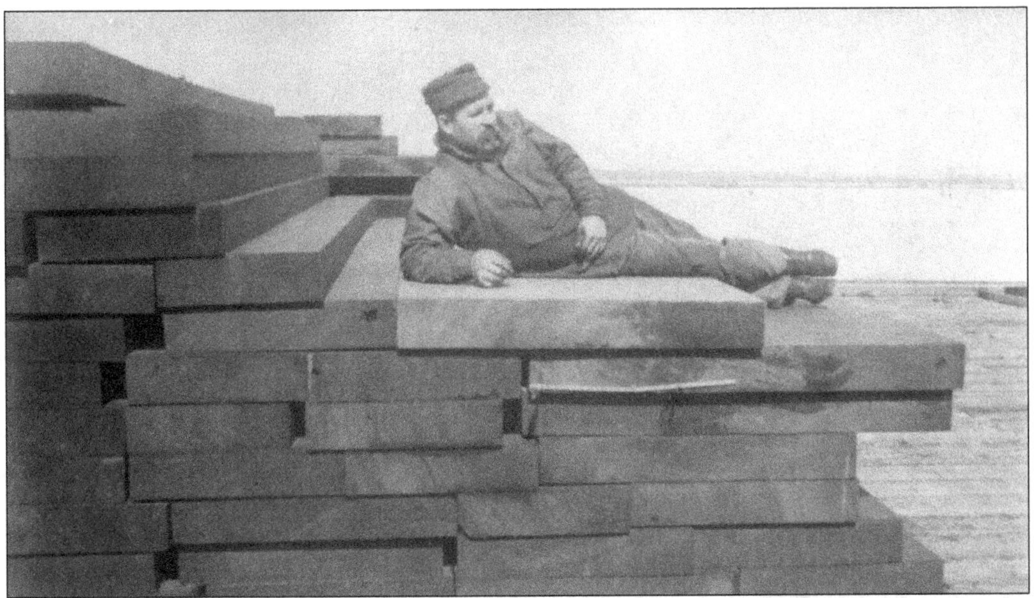

An unknown worker at Carson's Bay Mill relaxes on a stack of cants around 1884. He may be the grader, responsible for grading the quality of the lumber. Graders judged and marked each board for its future use. Cants were the transition between log and finished lumber. (HSU.)

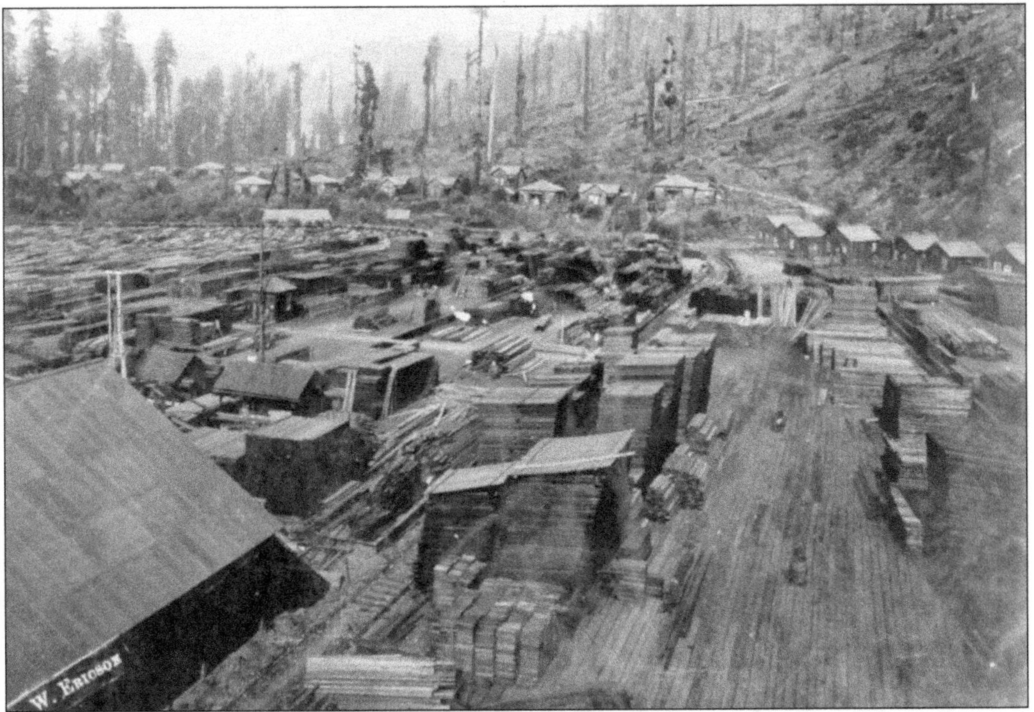

Redwood naturally contains moisture, and immersion in mill ponds added water content. Through experimentation in the late 1800s, mill owners learned that wood quality increased if it was air-dried for up to two years. This drying period, however, tied up valuable lumber, as shown here at the Pacific Lumber Company. In 1891, Dolbeer & Carson installed a kiln that dried lumber in two weeks, dramatically decreasing the time to market for lumber.

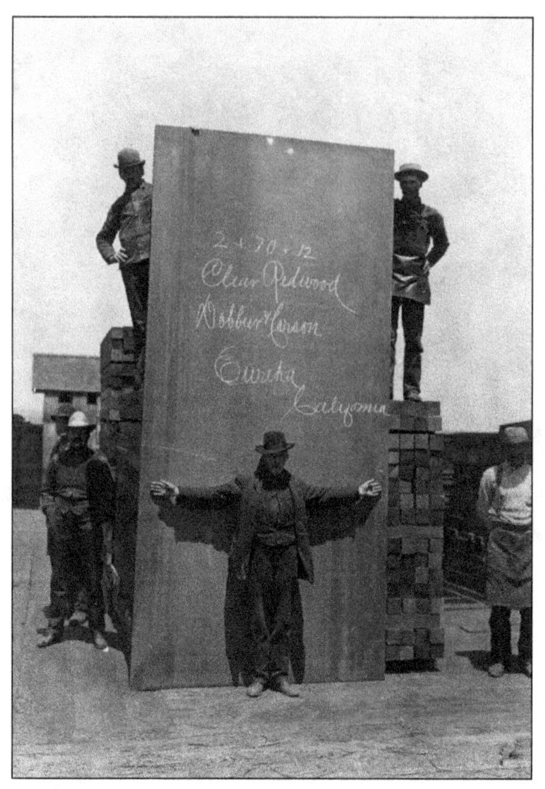

In 1897, Humboldt's mills had a combined output of 150 million board feet of lumber. Companies promoted their products using images such as the photograph at left of a board produced by Dolbeer & Carson from one log measuring 2 inches by 70 inches by 12 feet. The largest obstacle to success was shipping. From 1850 until 1914, when the Northwestern Pacific Railroad was completed, lumber transportation was limited to shipping by sea. Making transportation dangerous was Humboldt Bay's entrance, blocked by a hazardous, shifting sandbar that wrecked many ships. A captain of the era compared it to the rough waters around the Cape of Good Hope. Most lumber companies owned their own fleet of schooners. In 1905, the Humboldt County supervisors reported 1,500 ships arriving and departing annually. These ships were bound for local markets in California as well as ports in Australia, China, and England. (Left, HSU; below, HCHS.)

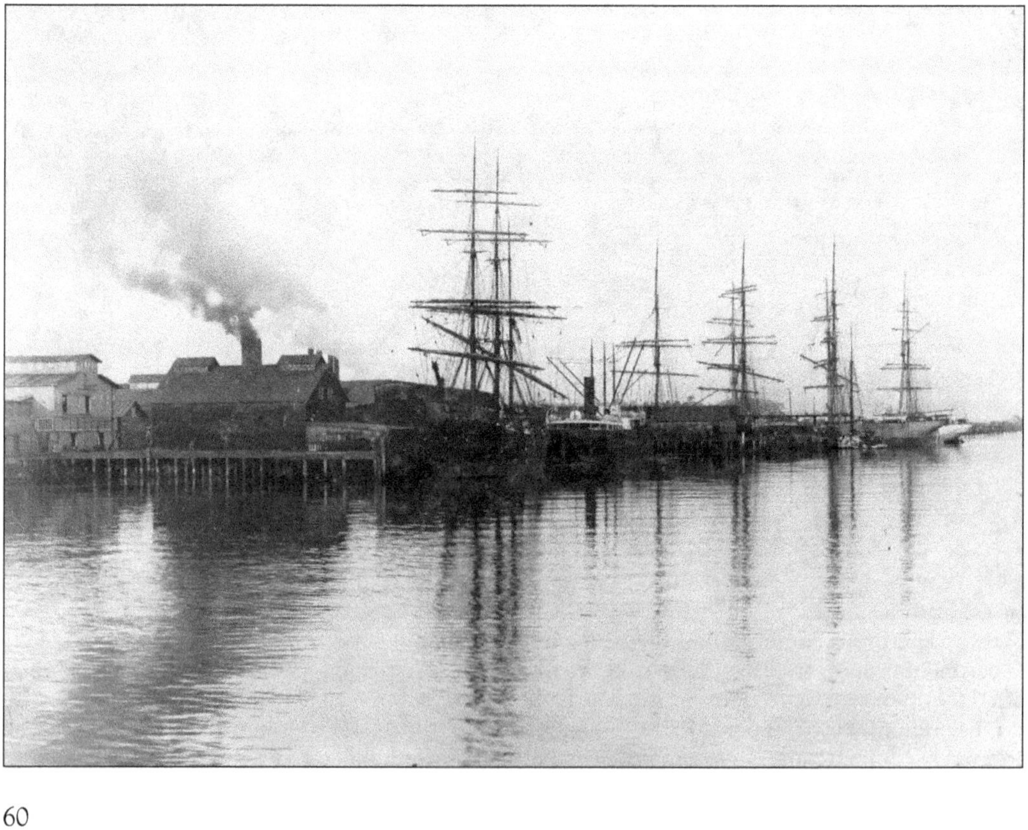

Three

Split-Products Industry

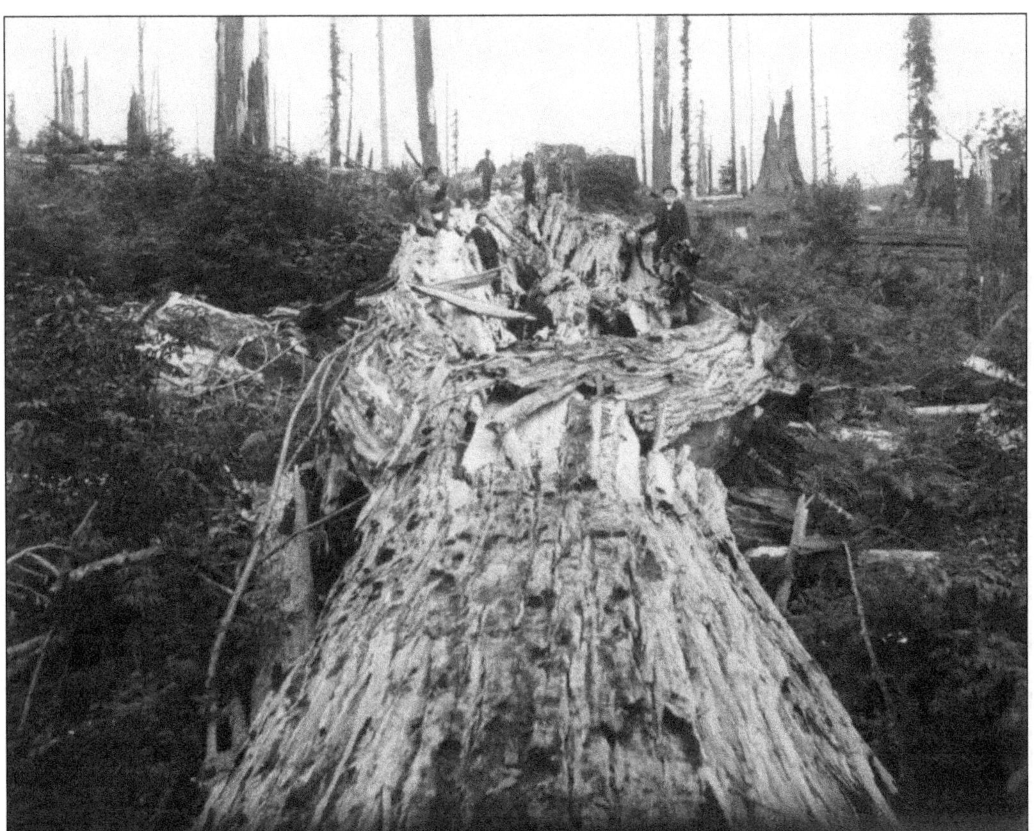

Although the primary use of redwood was lumber, another industry ubiquitous to the region took advantage of redwood's splitting characteristics. A straight grain allows redwood to split easily; in fact, this characteristic led to the care with which the tree was felled. Redwood could be split into "a plank two inches thick, twelve inches wide, and twelve feet long," according to the manufacturers association in 1897. (HSU.)

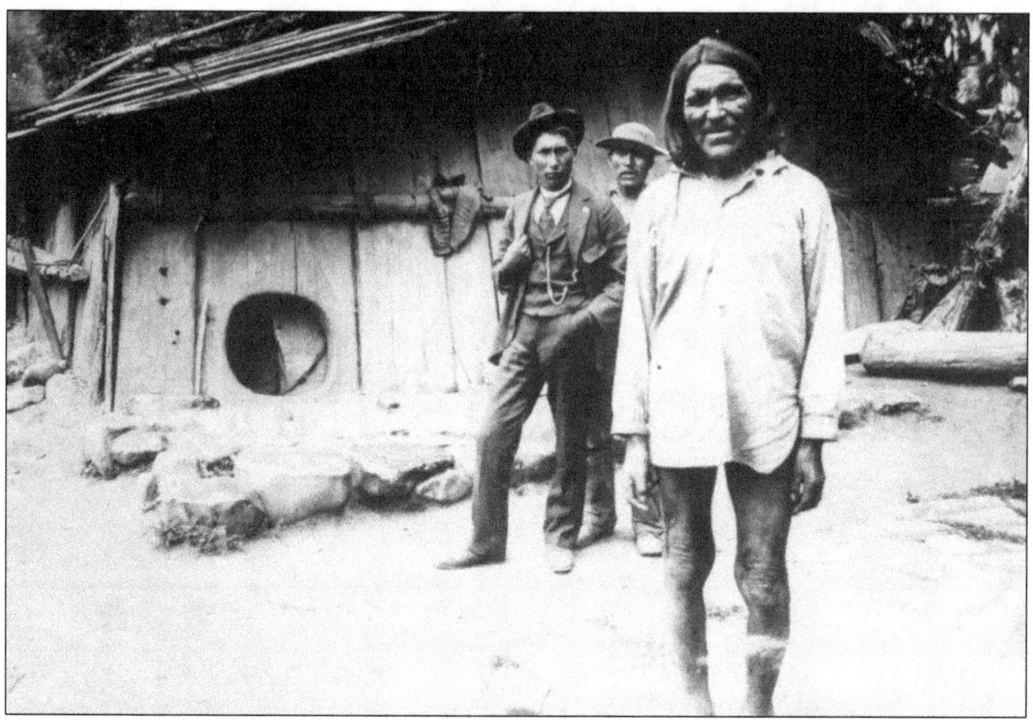

The Native Americans who lived among the redwoods utilized the trees' splitting characteristics, using the split boards to build their houses. Planks formed the building. The circular shape at left is the entrance. The native peoples also used redwood for building canoes. This traditional Yurok house was photographed in 1897 by local photographer A.W. Ericson. (HSU.)

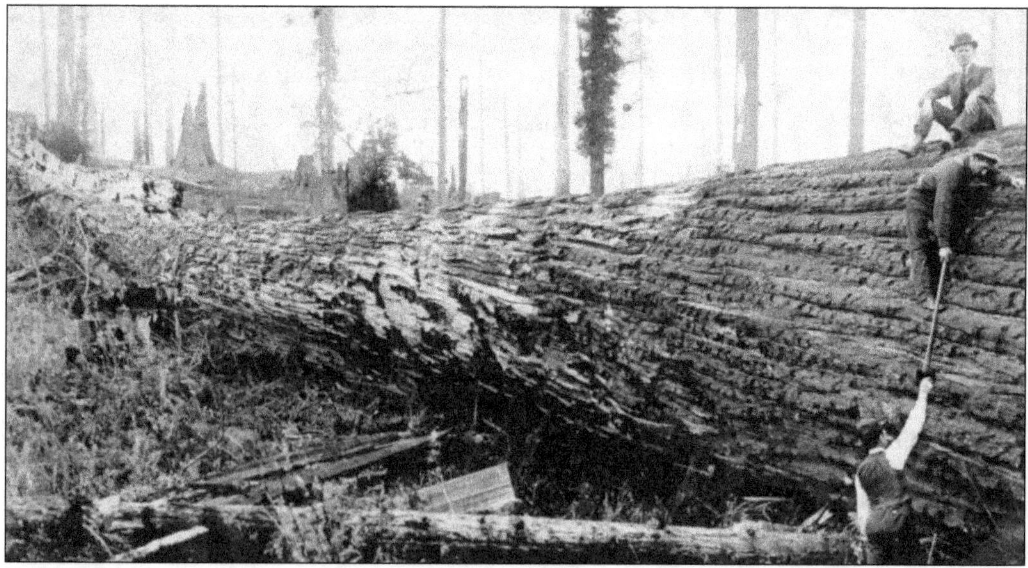

Redwood was split into shingles, grape stakes, railroad ties, and fencing. This tree, when felled by Henry Pollard and sons Roy and Lester at Fieldbrook in 1906, produced 96 cords of shingle bolts, making 900 square feet of shingles and 52 tiers of railroad ties. To ensure payment, ties and bolts were "branded" by hitting the end of the board with a metal rod that had a registered image on it.

Louis J. Thomas of the Loggers' Interpretive Association demonstrates how shingle bolts or large blocks of wood were split by hand into shingles. Using a wooden mallet, Thomas strikes a froe, driving it into the wood. As he pushes down on the froe, the handle is also pushed outward, splitting off the shingle. It was not until the late 1860s that shingle production became mechanized. (HSU.)

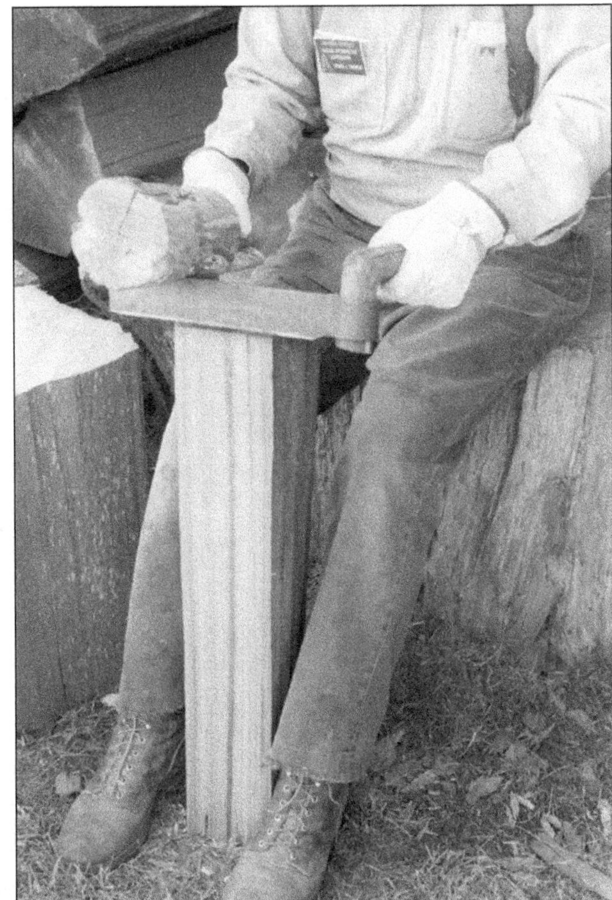

A hewing ax was used to shape ties after being split from the tree. By 1897, redwood railroad ties were being used on most of the railways along the Pacific Coast. Ties were also shipped to Mexico, Peru, Chile, and India. In addition to the wood being long lasting, its tannins helped deter insects.

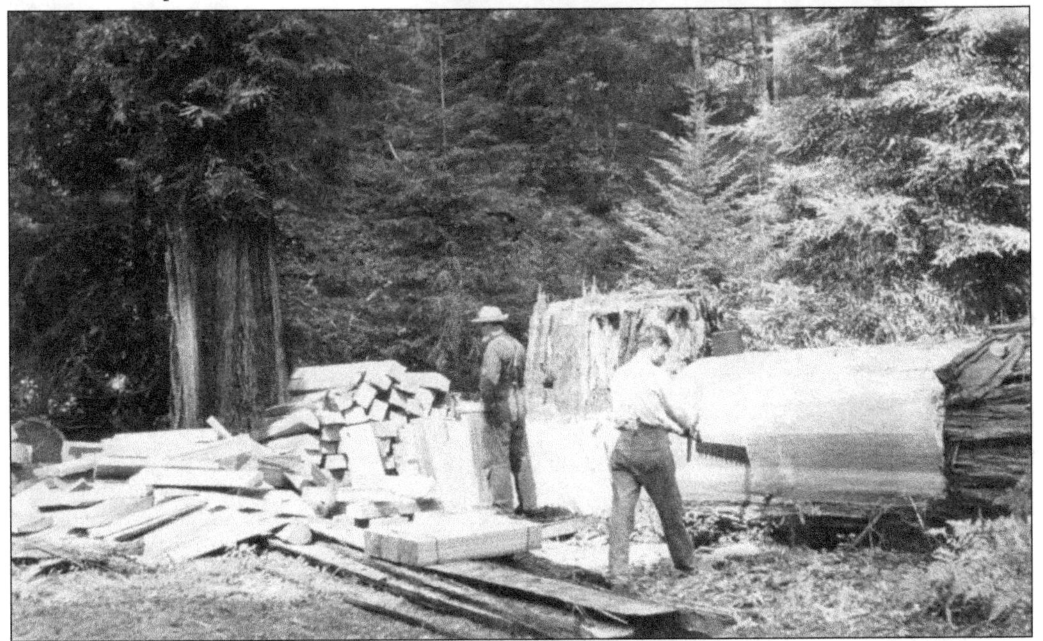

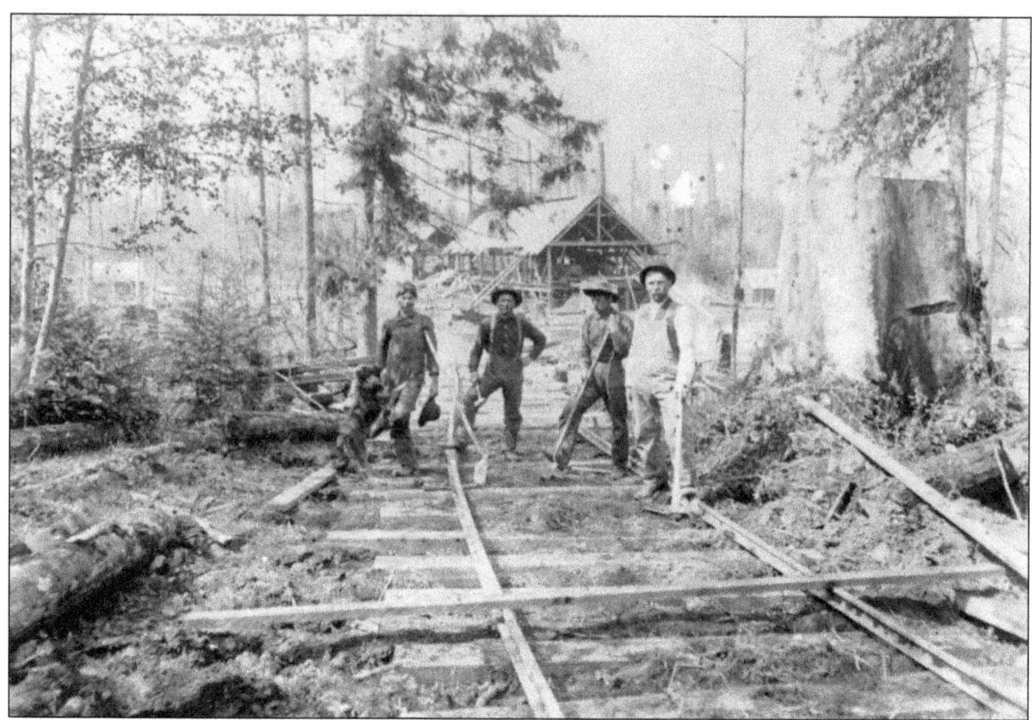

One advantage for smaller operations was that the split product could be made in the woods at the site where the tree fell, and no large equipment was needed. Redwood railroad ties were highly desirable, according to the Redwood Lumber Manufacturers, in that "the average life of a redwood tie is 12 years while a pine tie will hardly last four years, an oak tie six years."

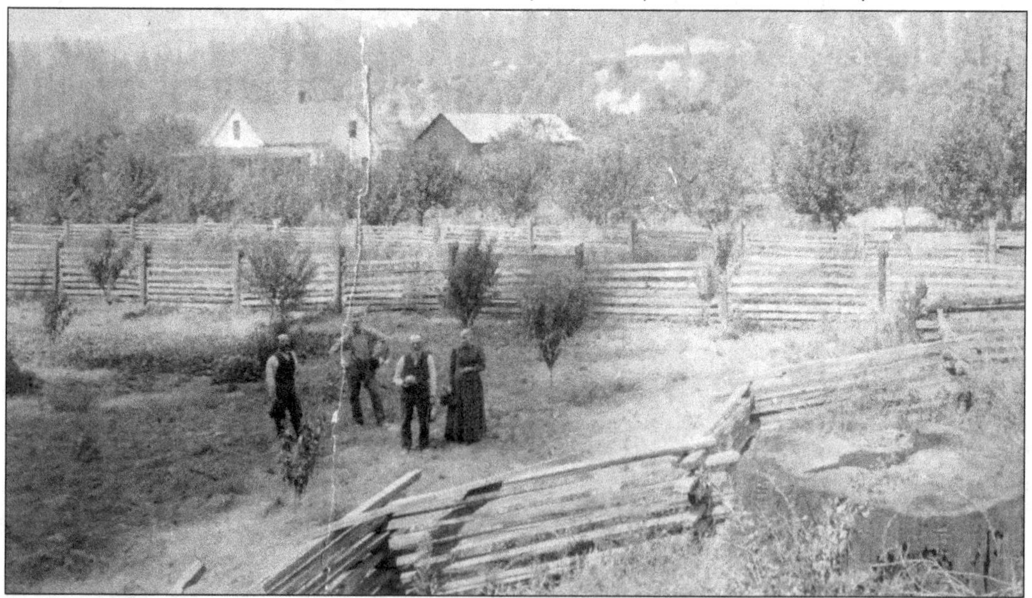

Other products often split from redwood were fence rails and posts. As shown in this photograph, the insect-resistant redwood was often used on farms and homesteads around Humboldt County. It was also shipped extensively from Humboldt Bay. Between 1888 and 1892, over two million redwood pickets and nearly 400,000 posts were shipped from the bay. (HSU.)

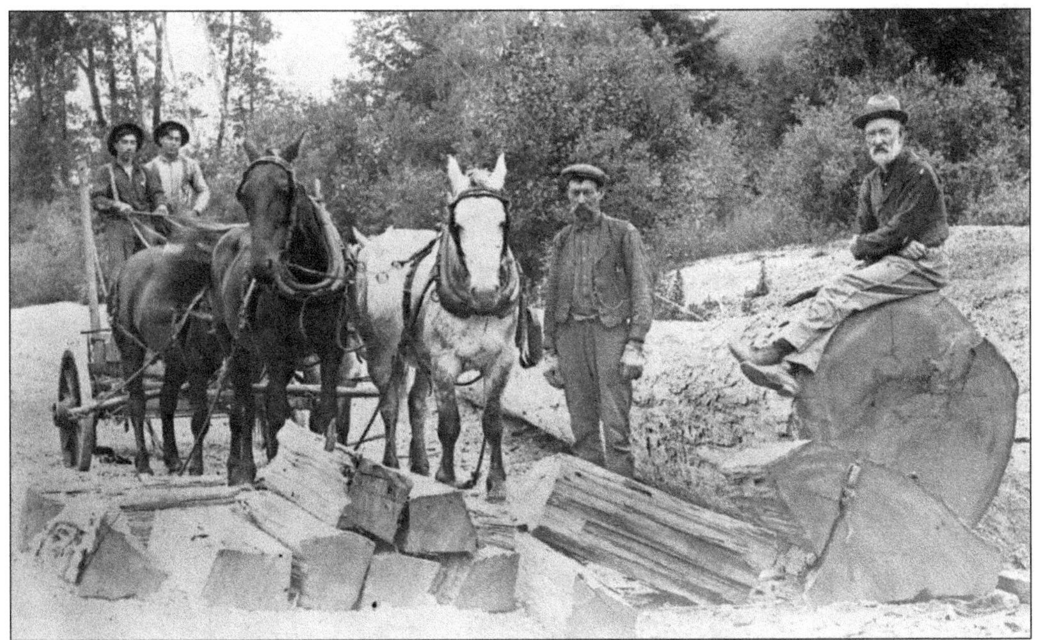

For the small entrepreneur, making redwood products was a great source of income. Working some distance from the shipping port at Eureka, shingle-makers made their product without a large outlay, hauling the finished product by wagon to the ports around Humboldt Bay. For many others, however, making split products was a big business. (HSU.)

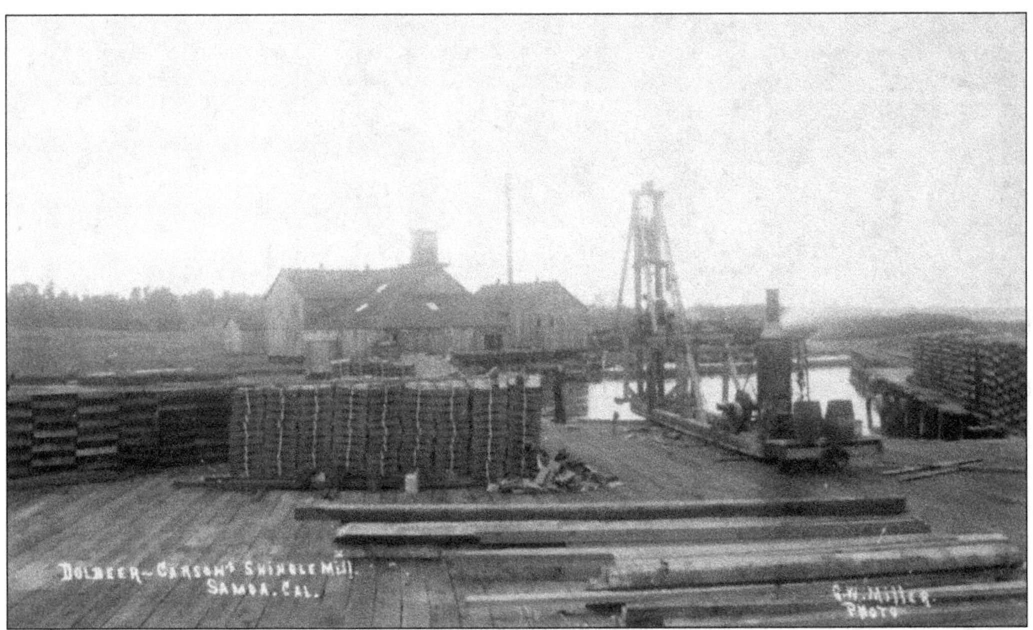

Redwood shingles, having the tree's attributes of durability and easy shaping, were the most popular and profitable of the split products. Architecturally, shingles were beginning to be used both for decorative siding of houses as well as for roofs. One shingle mill owner, J.G. Loveren, observed, "Redwood is, beyond question, superior to any other in this country." Between 1888 and 1892, 1.5 billion shingles were shipped from Eureka. (HSU.)

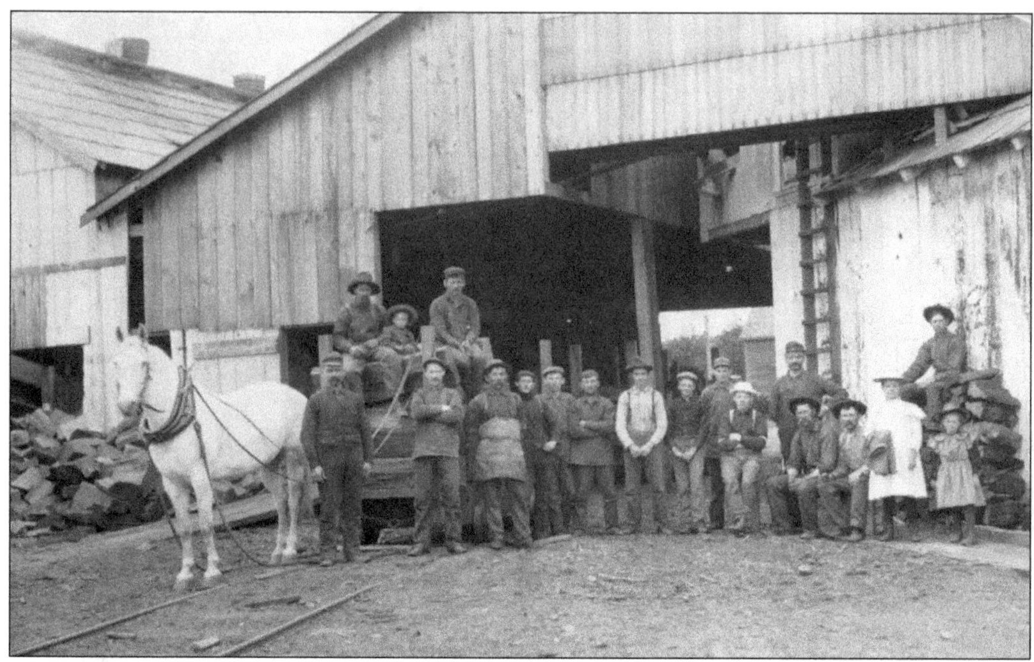

The *Humboldt County Souvenir* of 1904 notes that George M. Fay & Brothers built the first shingle mill on Humboldt Bay in 1867 at Fairhaven. By the 1890s, shingle mills could be found throughout the county. In 1896, there were 13 operational lumber mills and at least 26 shingle mills. (HSU.)

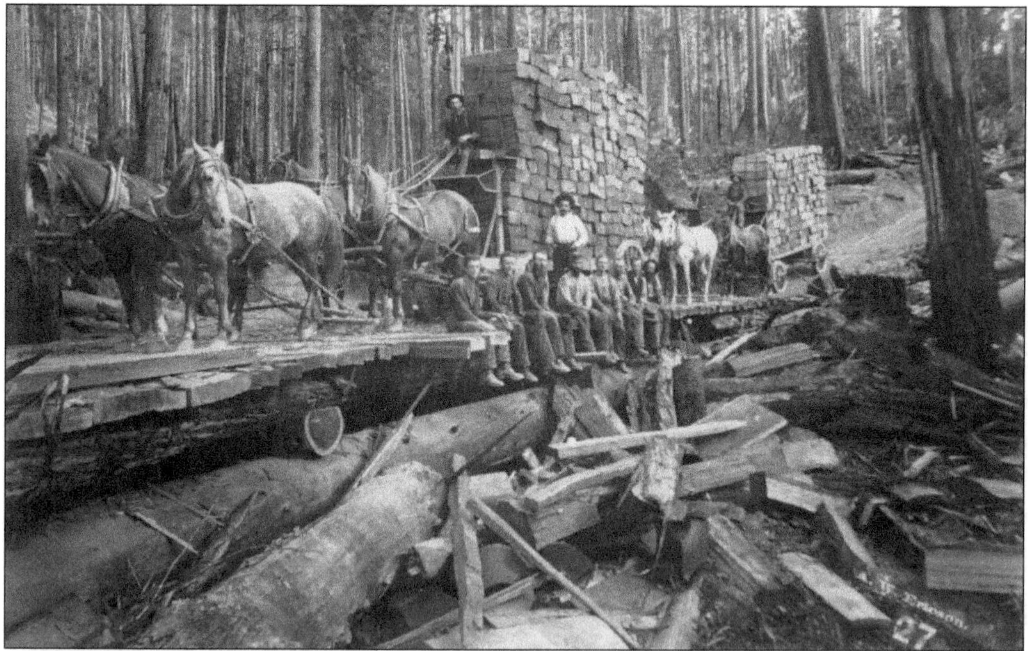

These large sections of redwood, or shingle bolts, are being hauled to Eureka from Ole Hanson's shake- and shingle-bolt claim at Freshwater. Hanson built a shingle-sawing machine that greatly enhanced production, thus increasing demand for bolts, which could be cut into shingles at the mill. His machine soon became the hallmark of a successful shingle mill. (HSU.)

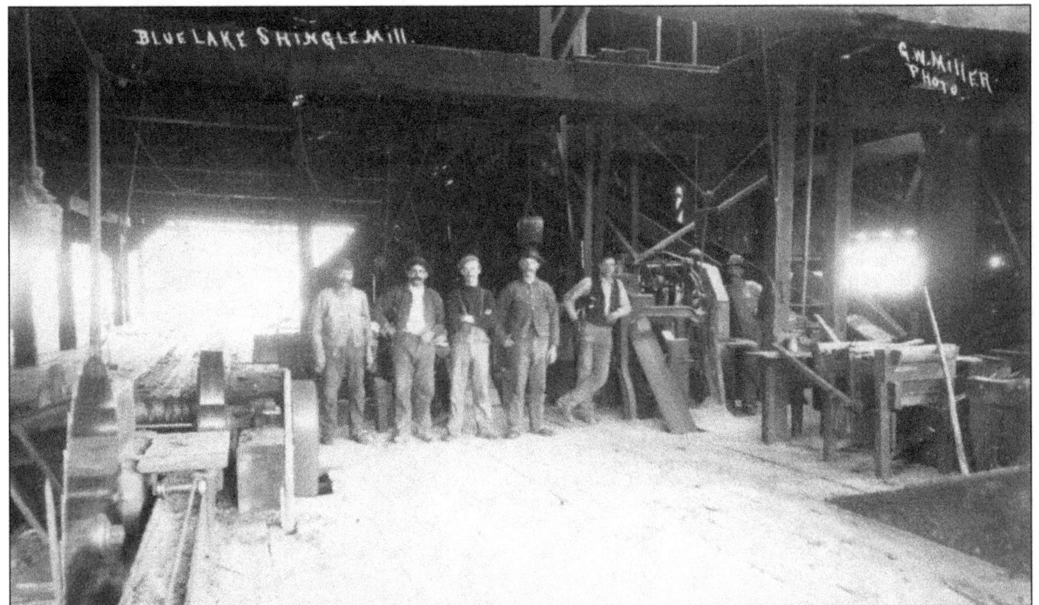

The *Humboldt County Souvenir* in 1904 noted that "the shingle mills of Humboldt range from plants of one machine up to five." Most shingle mills employed around 15 men, with filers and sawyers the highest-paid employees. The men in this interior view of the Blue Lake Shingle Mill are identified as Guy Dow, Lon Acorn, E.D. Atville, Jas. Buzzie, Jim Worthington, and Herb Acorn. (HSU.)

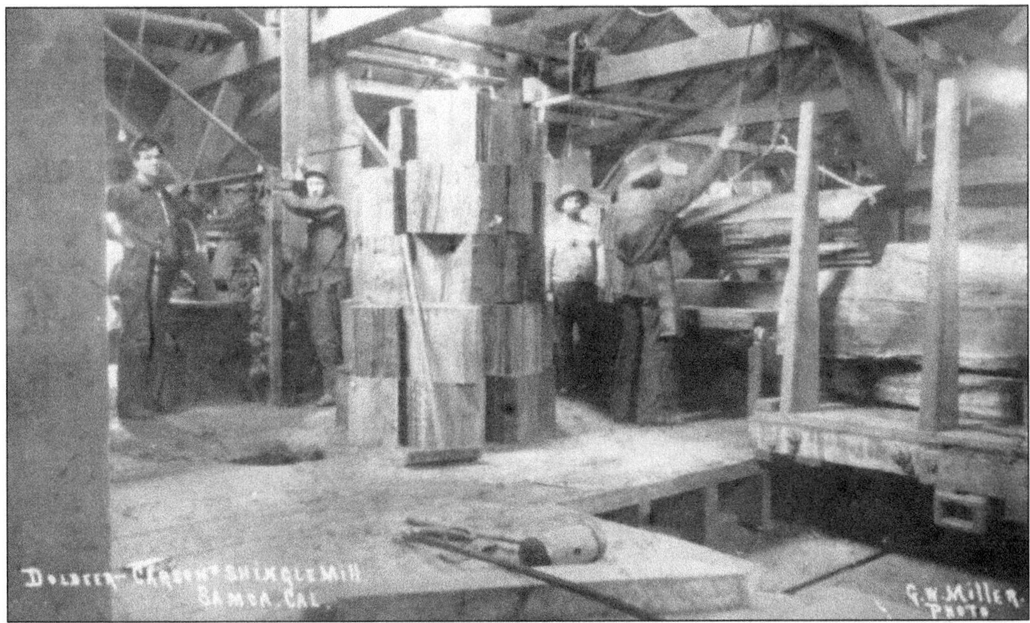

According to the *Humboldt County Souvenir*, the process of making shingles began with the bolt cutter using a cut-off saw, trimming one end of the bolt true, and cutting the bolt into three blocks. The sawyer placed these blocks one at a time into a shingle-making machine. The Dolbeer & Carson Company had three such machines in 1892, each one producing 12 million shingles a year. (HSU.)

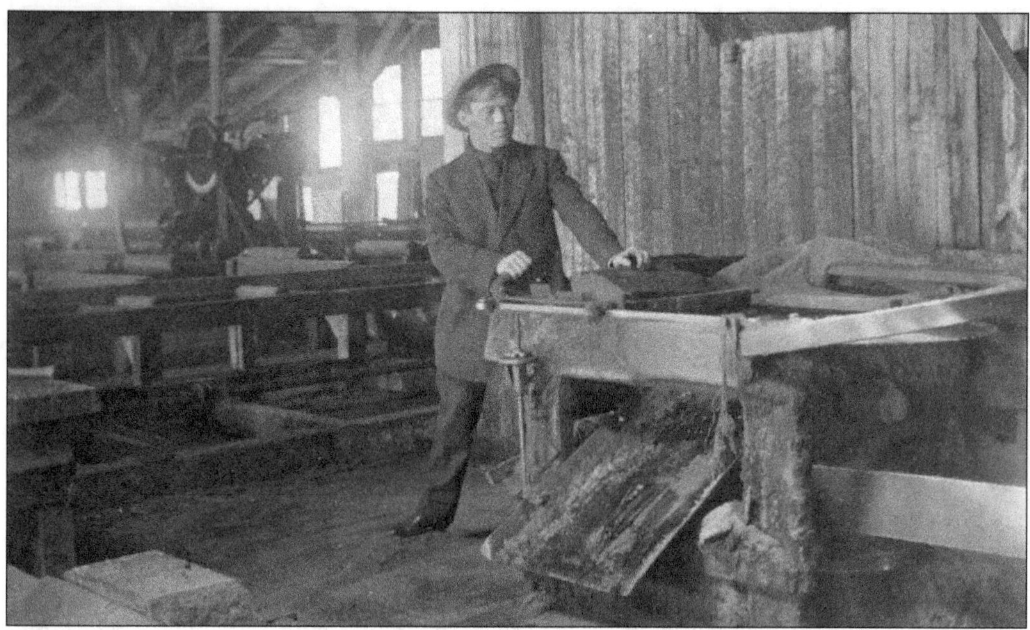

The shingle machine sawed the bolts into shingles of varying width. After removing the shingles from the machine, the sawyer smoothed the edges three or four at a time by holding them against the jointer. As described by the *Humboldt County Souvenir*, the jointer was a machine with "a revolving wheel, or cylinder, armed with eight blades similar to planer knives." William Everts is seen here at the Occidental shingle mill. (Clarke.)

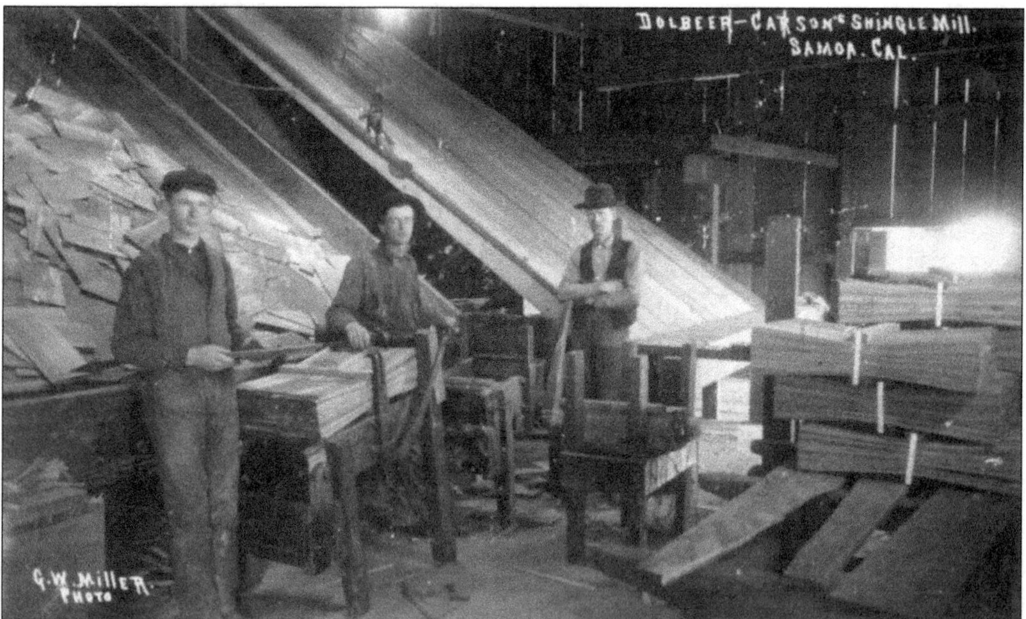

Once smoothed, the sawyer sent the shingles down a chute to the packers. The *Humboldt County Souvenir* explains it was their "duty to place [the shingles] in the packing horse and form them into symmetrical bundles of commerce, fastening them with sheet steel bands, nailing the ends of the bands." Once bundled into stacks of 200, the shingles were ready for market, although sometimes they were sent to a dry kiln. (HSU.)

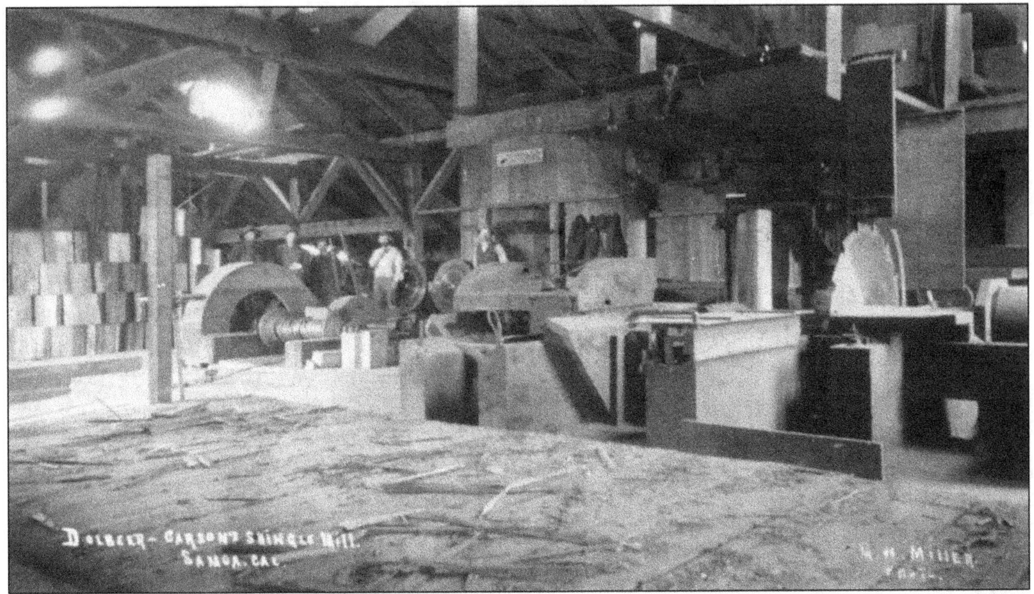

In 1888, the *Humboldt Times* reported that J.G. Loveren, owner of several shingle mills, "perfected a machine that will plane, bead, and snipe a shingle. He claims for the shingle so finished that the beading will carry the water off in a course without it running in between the shingles." The *Times* added, "Loveren deserves credit of solving the problem as a great many mechanics proclaimed it an impossibility." (HSU.)

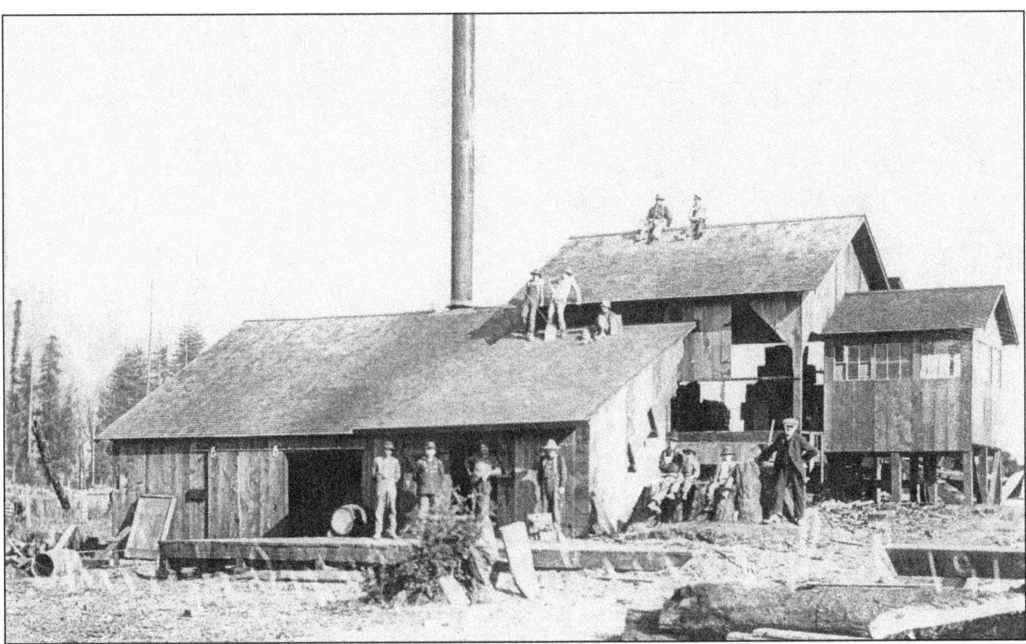

The Holmes Flat Shingle Mill was operated by the Holmes-Eureka Mill in Eureka. Its operators cut nearby redwoods, milling them before shipping, thus saving on transporting logs to Eureka and milling shingles there. Holmes Flat was logged several times, and the shingle mill also took advantage of prior logging by making shingles from tall stumps left by previous loggers, a common practice of large shingle companies. (HRIA.)

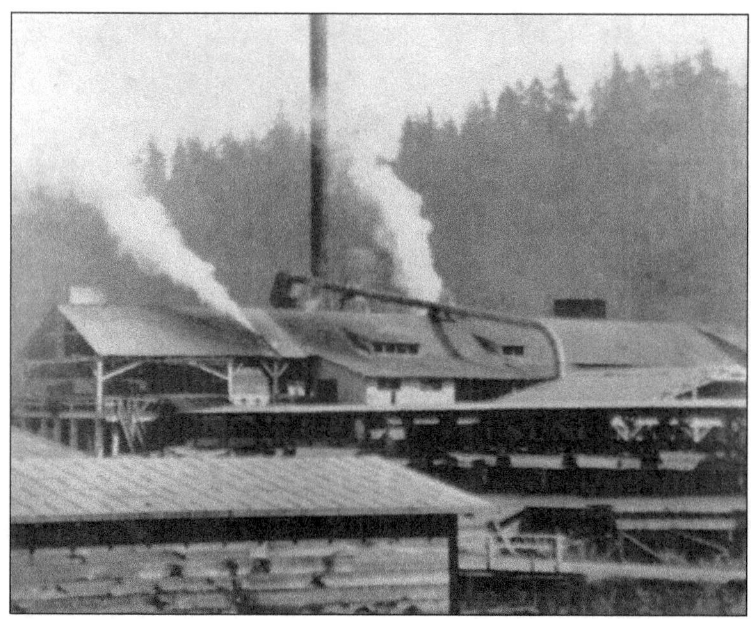

Brown's Mill, at Stafford, also took advantage of the groves of redwoods found near the river and the railroad extended south from Scotia by the Pacific Lumber Company. The mill was built in the early 1900s by Percy Brown and operated until the 1930s. In addition to making shingles, Brown produced doors, moldings, and finished redwood. He even had his own lumberyard selling his products. (HRIA.)

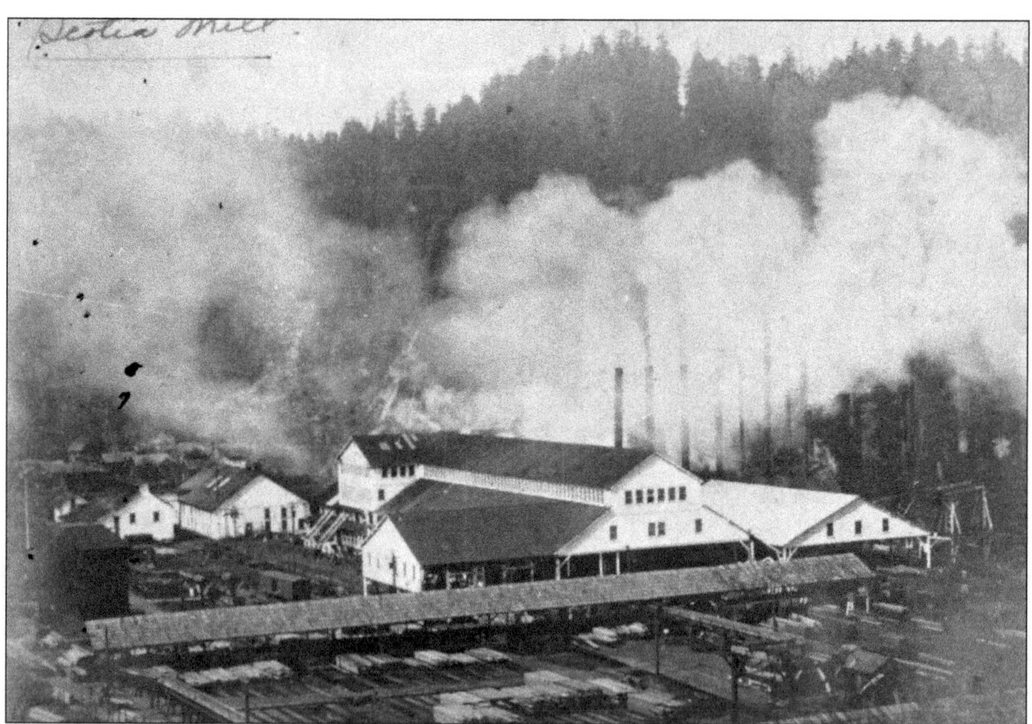

The Pacific Lumber Company devoted part of its operations to shingle production, as did many of the large corporate mills of the era. By 1904, the company had seven of Ole Hanson's shingle-making machines. The two hand-operated shingle saws and two shake machines "were in constant operation," according to the 1904 *Humboldt County Souvenir.*

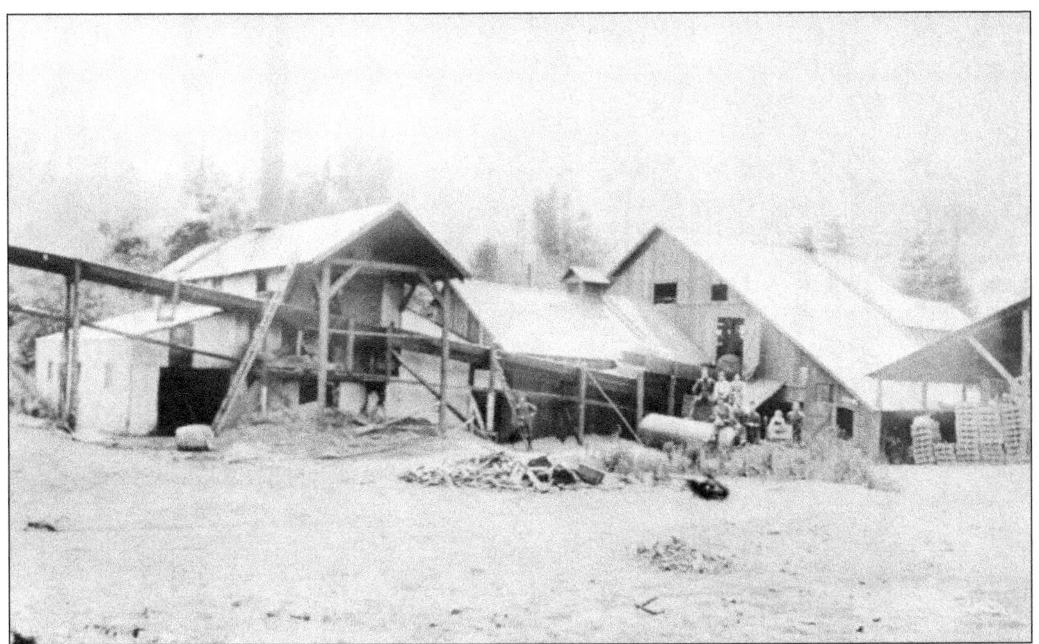

E.G. Ogle operated a shingle mill in Rio Dell, and his name still graces one of the streets in that community. Ogle opened his mill in 1901; by 1913, the facility employed 50 men and produced 120,000 shingles daily. His 1919 letterhead advertises that, in addition to shingles, Ogle's mill also produced shakes, posts, ties, and grape stakes. (HCHS.)

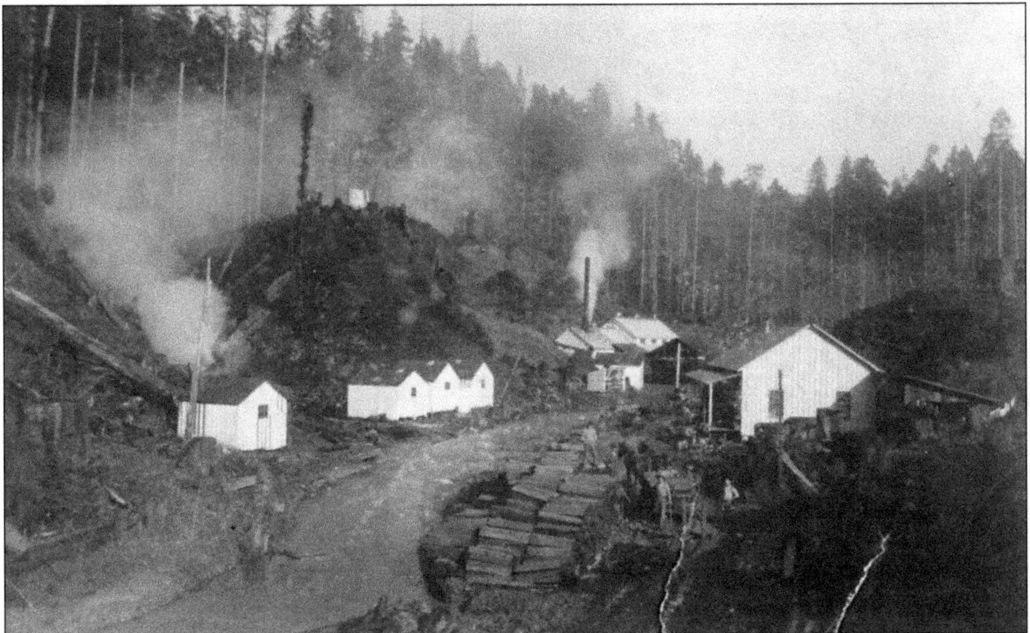

F.W. Beckwith had a general store and operated a shingle mill on the Van Duzen River near Hydesville. As with most shingle mills not connected to a large mill, Beckwith logged redwoods specifically for making shingles. A cord of shingle bolts, from 28 to 34 bolts, would be hauled to his mill to be made into shingles. In 1904, shingle bolts delivered to a mill were worth from $4.50 to $5.50 a cord.

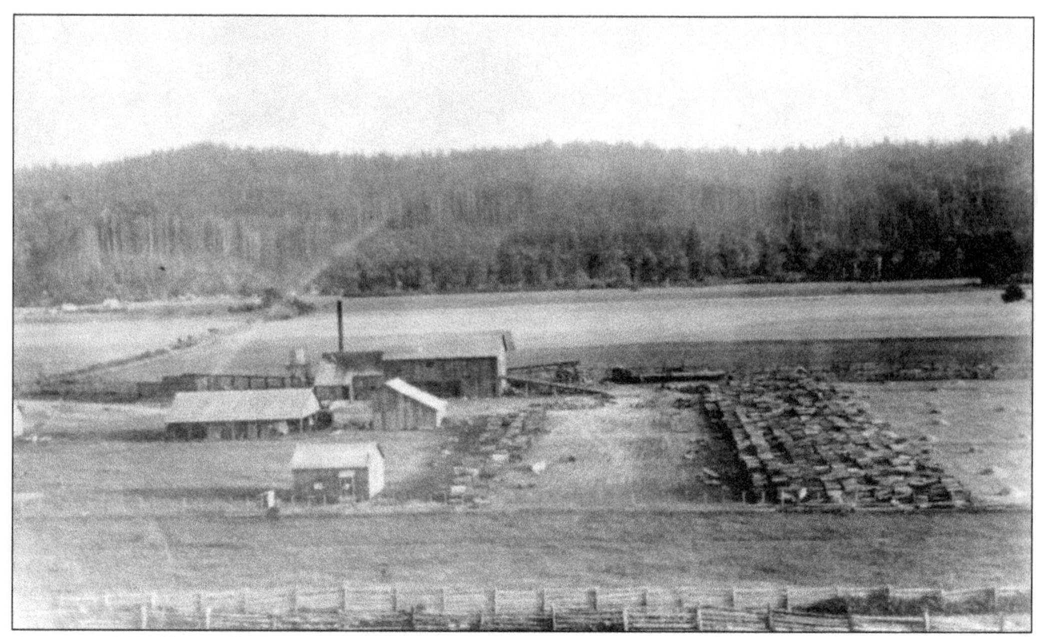

George W. Williams, born in Ohio, operated several shingle mills in the Eel River Valley. Pictured here is his Oil Creek Shake Mill along the Van Duzen River, which employed 40 men. In 1950, Charles Farrar noted in his *Growth and Development of Fortuna, California* that, when timber near Williams's Strong Creek Mill was exhausted, the facility was moved, as "it was cheaper to move the mill than to haul the shingle bolts the extra mile."

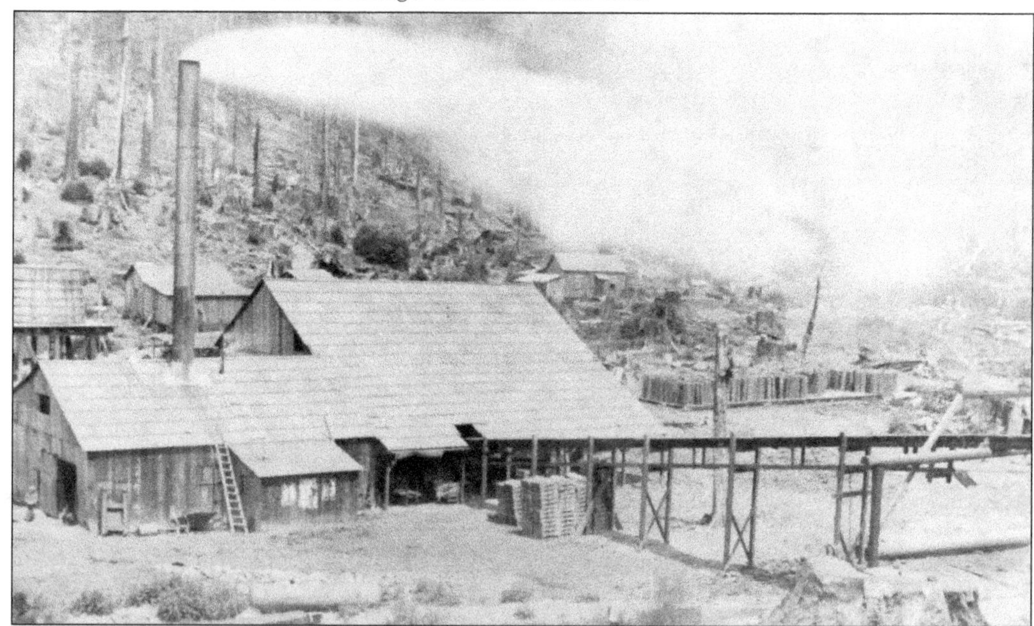

At Burnells, now called Alton, George Williams had another shingle mill. This facility was close to the tracks of the Eel River & Eureka Railroad, helping to keep down shipping expenses. Williams had access to trees across the Eel River and those from the Van Duzen River drainage. He served as Humboldt County supervisor for District Two, representing southern Humboldt in the early 1900s. (HCHS.)

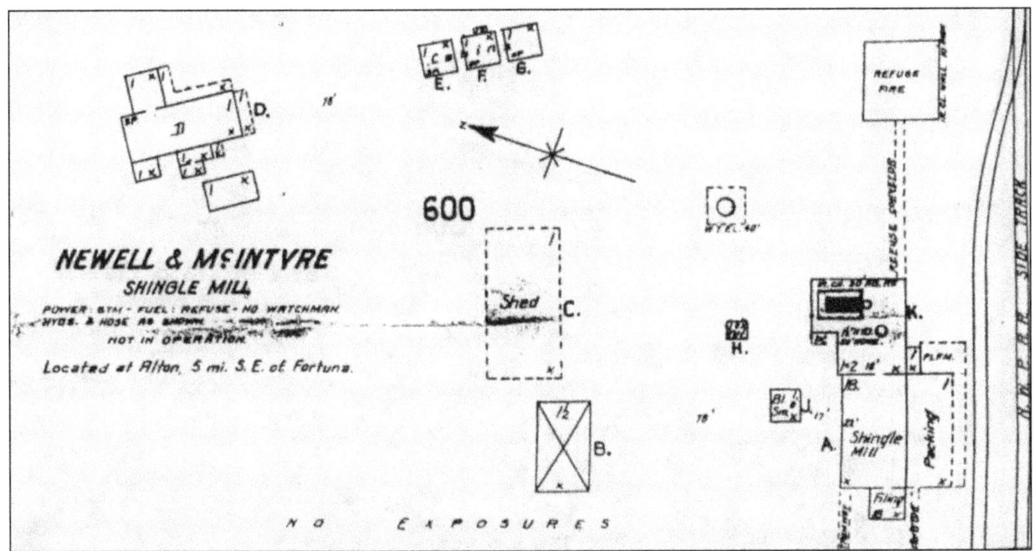

David S. Newell came to California from Maine in 1858 and worked in the logging industry around Mad River. In 1886, he moved to Fortuna and was involved in several businesses with his partner, Wallace McIntyre. These included a shingle mill at Alton, which closed in the early 20th century due to a glut in the shingle market in 1908.

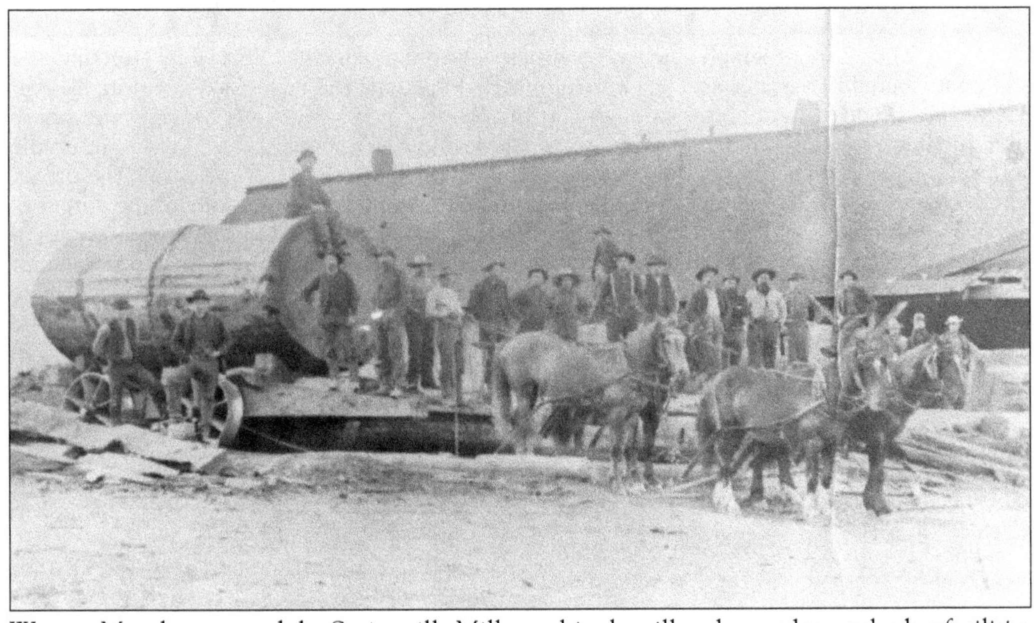

Wyman Murphy operated the Springville Mill as a shingle mill and owned several other facilities in the Fortuna area. The *Lumber World* of October 1, 1908, described the region as "the great Fortuna shingle making district." Here, a log is moved with horses to Murphy's Mill in 1885. William Chism of Rohnerville is the driver. (HCHS.)

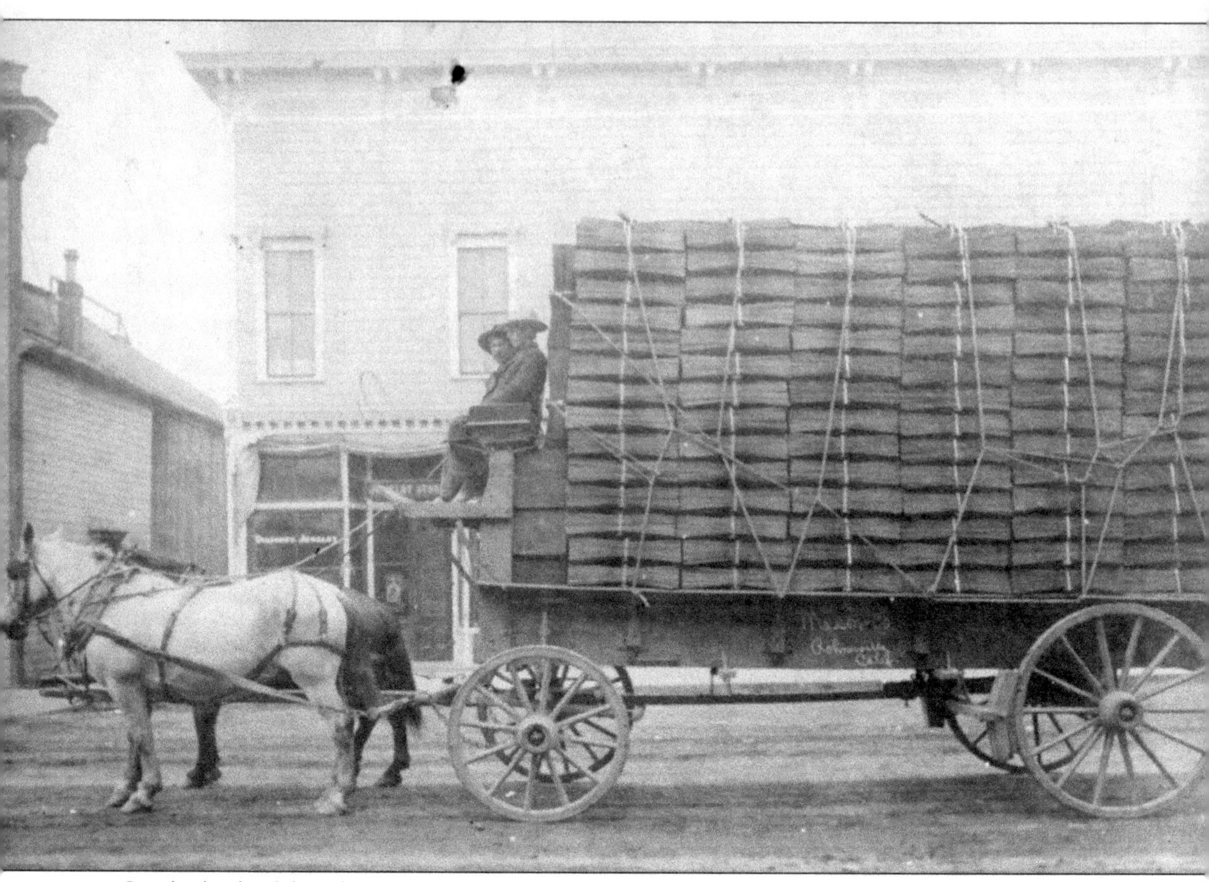

On the back of this photograph of a load of shingles in front of Fortuna's Star Hotel is an undated and unattributed newspaper article, explaining: "By long odds the largest load of shingles ever hauled by a single team of horses through Fortuna passed down Main street Monday afternoon. The shingles, 75,000 in number, were from the A. Masson & Co.'s shingle mill near Rohnerville and were loaded on the wagon direct from the hands of the packers. John Kennel, the driver, who by the way, is in the employ of Frank Barnam he having the contract to haul the output of the mill to the Fortuna depot, stopped in front of the Star Hotel and had Manager Bowman of the Skinner Duprey Drug Co. take a photograph of the immense load which towered in the air higher than some of the buildings on either side of Main street." The Star Hotel, built in 1876, was destroyed in a fire on January 28, 2015. Before being consumed by the flames, it was the oldest commercial building in Fortuna. (Clarke.)

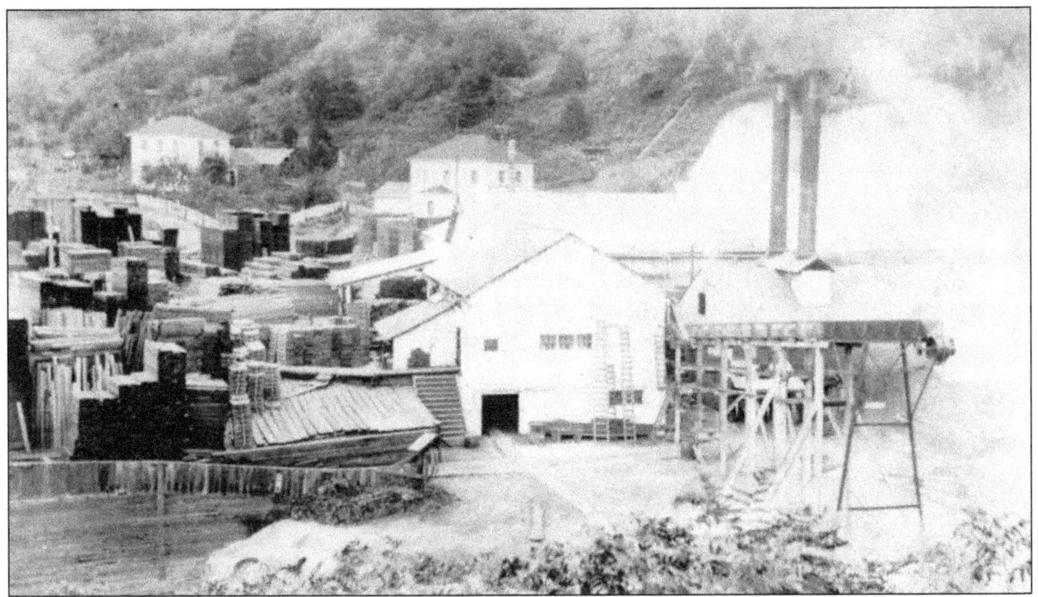

Another shingle mill in Fortuna was run by the Eel River Valley Lumber Company. In 1888, the shingle mill operated 18 hours a day and was cutting 75,000 shingles daily. The company owned its own railroad, vessels, and wharf. The wharf, at Field's Landing, was very busy, as the company exported most of its product. However, it did operate a mill yard, where it competed with TPL Co. selling lumber and shingles.

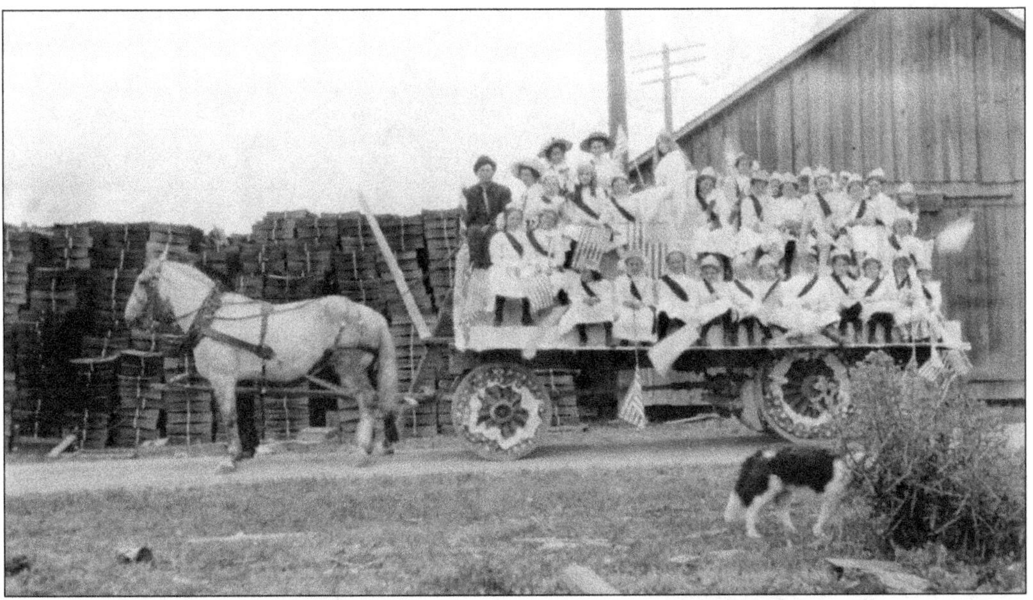

Virginian W.J. Swortzell and G.W. Williams purchased the Springville Mill in 1888, operating it as the Humboldt Milling Company shingle mill. The *Overland Monthly* observed in 1896: "these very enterprising people are large shippers over the Eel River & Eureka Railroad to San Francisco and the East. Their mills are complete and modern." The Swortzell & Williams Mill also provided electricity to Fortuna when it added a power plant in 1895.

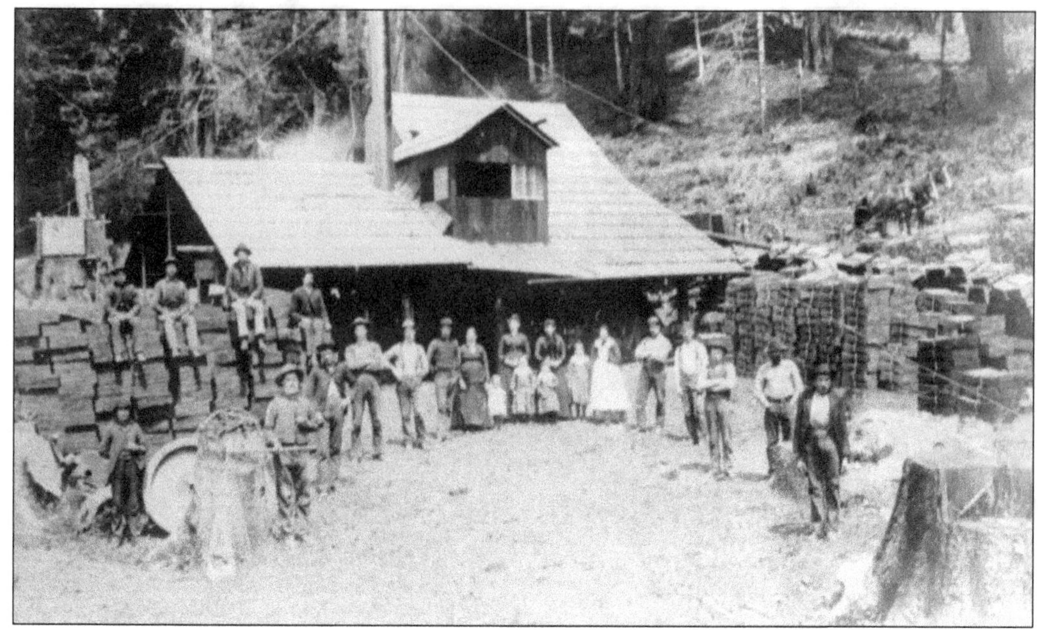

To the north of Fortuna, at Palmer Creek, Civil War veteran James Rowley from Iowa and his four sons started a shingle mill shortly after arriving in Humboldt in 1888. By 1892, they had produced 45 million shingles, using shingle bolts from lands owned by N. Tompkins. In the 1890s, Rowley and his sons also started making fruit boxes. James Rowley stands at far right with his large extended family. (Ross Rowley.)

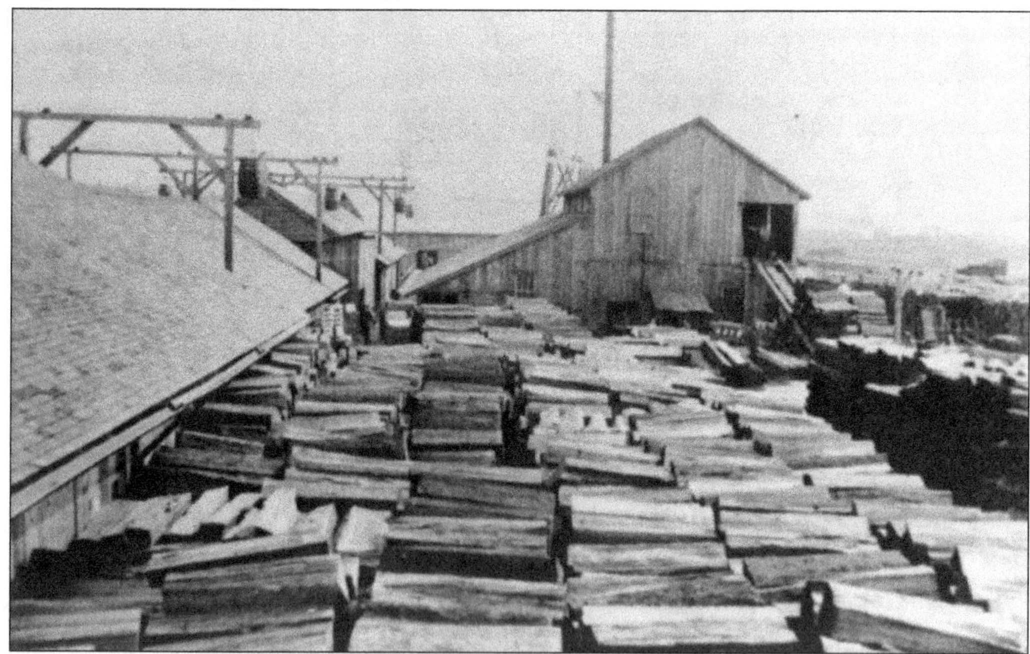

J.G. Loveren was a prominent shingle manufacturer in Eureka, operating one of the three stand-alone shingle mills in the city. His mill was located at the foot of U Street in Eureka. Loveren came to Eureka in 1874 and brought with him expertise gained in mill operations in Wisconsin. (HCHS.)

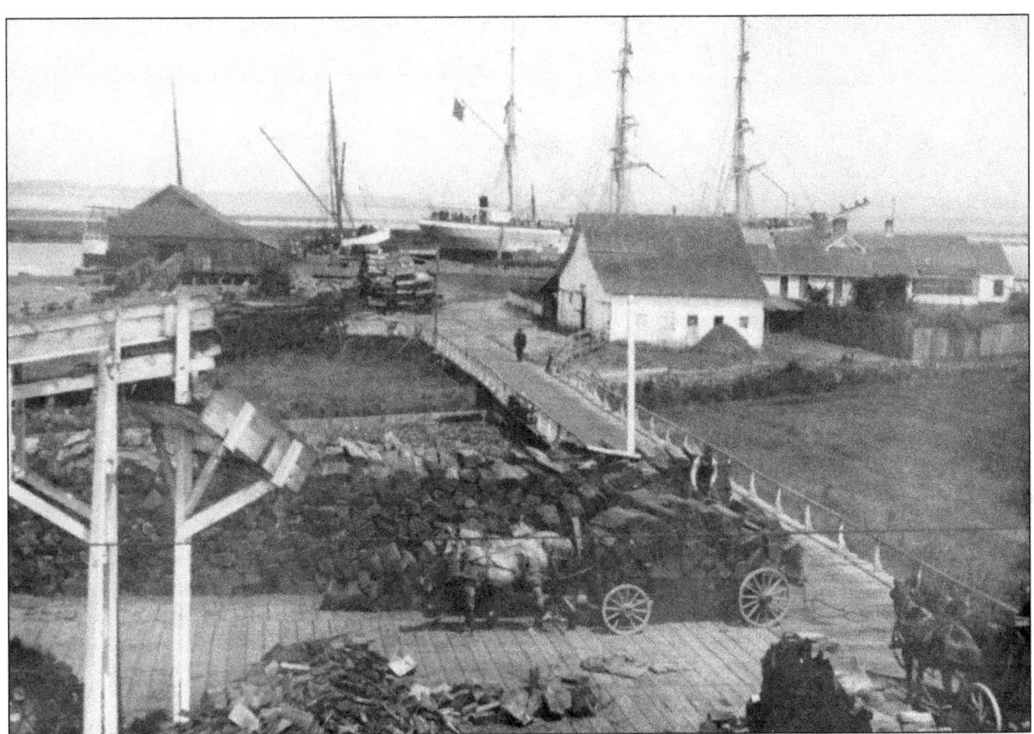

Robert Haughey operated a shingle mill in Eureka. It burned down in 1903. The *San Francisco Chronicle* reported that he rebuilt a "three machine shingle mill and in connection with it an up-to-date planing mill." Haughey also erected three drying houses, "fitted with the latest machinery." According to the 1904 *Humboldt County Souvenir*, Haughey was instrumental in making redwood shingles "recognized in the markets across the Rockies as superior to any other shingle." (HCHS.)

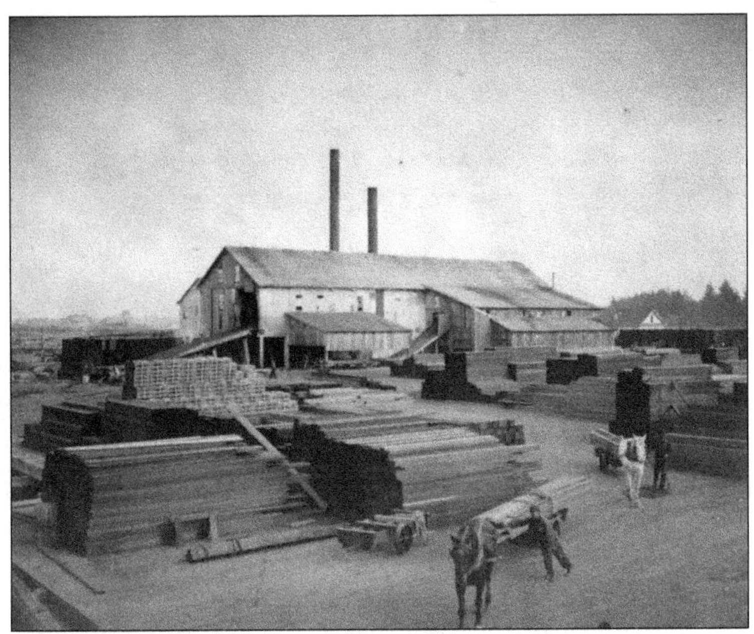

W.G. Press, a Chicago entrepreneur, came to Humboldt County at the turn of the 20th century, seeking a cool climate during the summer for his health. He became involved in the shingle business, building a large shingle mill with a capacity of 300,000 shingles per day at Bucksport in 1902. Press never permanently moved to Eureka, but spent his summers in Humboldt overseeing his mill and operations. (HSU.)

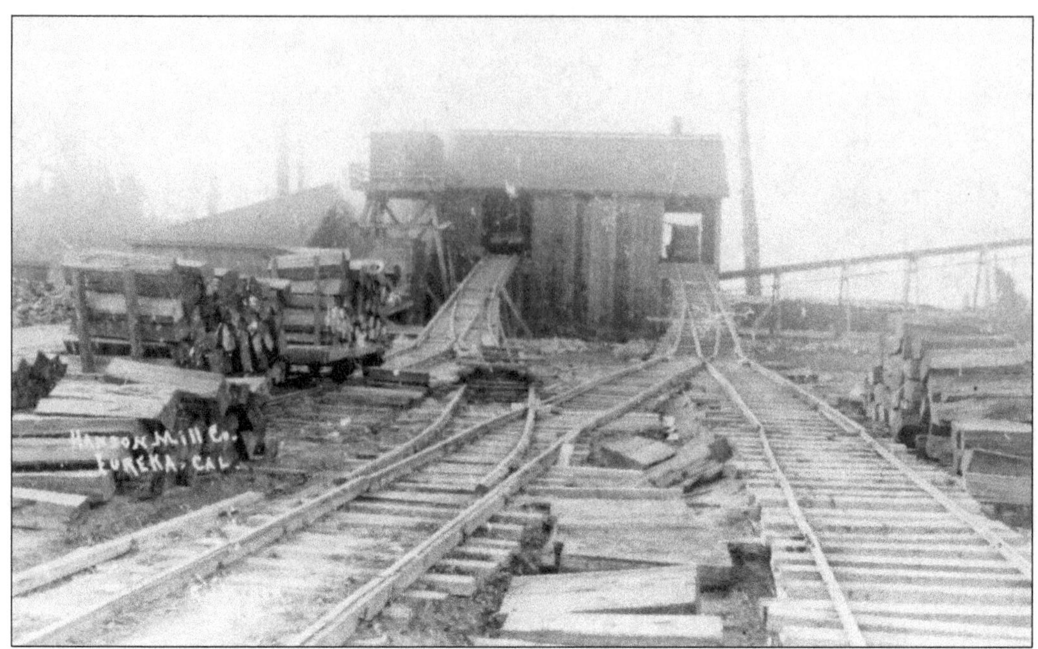

In addition to building the machine credited with revolutionizing the shingle business in Humboldt County, Ole Hanson operated his own shingle mill near Freshwater. Hanson came to Eureka from Denmark in the late 1870s. At the time of his death in 1915, he had been involved with the shingle business for almost 30 years. He had worked for many of the Eureka shingle mills while perfecting his shingle-making machine. (HCHS.)

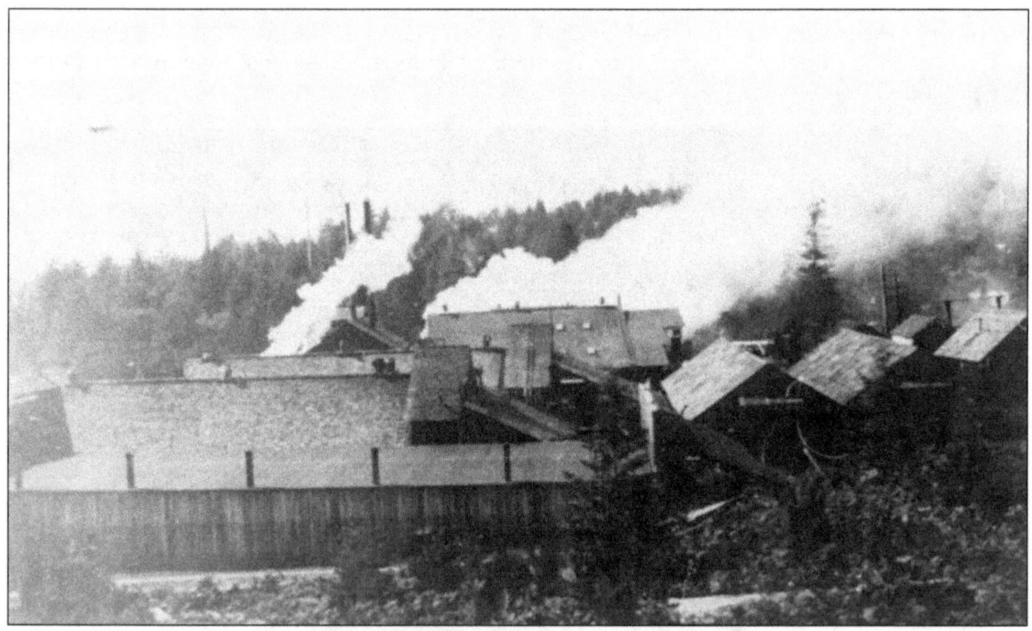

An article in the January 1909 *Overland Monthly* described the M.A. Burns Manufacturing Company of Eureka as one of the leading lumber interests of the community. The Burns company also owned and operated the Eastern Steamship Company. Beginning operations in the early 1900s, the company grew rapidly, and by 1918 was producing 200,000 shingles a day. (HSU.)

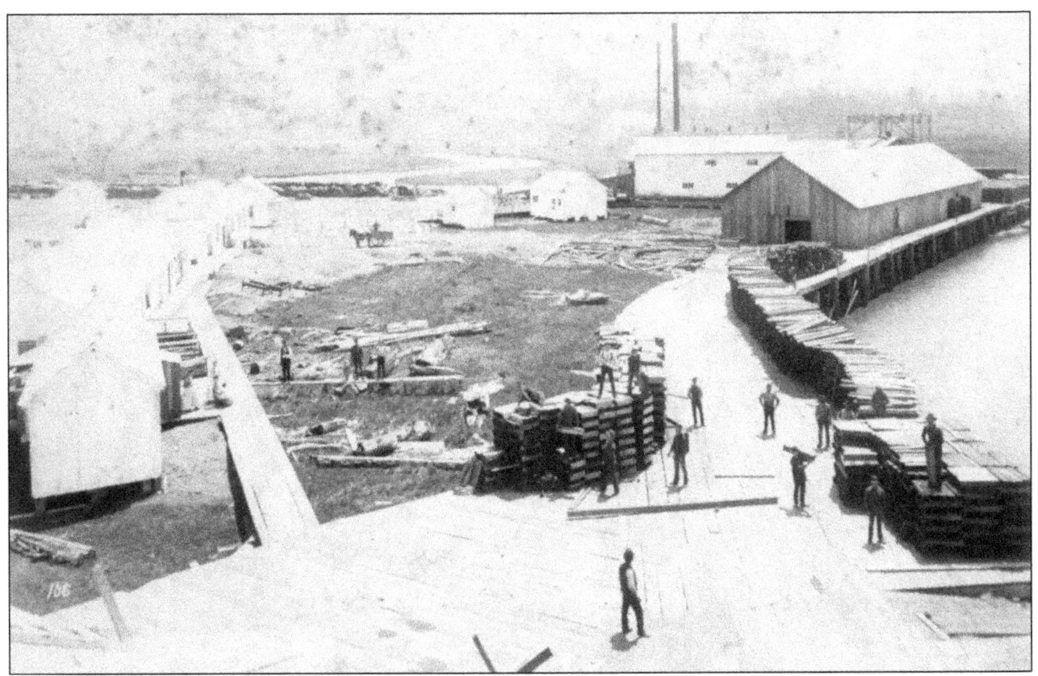

Cousins's shingle mill was part of the company's larger mill on Gunther Island. Later sold to Excelsior Redwood, the company continued to produce shingles, molding, doors, sashes, and, of course, lumber. The mill operations were described in *Memorial and Biographical History of Northern California* (1891) as "running day and night, sawing the gigantic logs. The operation is very interesting, many new devices being adopted to handle the enormous sticks." (HSU.)

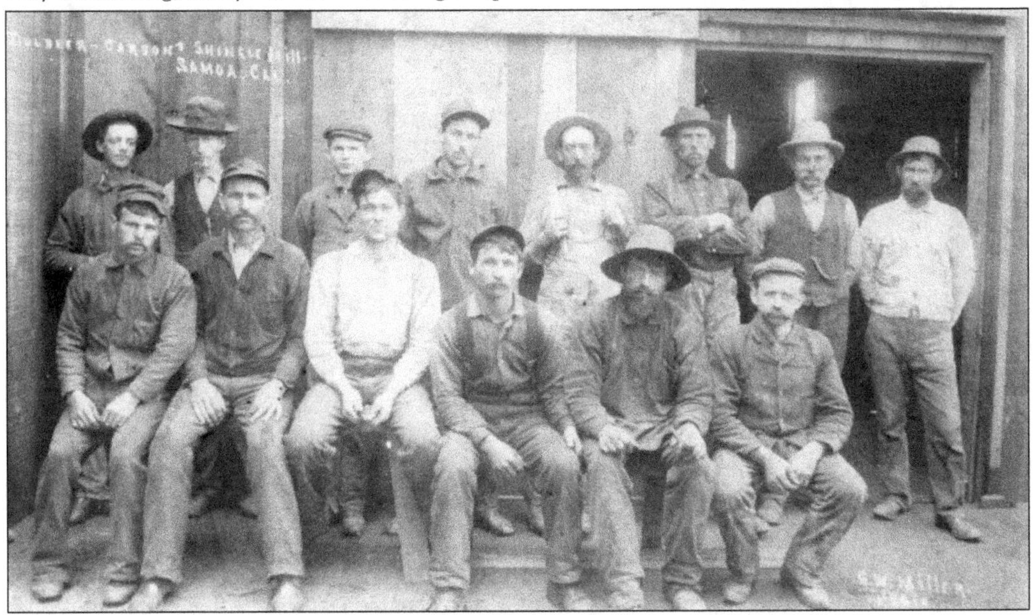

The Dolbeer & Carson Company built a shingle mill at Samoa to take advantage of the growing demand for redwood shingles. Its mill, with a capacity of 100,000 shingles a day, also produced laths and pickets. The mill had its own wharf, and the firm's product was shipped directly from the mill to consumers along the West Coast and to other markets. (HSU.)

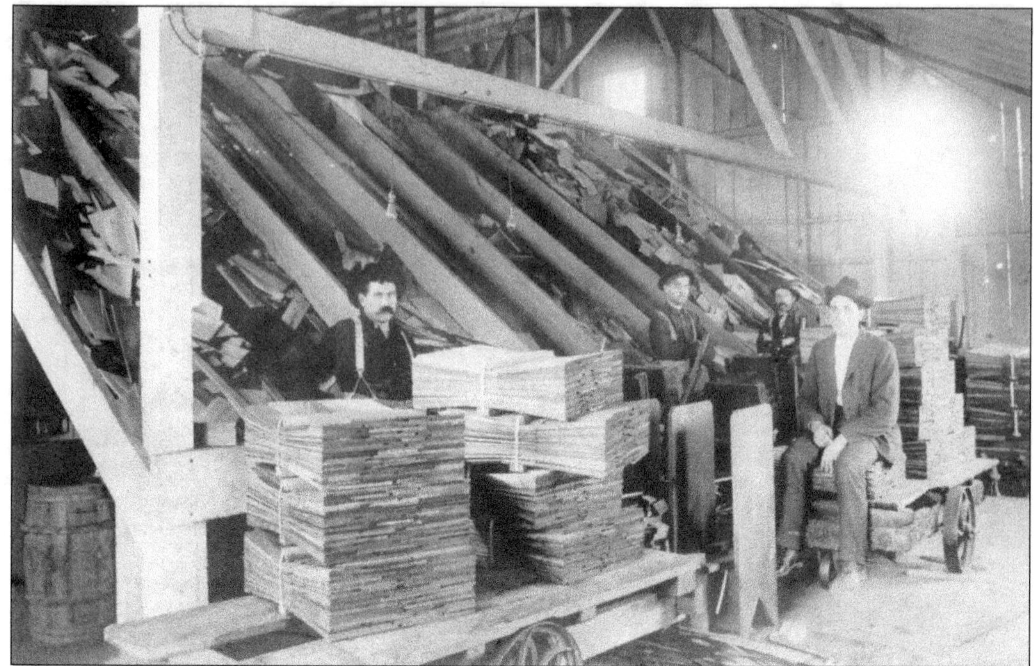

The Occidental Shingle Mill at Ryan's Slough was part of the McKay Company operations. The mill burned down in 1903 and, according to the *San Francisco Chronicle*, was "rebuilt at once upon modern plans." The new mill had three Hanson machines and a new drying shed that could dry 200,000 shingles every 24 hours. (HCHS.)

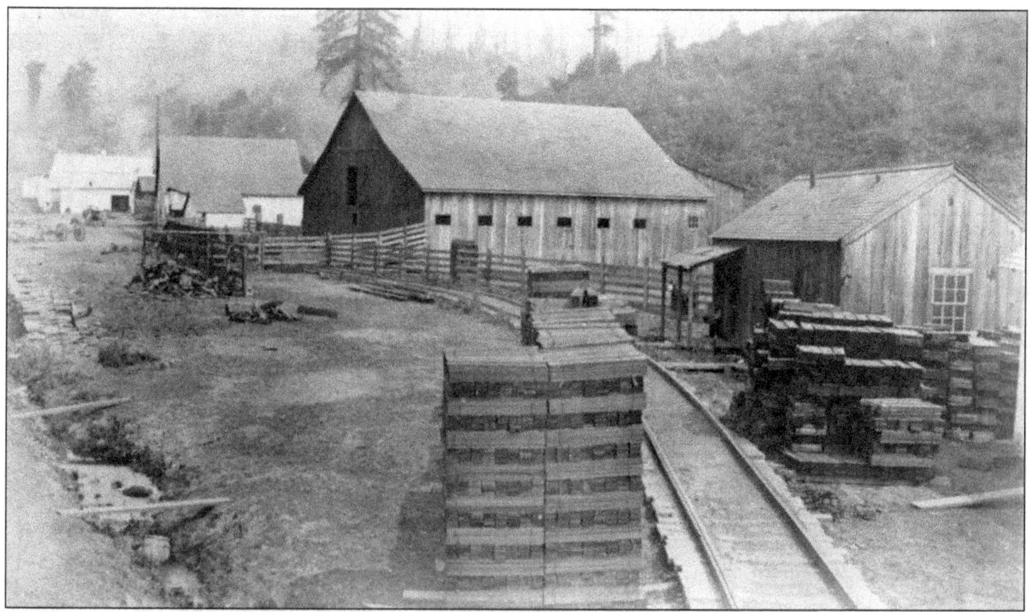

The Union Mill of Flanigan, Brosnan & Company, a shingle mill on Jacoby Creek, was also known as the Harpst or Bayside Mill. The firm Harpst & Spring partnered with Flanigan, Brosnan & Company to open the shingle mill in 1882. Flanigan, Brosnan's logging railroad brought the shingle products to the bay, where they were loaded directly onto vessels docked at its wharf near Bayside (HSU.)

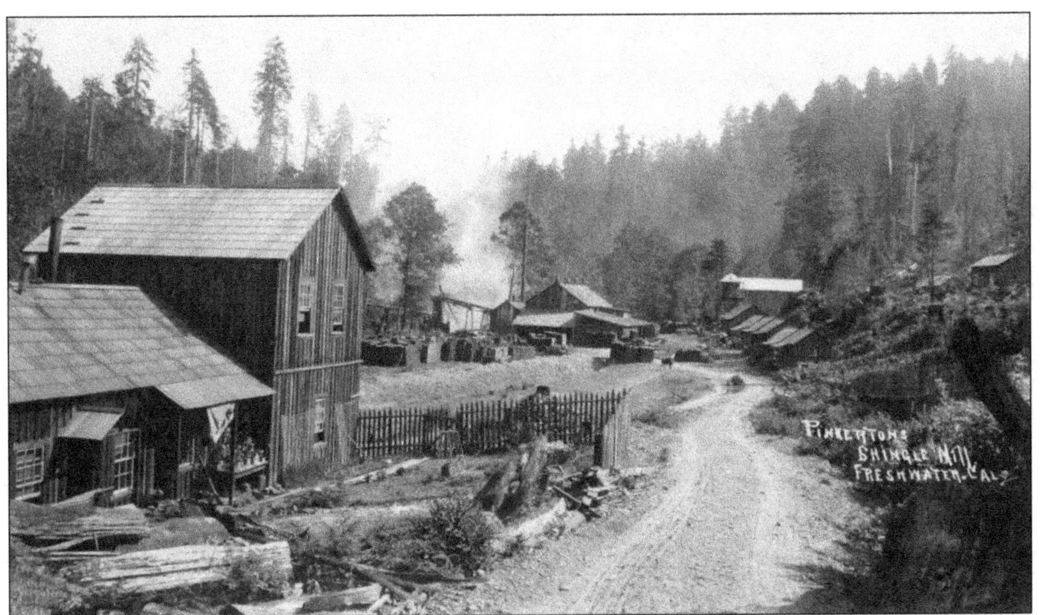

George Pinkerton began his shingle mill at Freshwater shortly after his arrival in Humboldt County in 1875. His facility had two shingle machines and one shake machine. One of his 11 employees, Gilman C. Knapp, invented the Knapp Shake Machine for sawing shakes. Pinkerton also served as superintendent of the woods for the Little River Redwood Company. (HSU.)

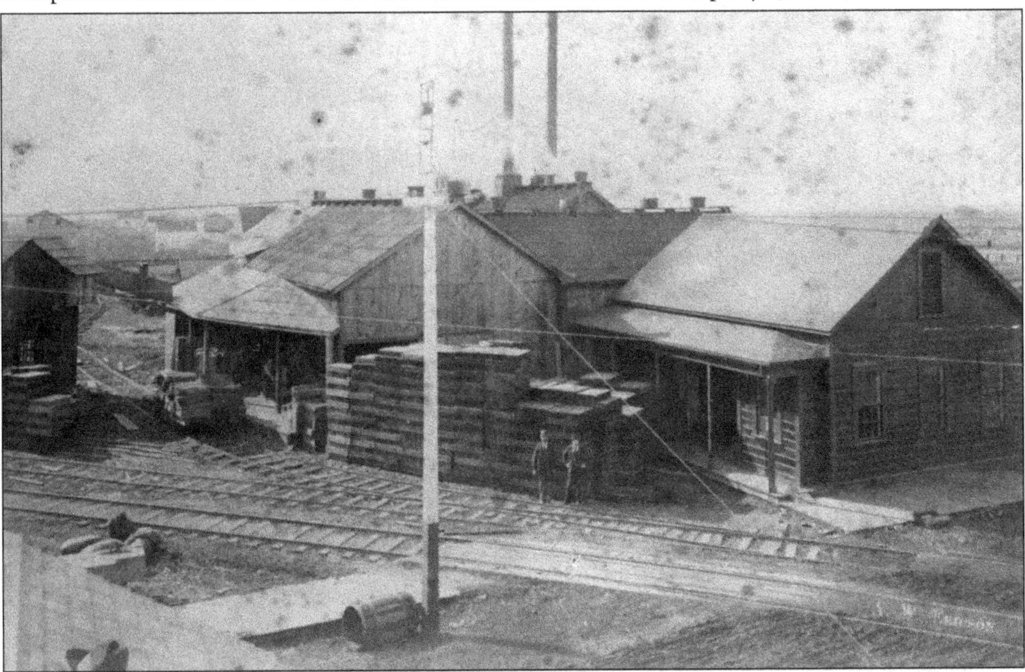

The Humboldt Manufacturing Company of Arcata, owned by Swedish immigrant Isaac Cullberg Jr., began operations in 1894 near Eighth and K Streets. In 1895, the *Blue Lake Advocate* reported that the company was "running in full blast on a schedule of eighteen hours. The cutting capacity of the shingle mill averages about 80,000 while the shake machine cuts about 15,000 per day." In 1905, the company began to produce electricity for the city of Arcata. (HSU.)

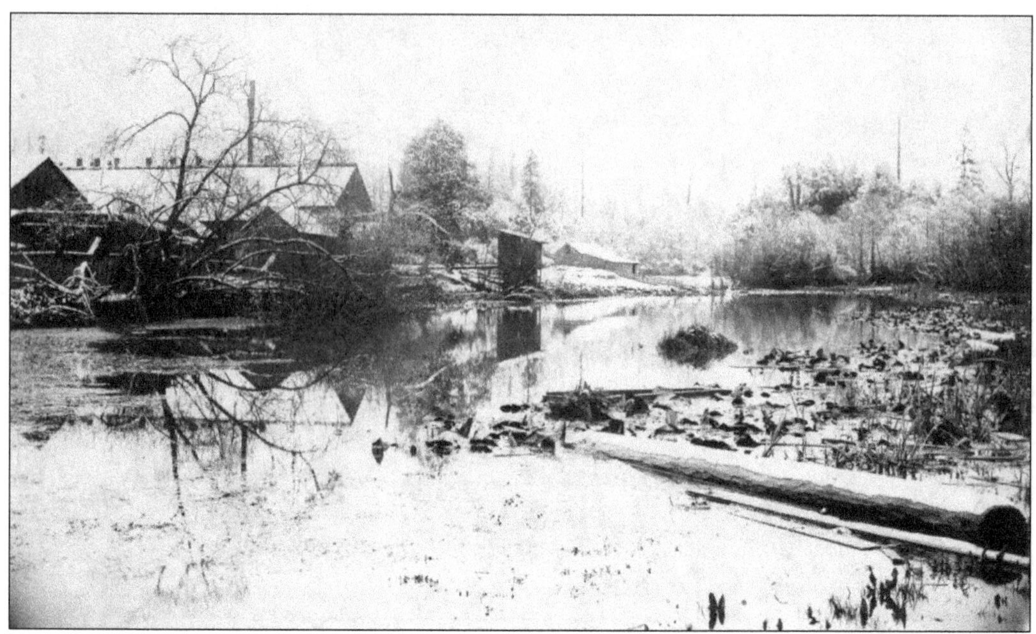

The Blue Lake Manufacturing Company, like the Humboldt Manufacturing Company, also produced electricity as a by-product of making shingles. The company used a steam engine to power both the mill and 600 incandescent lights for the town of Blue Lake. The mill was in operation from 1902 until 1912, when it sold out to the Western Gas & Electric Company. (HSU.)

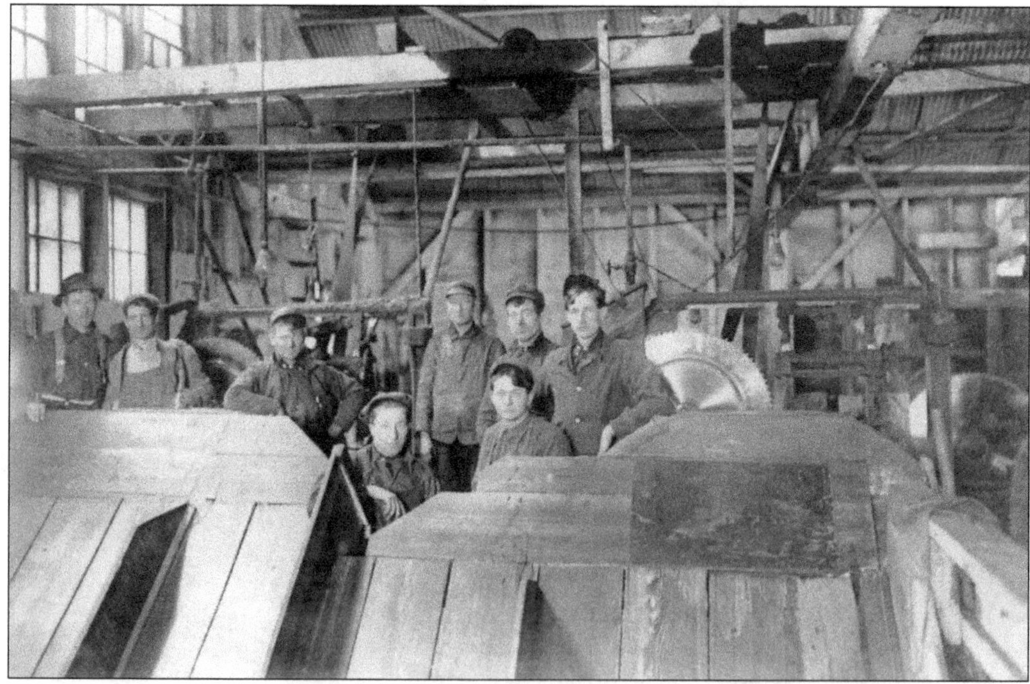

In 1910, C.J. McConnaha and his brother Burr opened a shingle mill at Trinidad. They also had a mill at Patrick's Point. However, in 1918, they had to move their workers to the Trinidad plant, as they were encountering difficulties in hauling the shingles to Trinidad. The company also had a bolt camp near Essex. (HCHS.)

Four

SPECIALTY MILLS

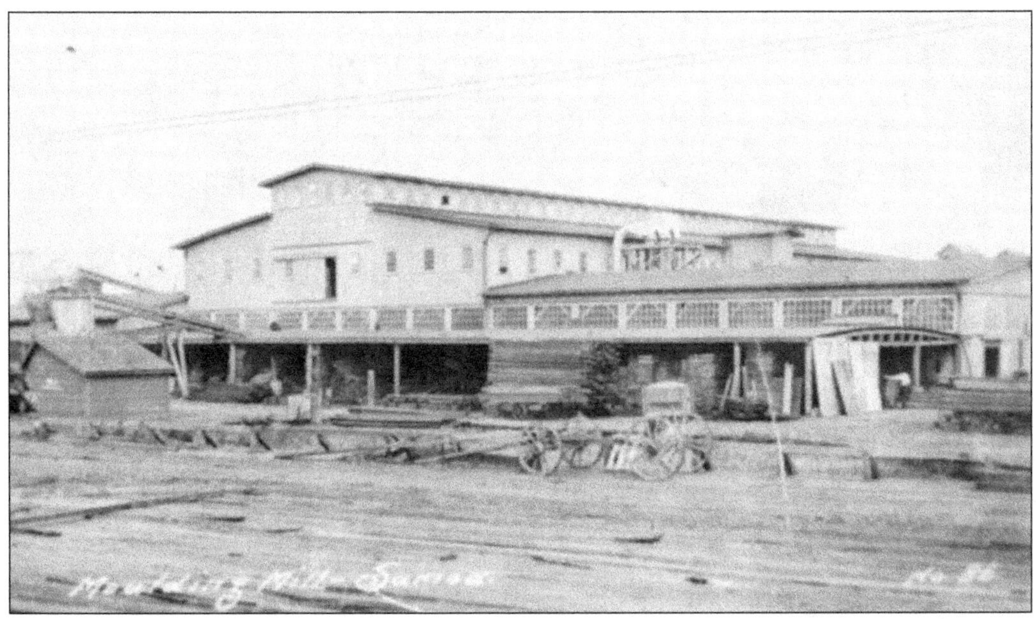

In the late 1800s, redwood was logged primarily for lumber and shingles. Other uses, however, were also being explored, including the production of moldings for houses. Redwood molding was desirable, as it was easy to cut into the many patterns used in Victorian houses, both for the exterior and interior. This is the Hammond molding mill at Samoa. (HSU.)

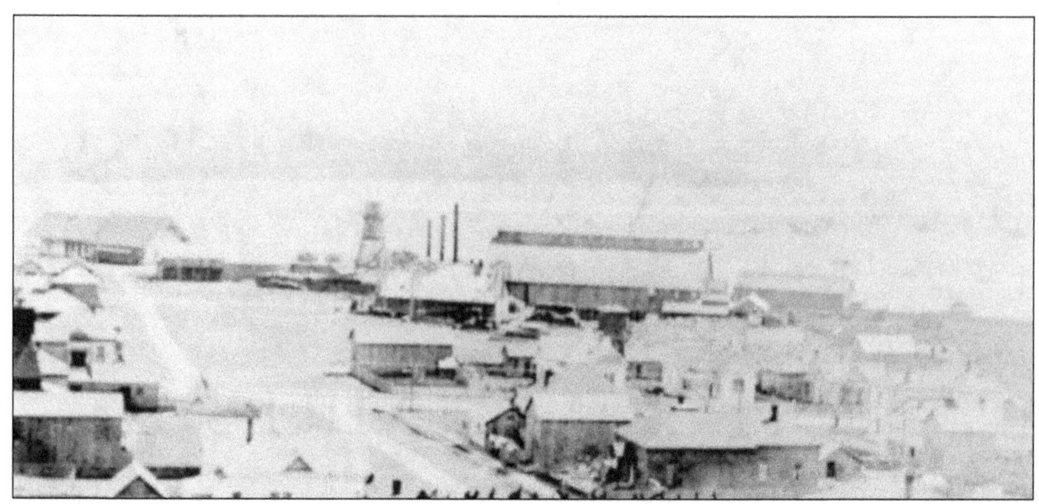

The Humboldt Milling Company operated the shingle mill at Fortuna, with William Swortzell as president. In addition to making shingles, they also specialized in moldings and making redwood doors. In 1913, the firm won an award at the California State Fair for "producing the best redwood doors turned out by any firm in the state." The *Humboldt County Souvenir* believed the Humboldt Milling Company operated the "largest door, moulding, sash, shingle and shake mill in the county." In 1896, George Hooper, vice president of the Excelsior Redwood Company, noted that the firm sold many redwood doors and that builders desired redwood doors since "once put in place, they are never called upon to repair them." Hooper also observed that doors made "in the proper manner will stand the test of age and wear against other soft wood."

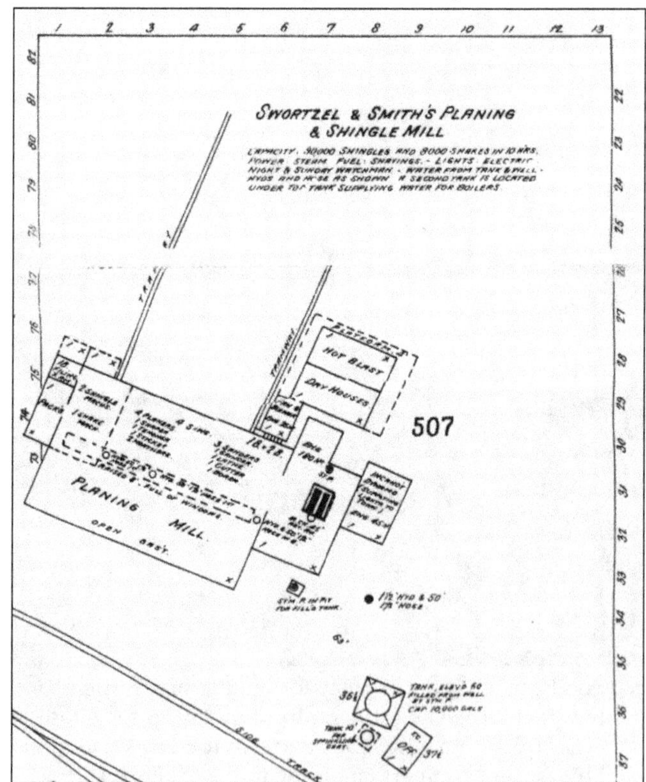

One use touted for redwood was in the production of water tanks and pipes. Here, redwood pipes made for the Oregon & Eureka Railroad leave the Bay Mill. Redwood pipes, according to the Redwood Manufacturers, were a constantly growing market in 1897. They claimed that "where water pressure is steady . . . there is no pipe more economical." (Clarke.)

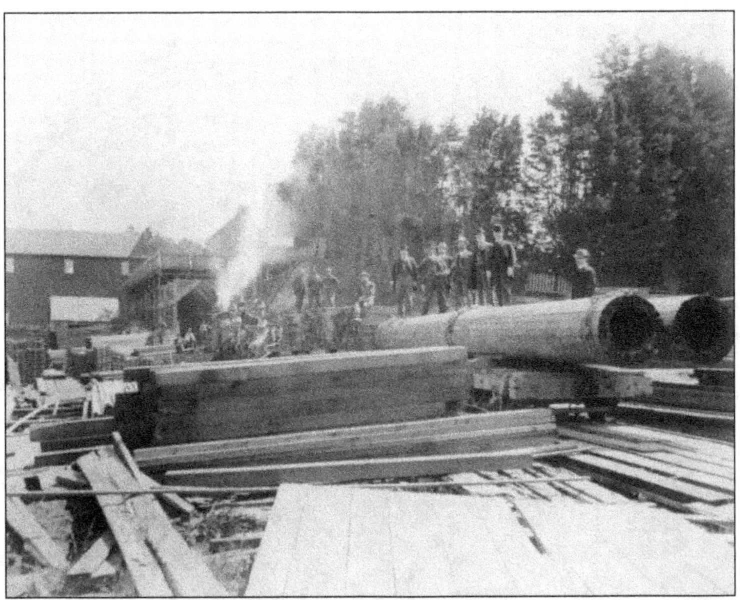

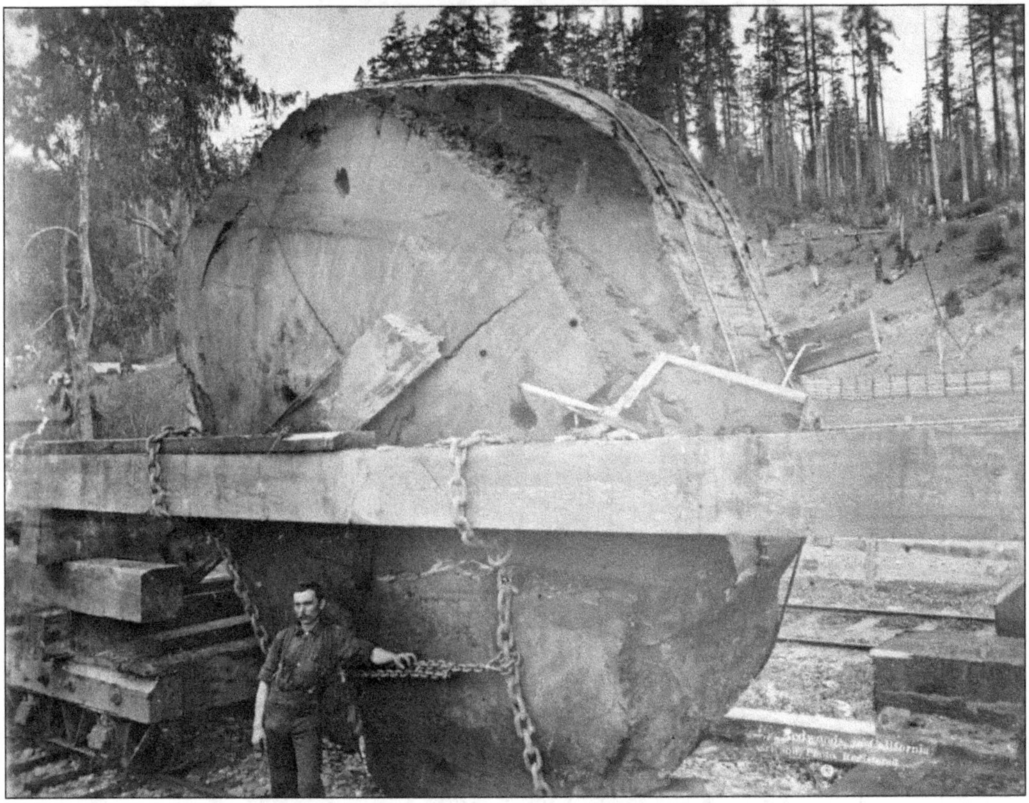

The "Astor cut" represents the endeavors of redwood lumber manufacturers to find new markets by promoting redwood products. In 1898, William Astor allegedly bet the Prince of Wales that a single redwood section would create a table with seating for 45. Cut in Fieldbrook, in the Vance logging operations, the section was shipped to England. The sixteen-foot, six-inch section remained outdoors, being too large to be moved into Astor's mansion. (Clarke.)

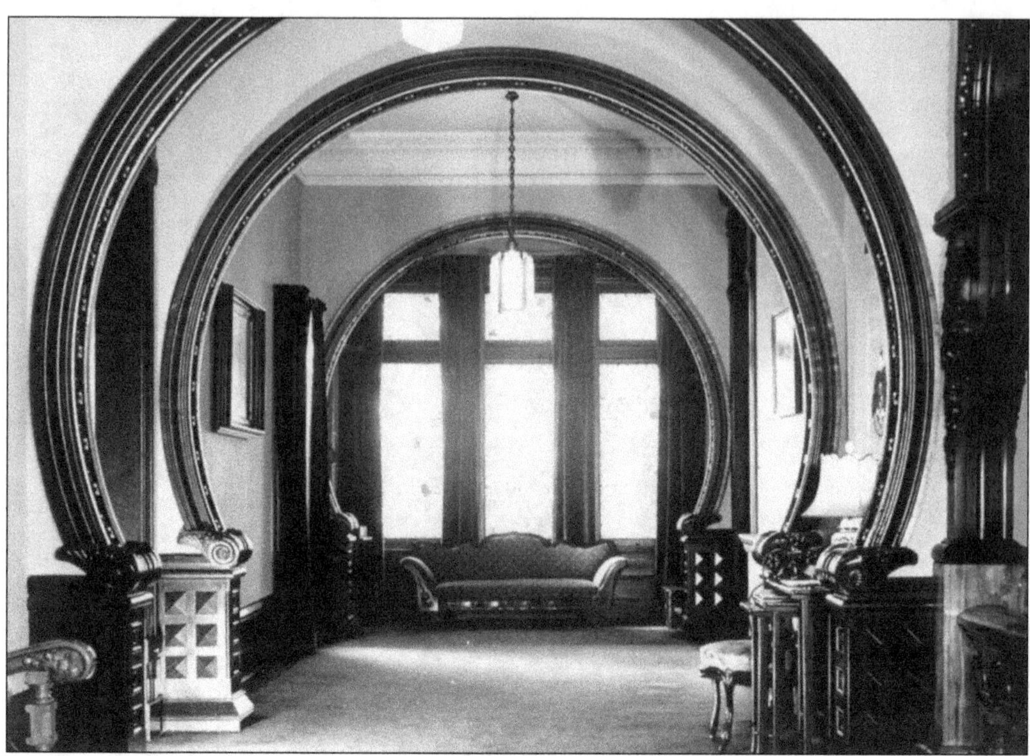

William Carson built a mansion in 1884–1885 above his Bay Mill to show off the qualities of redwood. He was able to keep many of his mill's workers employed during a recession in the lumber business by hiring those same workers to build his house. Carson hired wood carvers from around the world to work on the interior. Another impact of Carson's mansion was that it inspired many others to build houses that mimicked the architecture and use of redwood. Several businesses in Eureka were specialty mills that focused on finished redwood. In 1890, Charles Richardson was the proprietor of the Eureka Moulding Mill, which specialized in redwood furniture and ornamental house finishes.

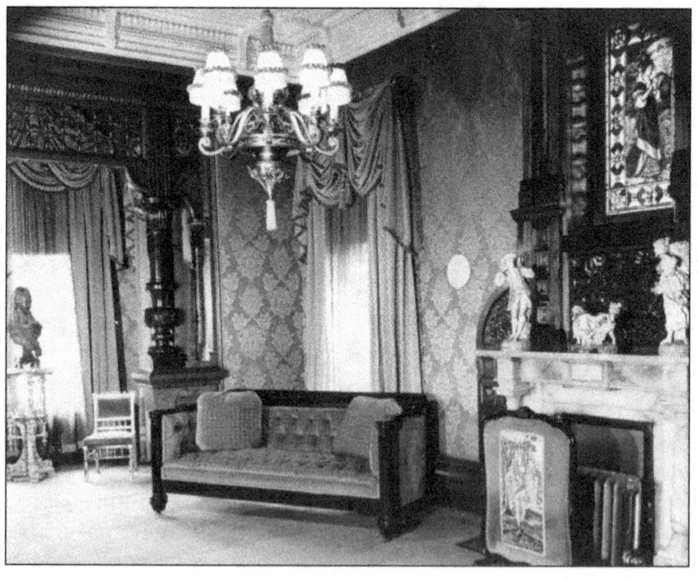

One ornamental feature used extensively in the Carson Mansion is wood from redwood burl. Burls are growths found naturally on redwoods, often at the base of the tree, as shown here. Some burls are found higher along the trunk. Burl wood is often curly and has intricate designs due to unsprouted buds forming the burl.

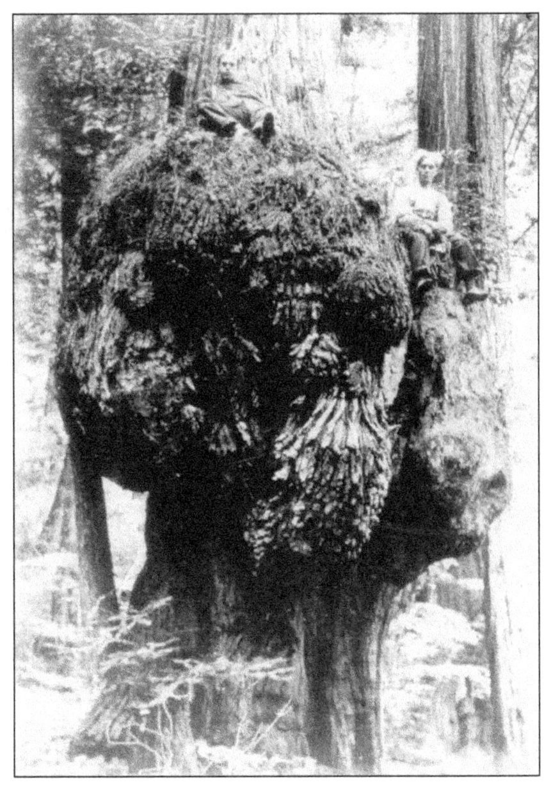

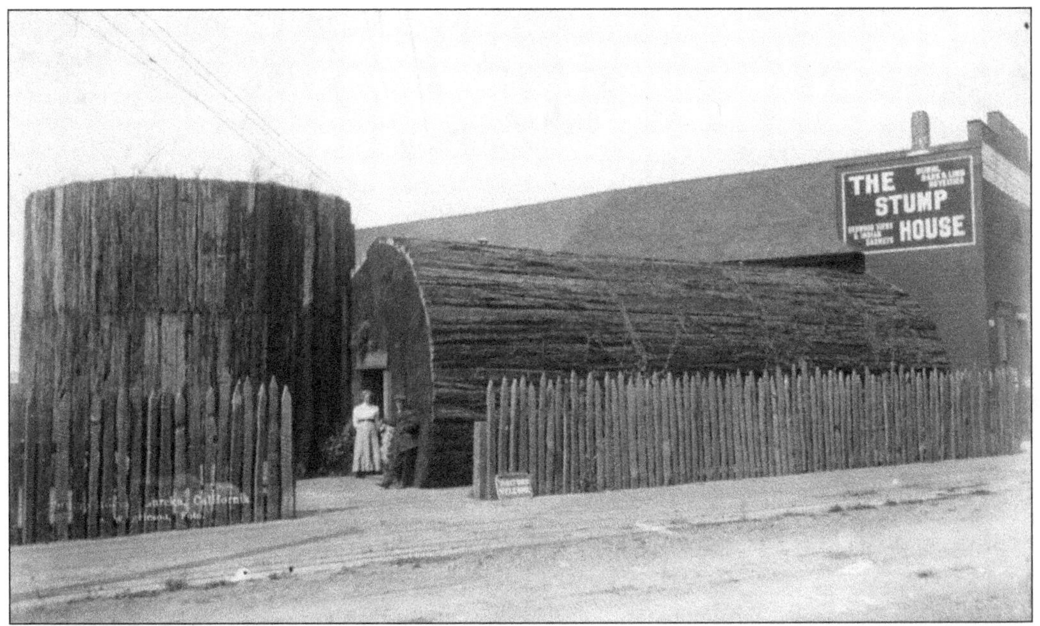

A small industry centered on redwood burls. In 1902, Rodney Burns opened the Stump House, which included a factory to produce burl cups, dishes, plates, and other memorabilia. Leigh H. Irving notes that it was housed in "a structure resembling a mammoth redwood log as it lies in the forest after being felled. Within . . . is an array of manufactured articles such as can be found nowhere else." (HSU.)

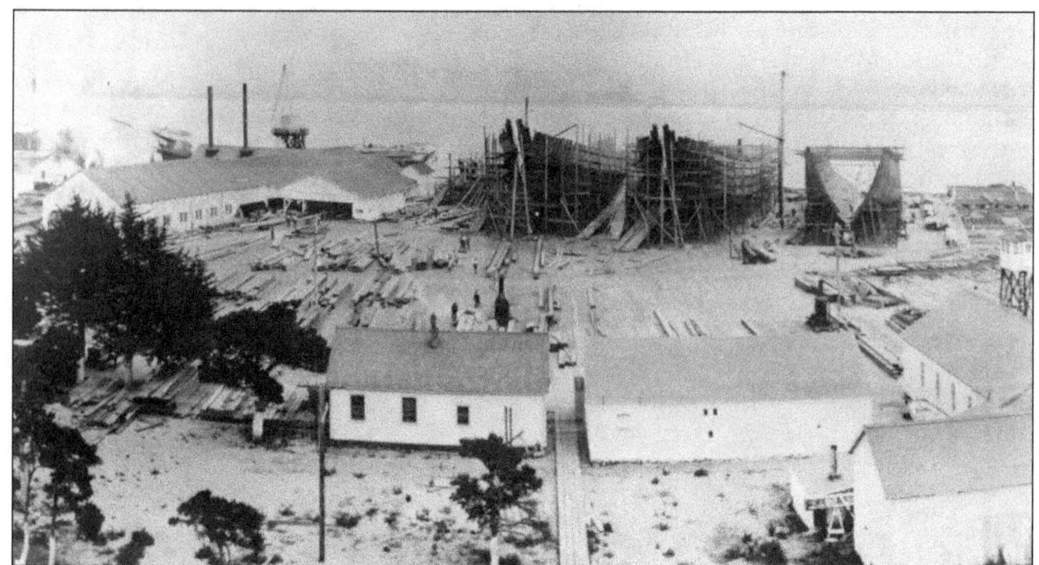

Although redwood was the predominant tree logged in Humboldt County in the 19th century, it was not the only variety of tree harvested. Douglas fir, or Oregon pine, as it was known at the time, was logged specifically for building ships. Shipbuilding was a critical adjunct to the redwood lumber industry, as mill owners depended on seagoing vessels for transporting their product. (HSU.)

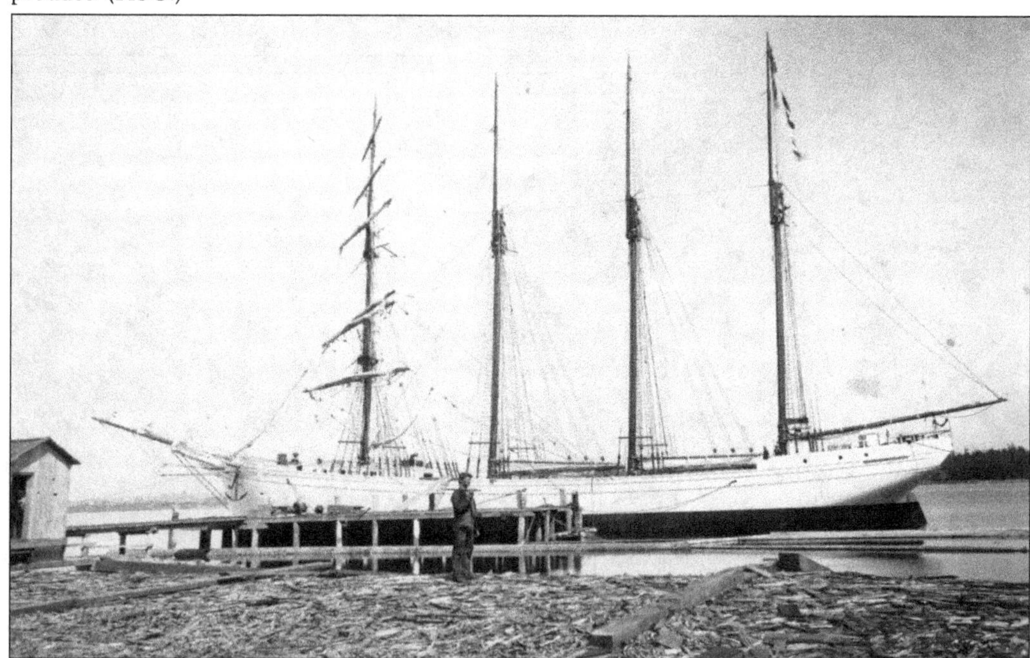

The Redwood Lumber Manufacturers Association explained the importance of ships to the industry in 1897: "Engaged in carrying to market the output of these redwood mills are nearly one hundred different sailing vessels, and about half as many steam schooners employed the year round. . . . The largest craft are generally three, four, and five masted and are employed in the direct trade with Central and South America, the islands of the Pacific, and Australia." Pictured here is the four-masted *William Carson*, launched in 1899. (HSU.)

One of the first shipbuilders on Humboldt Bay was Euphronius Cousins. His Eureka shipyard was near the Dolbeer & Carson mill. The first vessel built by Cousins was the brig *Hesperian* in 1865. One of the last ships built by the firm was *Ruby Cousins* (pictured) in 1882. Cousins is credited with building 11 ships between 1865 and 1883. (HSU.)

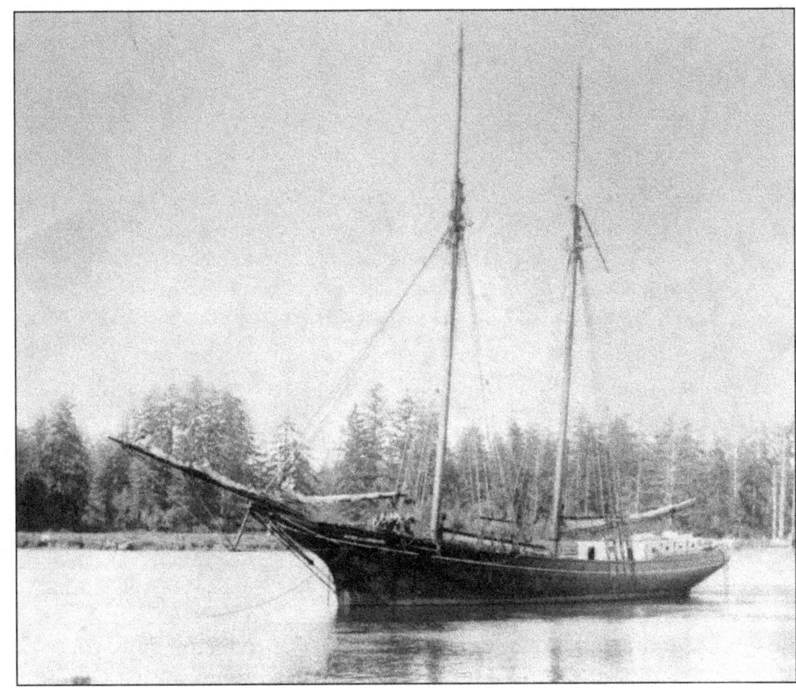

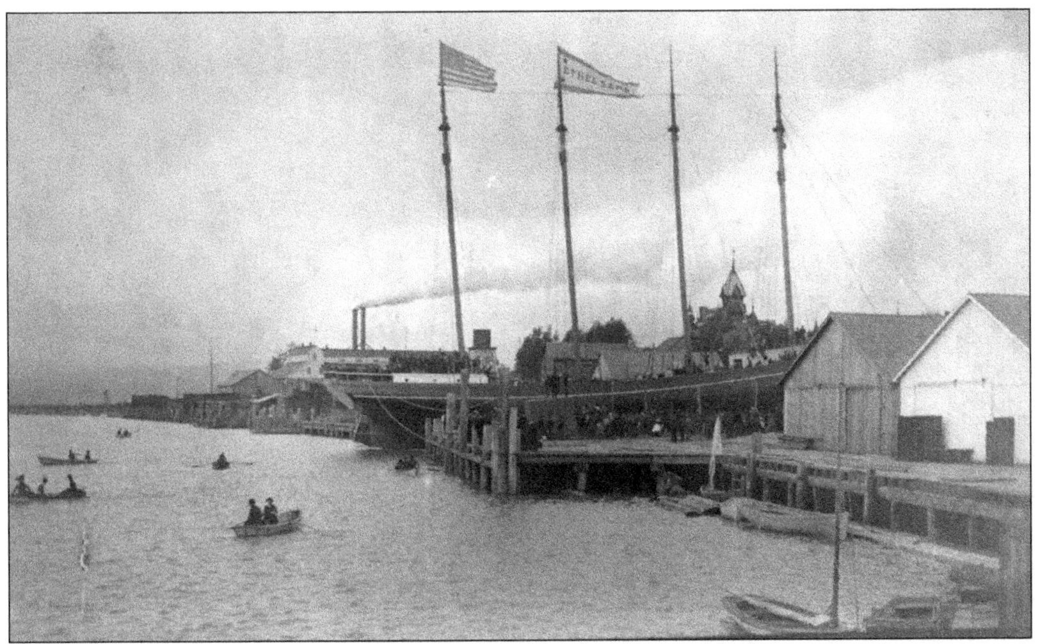

Also using Cousins's shipyard facility in Eureka at the foot of K Street was the firm Cutten & McDonald, which built three vessels between 1881 and 1883. The firm J. Farnum next used the facility, building one ship in 1887. From 1889 to 1893, Peter Mathews used the site to build five schooners. One of his ships, the *Ethel Zane*, is shown being launched in 1891. (HSU.)

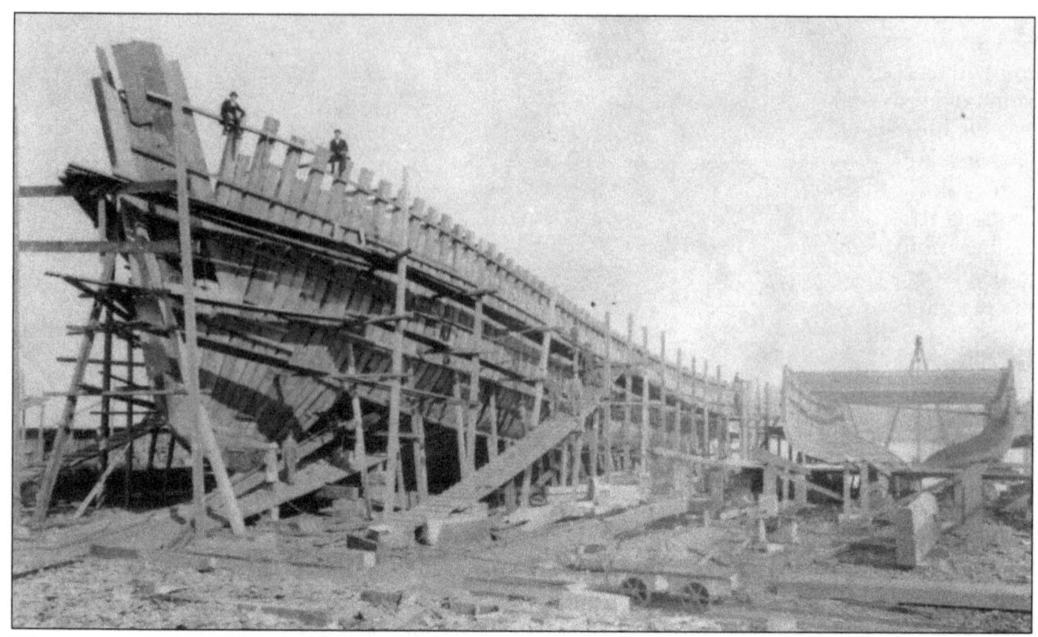

The most prolific of Humboldt Bay shipbuilders, producing more than 100 vessels between 1867 and 1902, Hans Bendixson came to Eureka in 1867 from Denmark. Observing that the hazardous sandbar at the bay's mouth prevented many ships from sailing safely into the harbor, Bendixson designed and built ships with a shallower draft than those of other ship-makers along the coast. His ships' structure allowed lumber to be stacked on the deck. (HSU.)

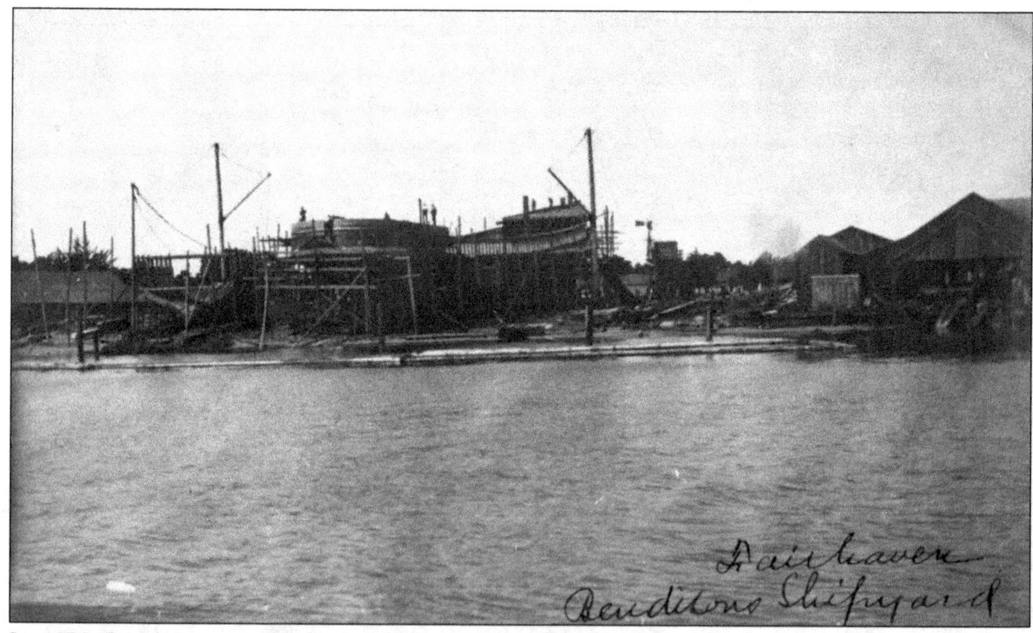

In 1873, Bendixson established a shipyard at Fairhaven. There, he had his own mill, cutting lumber to specifications for shipbuilding, shops, and lumberyard. He also had cottages for his more than 150 employees. Bendixson used Douglas fir, as it was well suited for shipbuilding. Unlike redwood, it did not reabsorb water, had a higher tensile strength, was not as brittle, and could better withstand the marine environment. (HSU.)

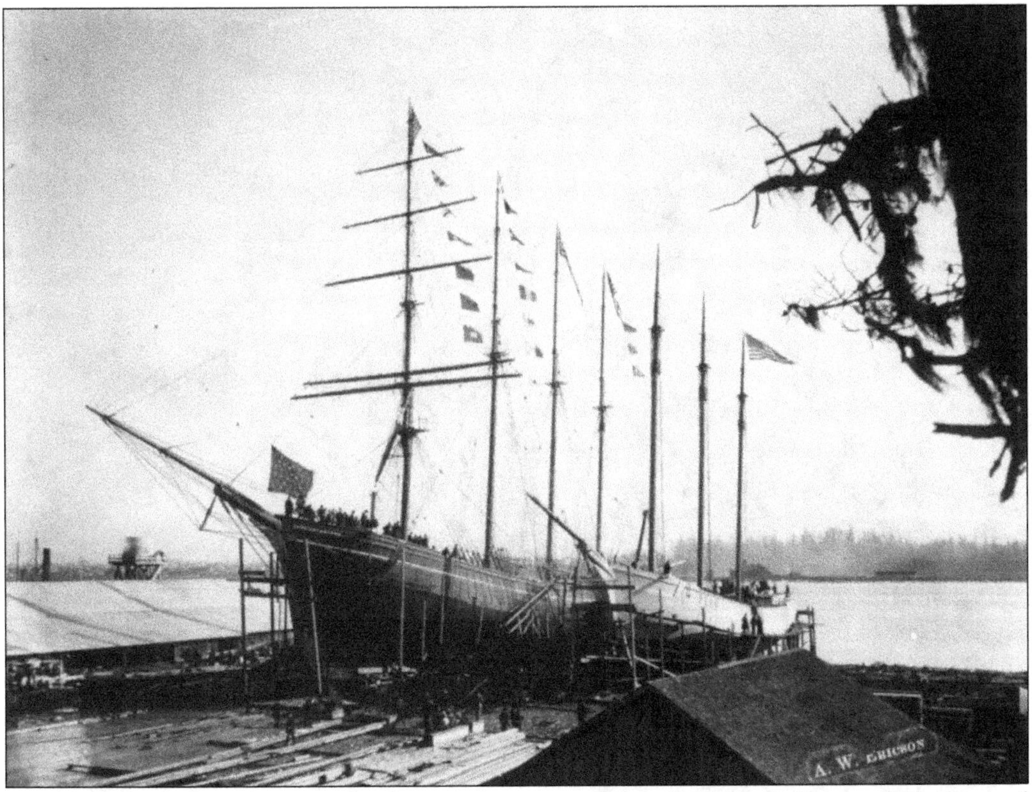

Bendixson built ships for many lumber companies, including Dolbeer & Carson, TPL Co., and the Elk River Lumber Company. He built the largest wooden vessel ever launched in California at that time, the *Jane L. Stanford*. A barkentine, she was 215 feet long and had a 41-foot beam. Bendixson built the ship in 1892 for J.J. Smith of San Francisco for use in shipping lumber. She sailed to China, Australia, and Hawaii. (HSU.)

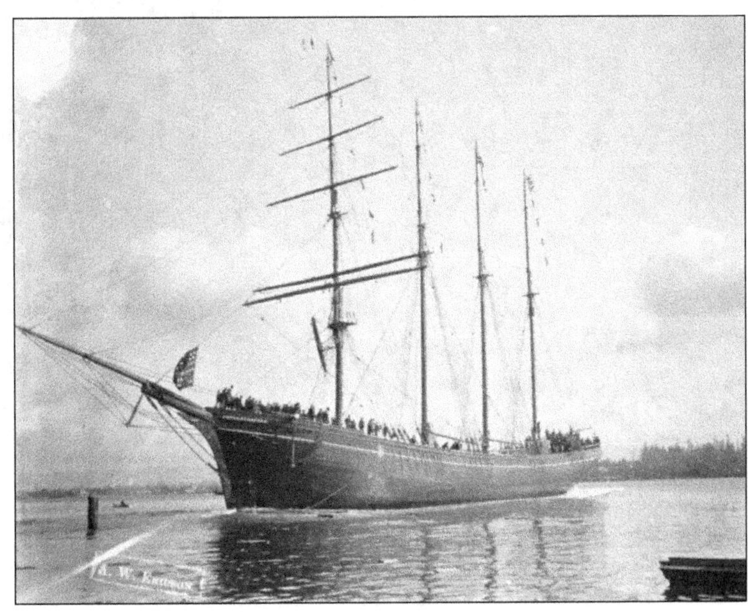

The *Jane L. Stanford* was hit by a steamer in 1929. The Coast Guard declared her a navigational hazard, dispatching a demolition team to destroy the vessel. Due to Bendixson's sturdy construction, the ship resisted the Coast Guard's efforts. Instead of sinking, she broke into two large sections that washed ashore on Santa Rosa Island, near Santa Barbara. (HSU.)

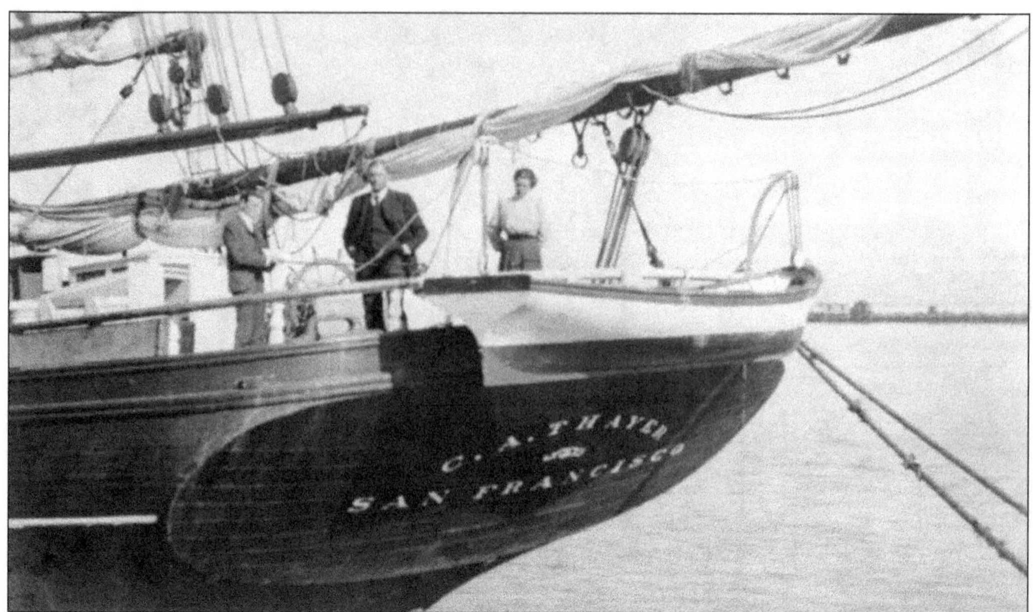

The only one of Bendixson's ships still in existence in the 21st century is the C.A. *Thayer*. Built in 1895 for the E.K. Wood Company of San Francisco, she was named for Clarence Thayer, one of the company's partners. She hauled lumber from the company's mill in Grays Harbor, Washington, to San Francisco, Hawaii, and Fiji. Pictured are Capt. and Mrs. G.T. Peterson. (San Francisco Maritime National Historic Park.)

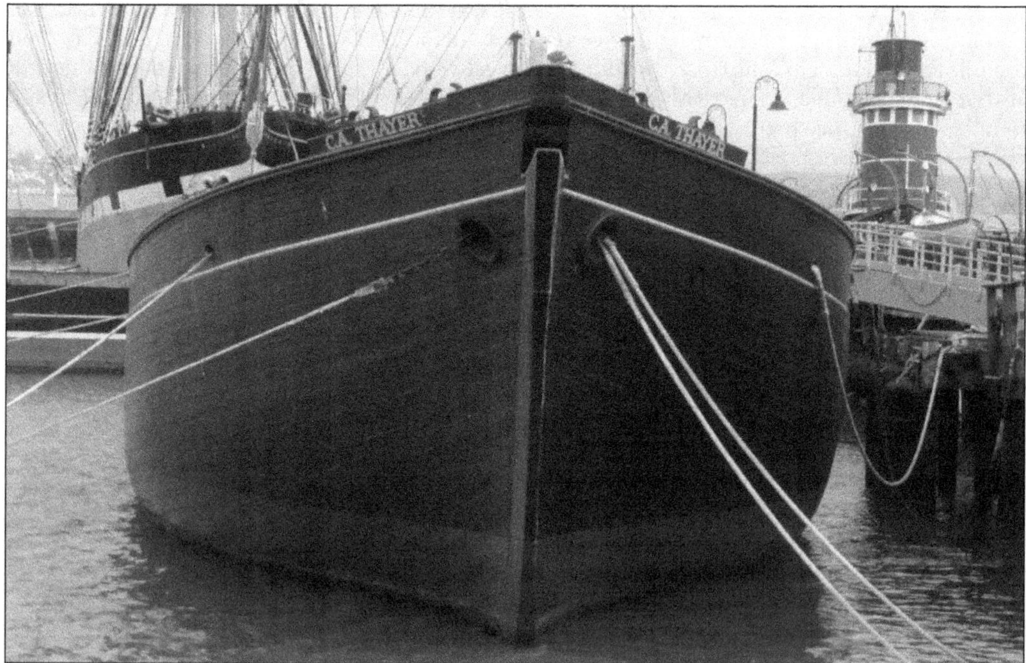

After 1912, the C.A. *Thayer* worked in the salt/salmon trade, hauling salt to Alaska for use in packing the salmon she hauled back to San Francisco. When purchased by the state of California in 1957, she was the last commercial sailing vessel on the West Coast. Following extensive repairs, the vessel was put on display at the Maritime Museum in San Francisco. (Bart Sears.)

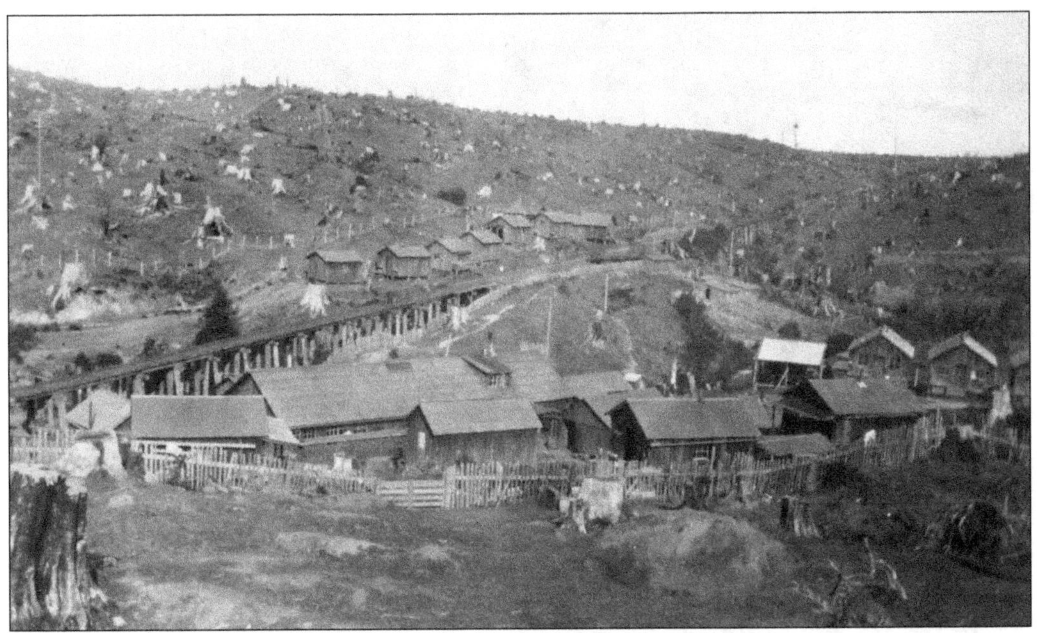

The Arcata Barrel Company opened in 1902 as a subsidiary of the San Francisco–based California Barrel Company, founded in 1859. The company imported fir, hemlock, and spruce from Humboldt County bolt camps at Essex, Strawberry Creek, and Dow's Prairie. By the turn of the 20th century, the company established the Arcata Mill to better meet demand. (HSU.)

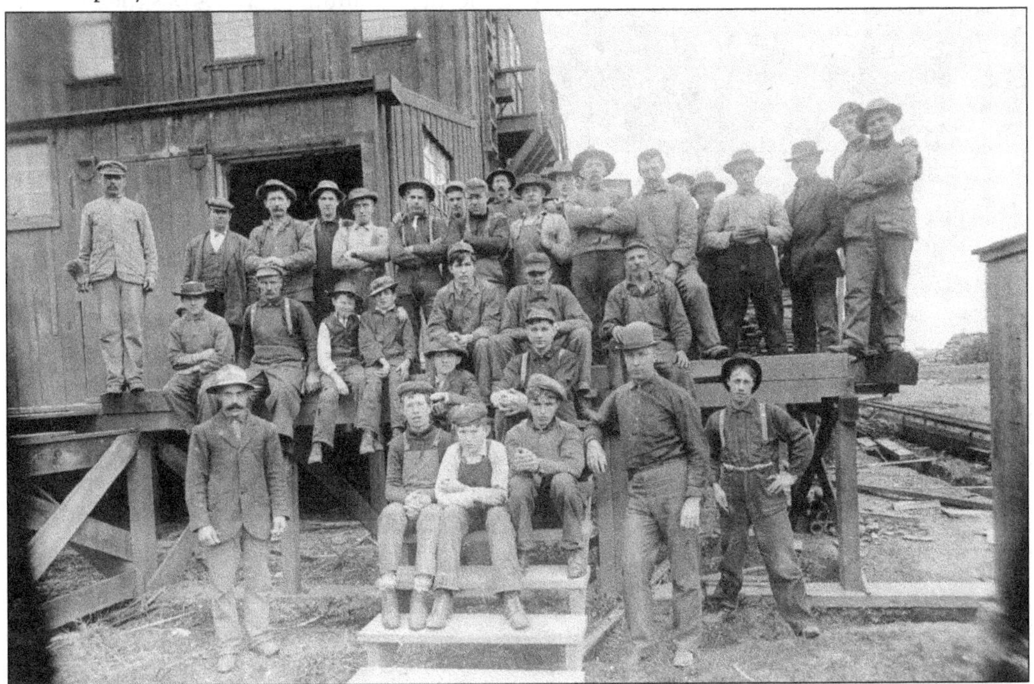

In 1915, the Arcata Barrel Company was considered "the best equipped mill of its kind." That year, a new market for the company's barrels was found, as they began being shipped to China. The Arcata Barrel Company was one of the largest employers in Arcata until it was sold in 1956. (HSU.)

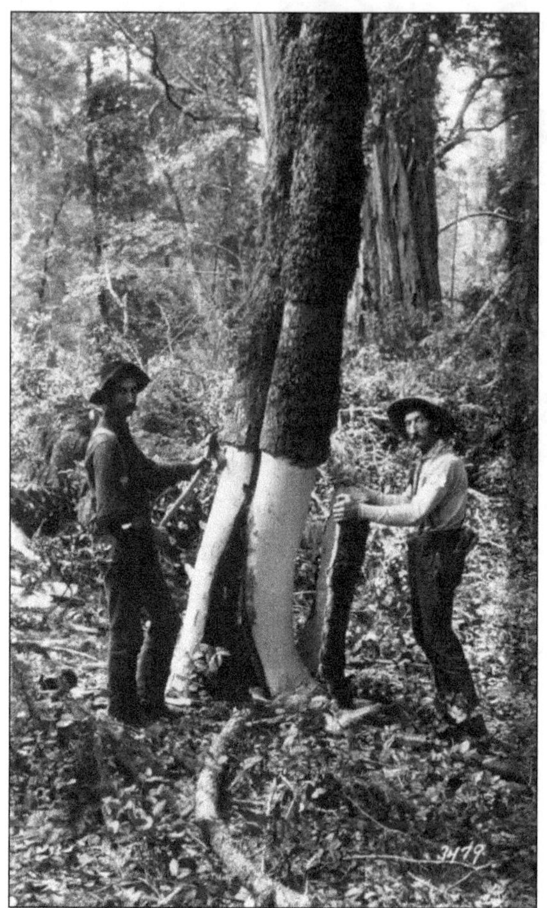

Another wood-product industry in Humboldt County in the late 1800s was based on the tannic acid found in the bark of another tree in the region, *Lithocarpus densiflora*, commonly known as tanoak. Tanoak grows both among the redwoods and on the drier hills above the redwood belt. Tanoak was first harvested in the Bald Hills region of northern Humboldt, though it was also peeled extensively in southern Humboldt. (HSU.)

Tanbark was used in tanning cowhides for leather. By the middle of the 19th century, tanning of hides was the fifth-largest industry in the United States, according to author Gordon C. Whitney. Tanneries were found locally near Rohnerville, Eureka, Arcata, and at Freshwater, pictured here in 1890. (HSU.)

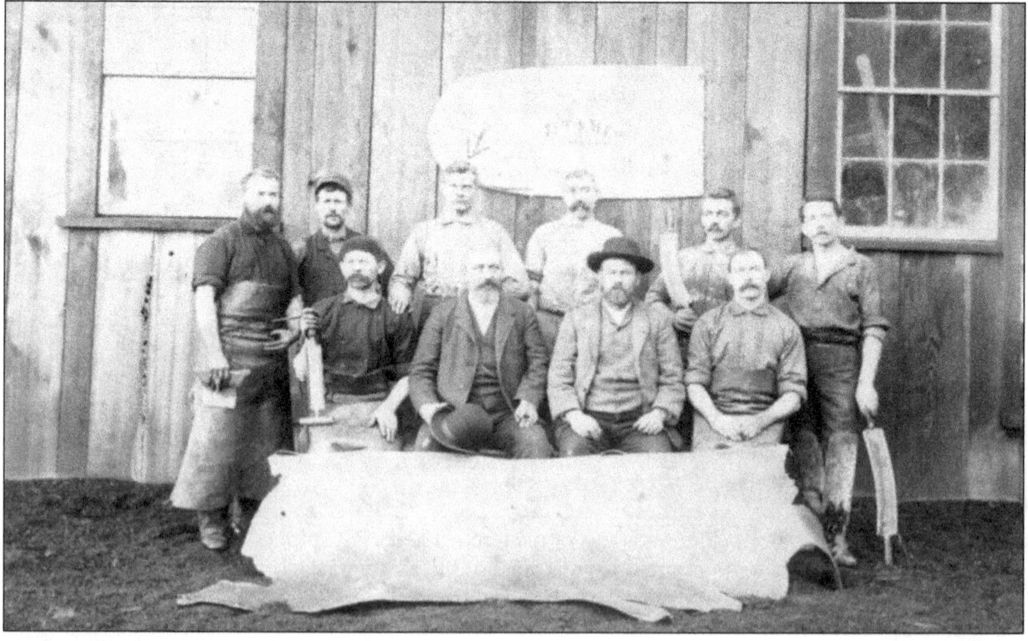

The tanbark industry was connected to the redwood lumber industry, as large lumber companies would send men into the forest to harvest tanbark before the area was logged for redwoods. Otherwise, when loggers burned the forest to make removal of redwood logs easier, the fire would damage tanoak, and the profitable bark could not be removed. (HSU.)

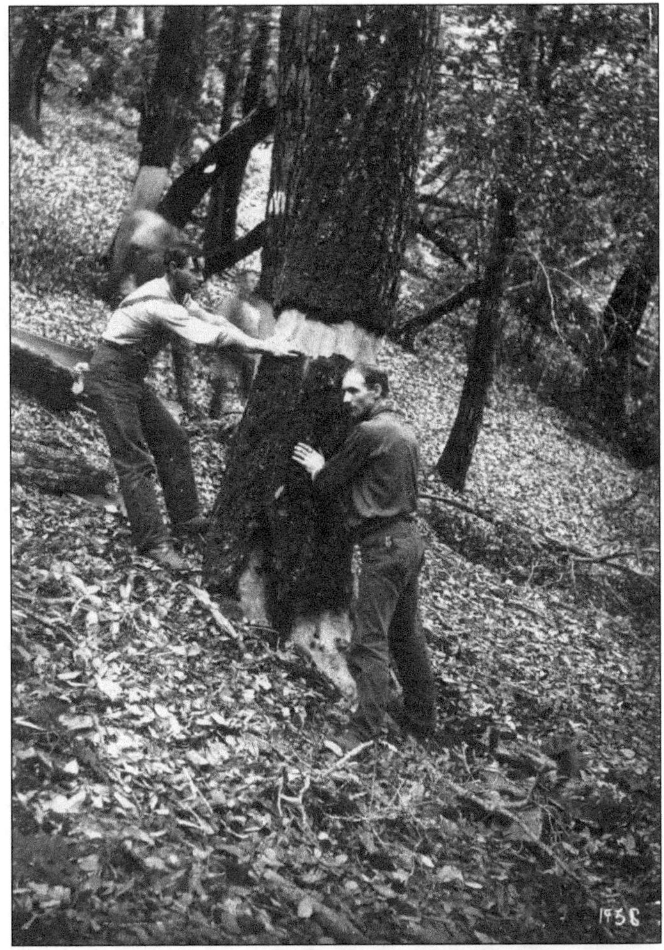

The tannin-filled bark could be most easily removed between late May and mid-August. A large tree could be peeled in half a day by two men using a one-edged ax. Peeling began with workers ringing the tree at its base and, again, four feet above the initial ring. This thickest and most valuable section of bark was then slit between the marks, and the bark was removed in one to four sections. (HSU.)

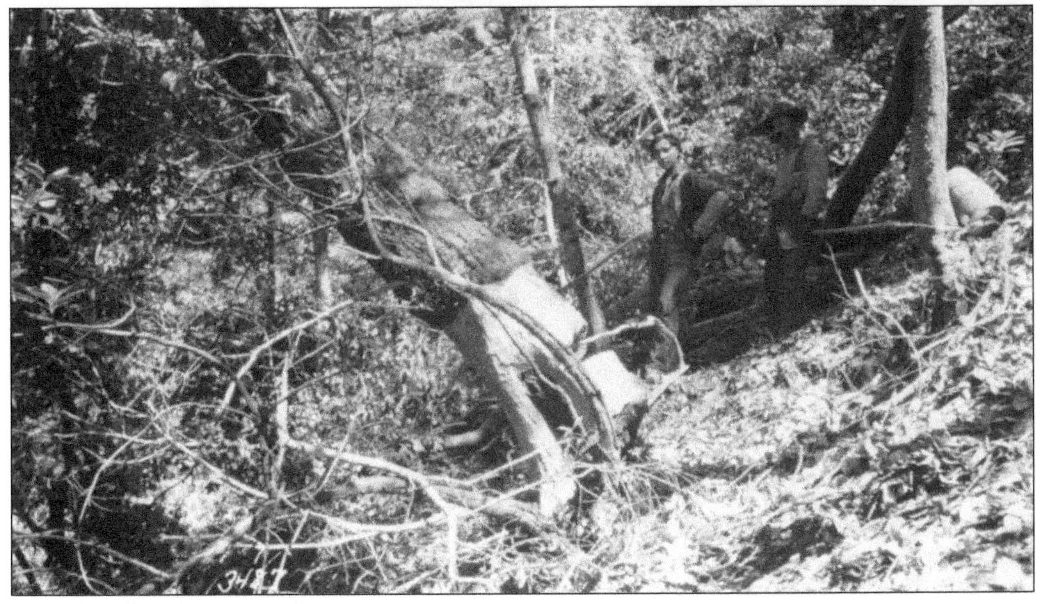

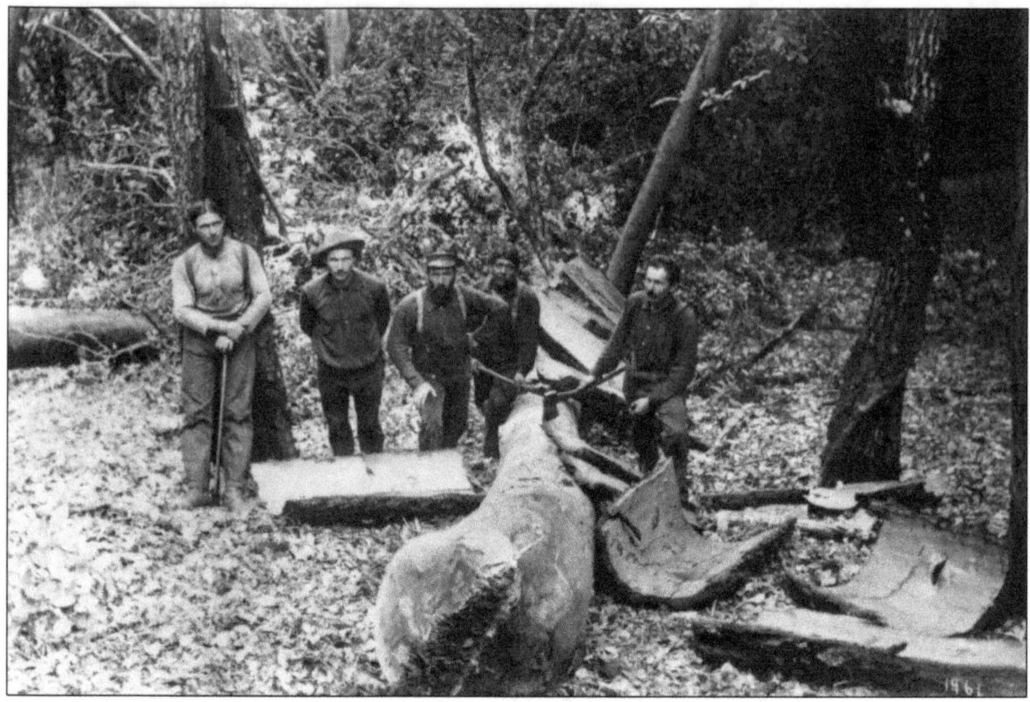

After this lower section was peeled, the tree was cut down, more bark was removed, and the wood and treetop were left in the forest to decay. According to Warren Ormsbey, a tanbark peeler in the late 1890s, "it was considered a day's work if a team could peel two cords of bark per day. In those days we worked six days a week from 6 o'clock in the morning until 6 o'clock at night." (HSU.)

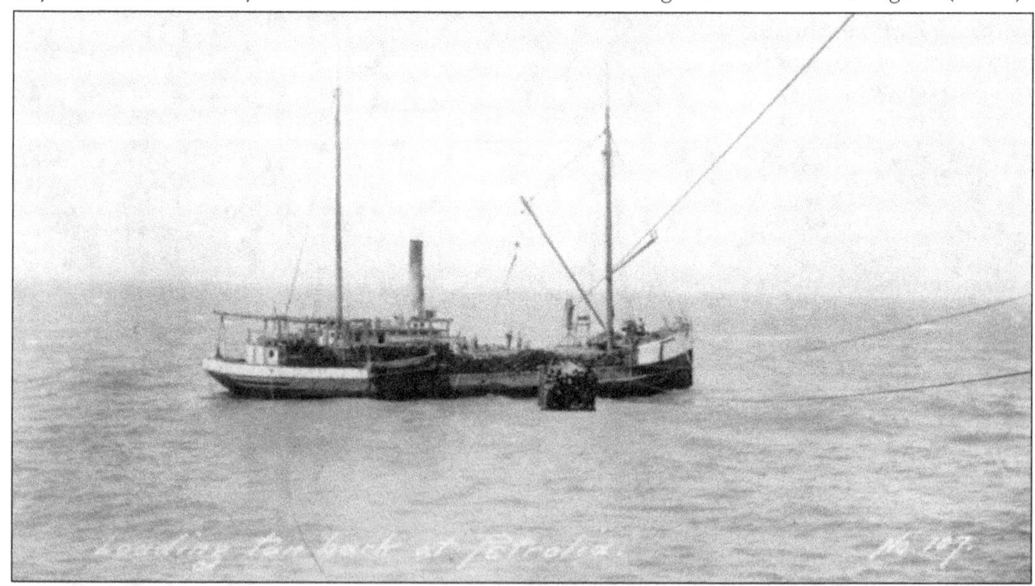

Dried tanbark was hauled by mule train or wagons to shipping ports. While some of Humboldt County's tanbark was destined for local tanneries, the majority was shipped to facilities near San Francisco. In 1889, 3,840,000 pounds of tanbark shipped from Humboldt Bay and from a port at the mouth of Bear River. There, a railroad from Petrolia brought the tanbark that was loaded onto ships by a cable system.

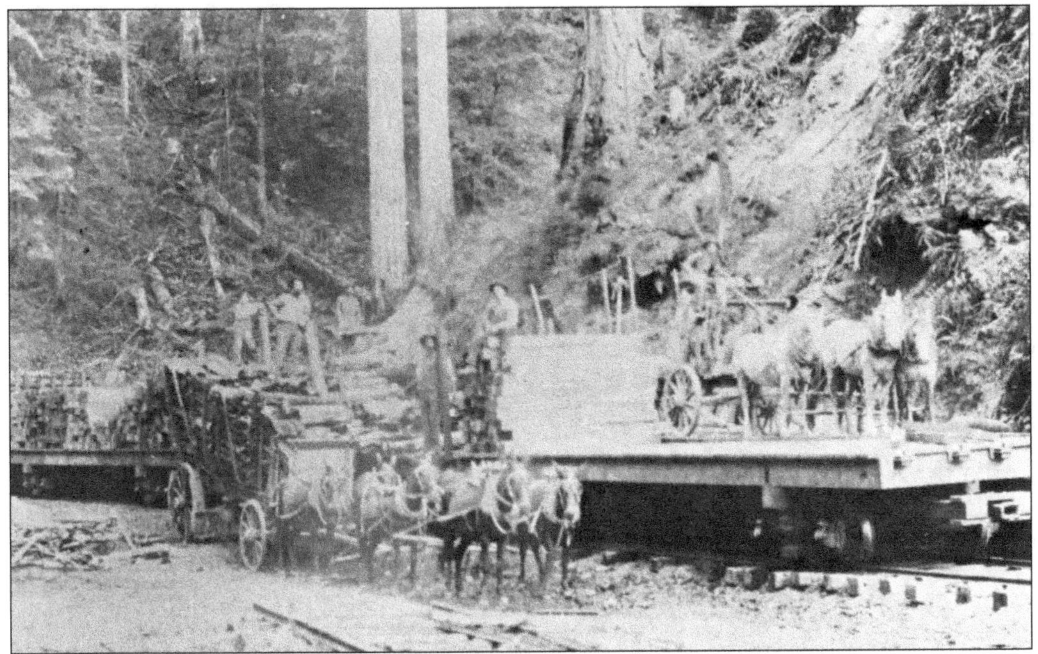

Tanbark and split products such as railroad ties were sometimes combined in railroad shipments, as shown at Stephenson's siding near Metropolitan. Curling up as it dried, tanbark formed distinctive rolls. From 1889 to 1893, over $33,000 worth of tanbark was peeled and shipped from Humboldt County.

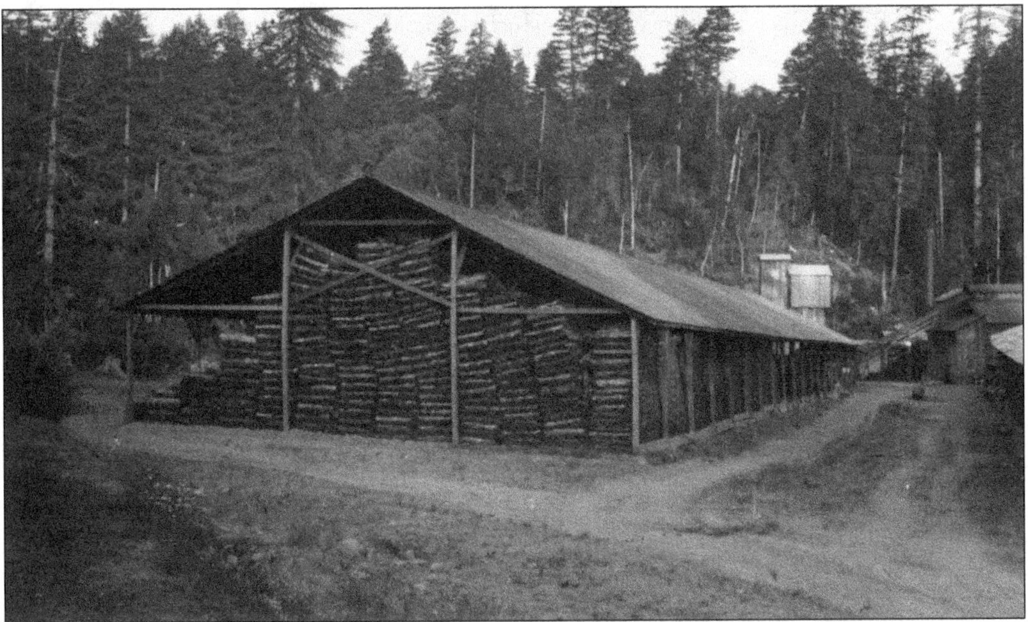

At Briceland, in southern Humboldt, another tactic was explored. In 1904, the Wagner Leather Company of Stockton built a $25,000 mill to extract acid from the bark. Only the resulting resin was shipped. Willis Jepson noted in *Tanbark Oak and the Tanning Industry*: "A cord of dry bark, 2,200 pounds, is reduced to 50 gallons of extract, which weighs about 550 pounds. The extractor has a capacity of 12 cords a day." (HSU.)

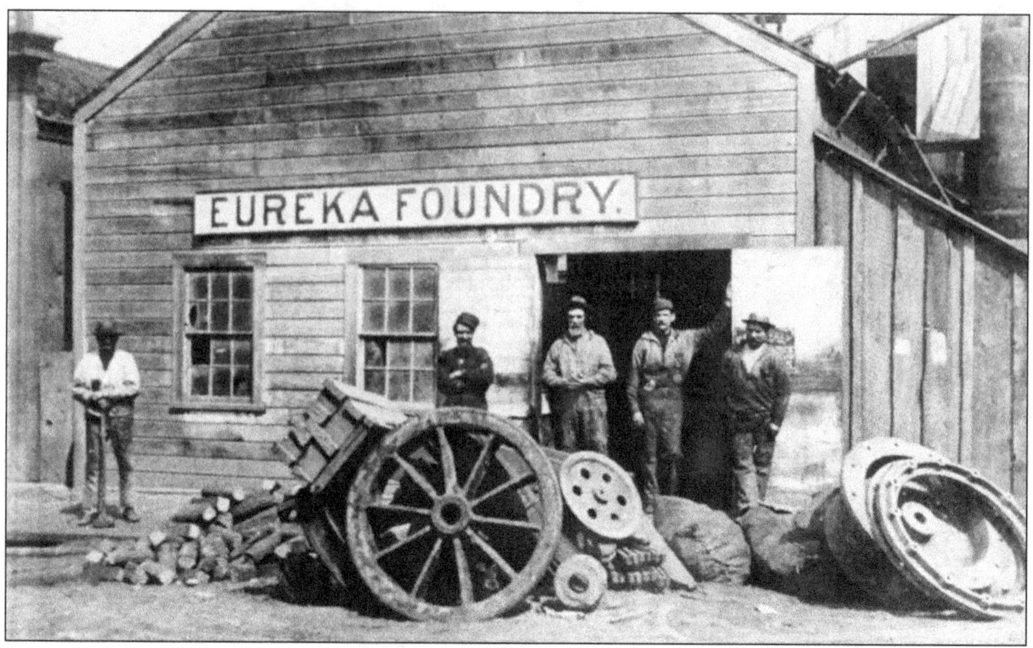

One specialty mill not directly tied to wood production in Humboldt County, yet indispensable to the many lumber mills, was the Eureka Foundry. As the *Humboldt County Souvenir* of 1904 explained, the company "owns and operates a plant of large size, and [is] capable of caring for all the heavy work of the lumber mills and logging camps. It builds and rebuilds locomotives and engines of all descriptions. It constructs all the heavy 'bull-donkeys' that are used in the logging operations of this county and the invention of which practically revolutionized the lumber business here." The foundry opened in 1883 and incorporated in 1899, with principal stockholders M.C. Wells of San Francisco and M.H. Pine, Charles Ehemer, Euphronius Cousins, E.J. Shepardson, and W.S. Gibbard of Eureka. (Both, HSU.)

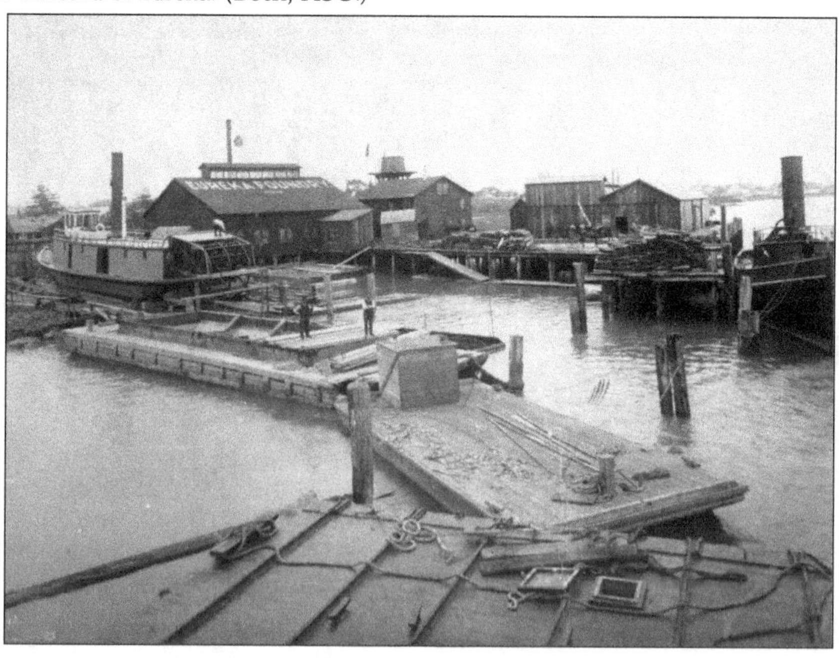

Five

Woods Camps and Company Towns

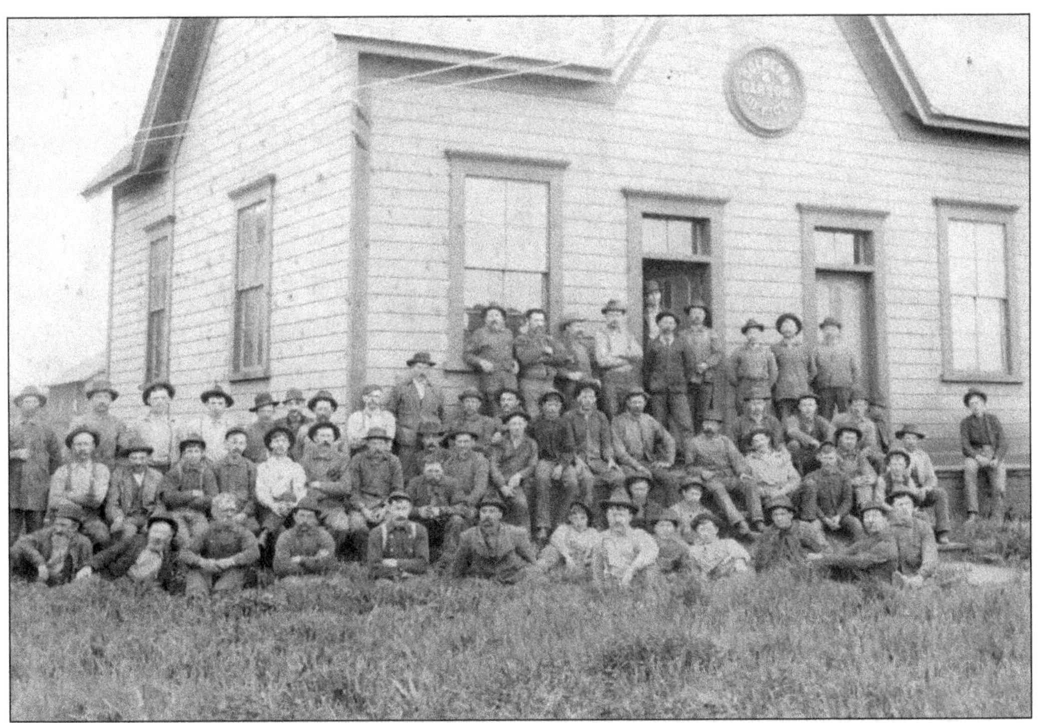

As one of the earlier lumber companies, founded when redwood forests were still close to Humboldt Bay, Dolbeer & Carson never had its own company town. Most of its workers, like these men photographed outside the company office, lived in Eureka. In 1880, Eureka, the largest town in Humboldt, had only 2,639 inhabitants. Company owners and their workers were often neighbors. (Clarke.)

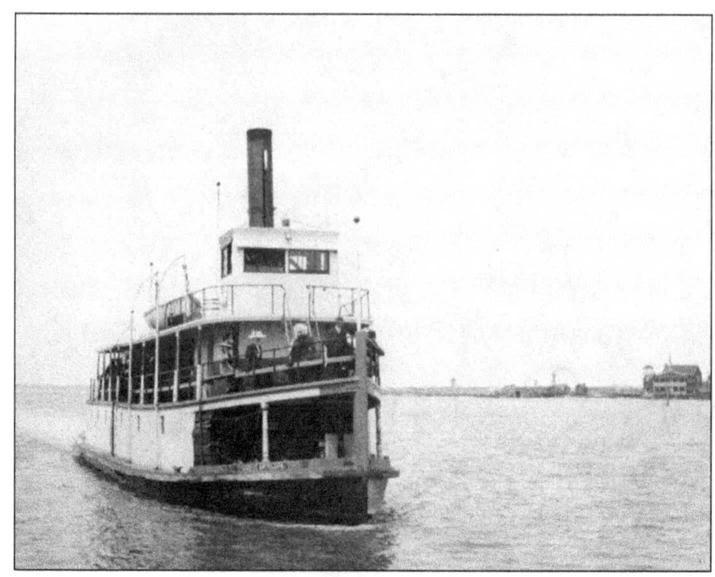

The original stern-wheel steamboat *Antelope*, built for John Vance at Cutten & McDonald's Eureka shipyard, launched with great fanfare in July 1888. As part of Vance's Arcata & Mad River Railroad, the *Antelope* made regular trips from Eureka to Arcata. The second *Antelope* reused the machinery from the first and was launched in 1910. It ferried Hammond Lumber Company workers from Eureka across the bay to the Samoa Mill.

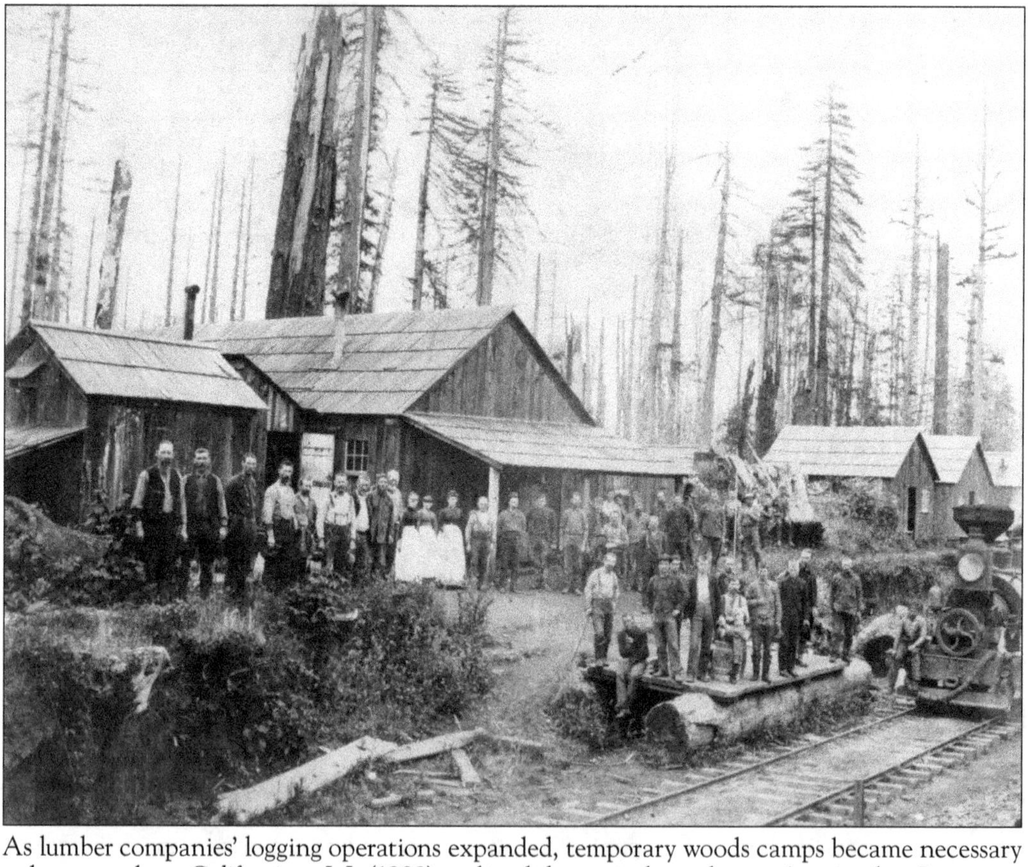

As lumber companies' logging operations expanded, temporary woods camps became necessary to house workers. *California as It Is* (1888) outlined the typical woods crews' pay scales. Swampers (road construction crew) earned $60–$100 a month, choppers $65–$75, sawyers and chain-tenders $65–$100, and teamsters $125–$150. The pay scale for cook and cookhouse workers was not listed. (HCHS.)

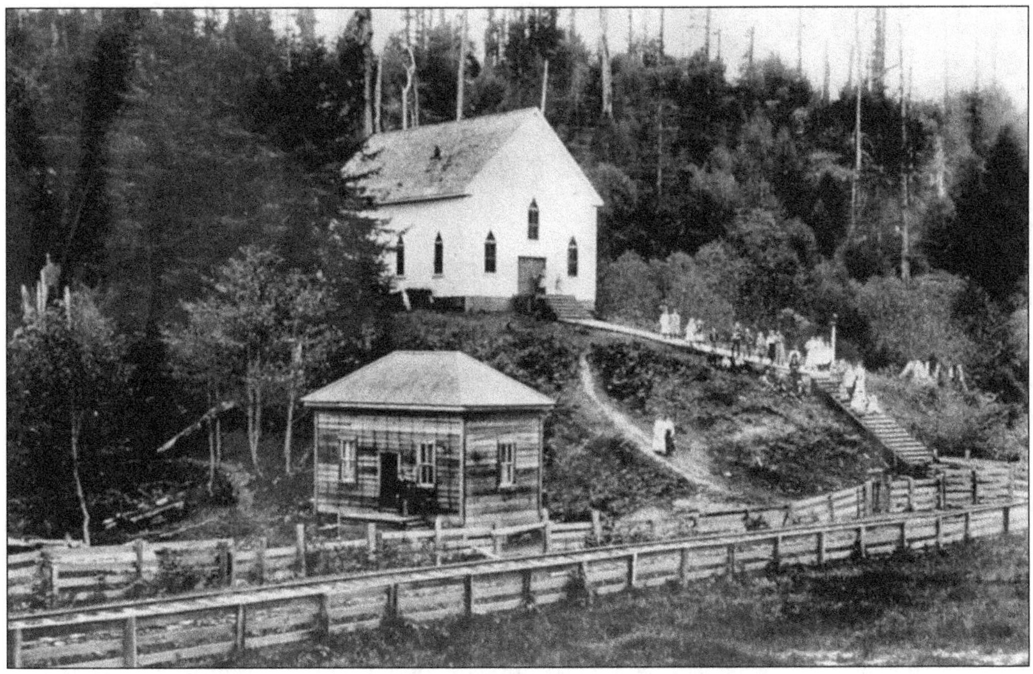

One of Humboldt's first company towns was Falk, where the Elk River Lumber Company mill was constructed in 1882. Falk historian Jon Humboldt Gates noted that the new town required "homes, bunkhouses, a general store, a cookhouse, a blacksmith shop, a community hall, the mill itself, and a railroad to connect it to Humboldt Bay." Shown is Falk's First Congregational Church, constructed in 1895, with the minister's house in the foreground. (Greg Rumney.)

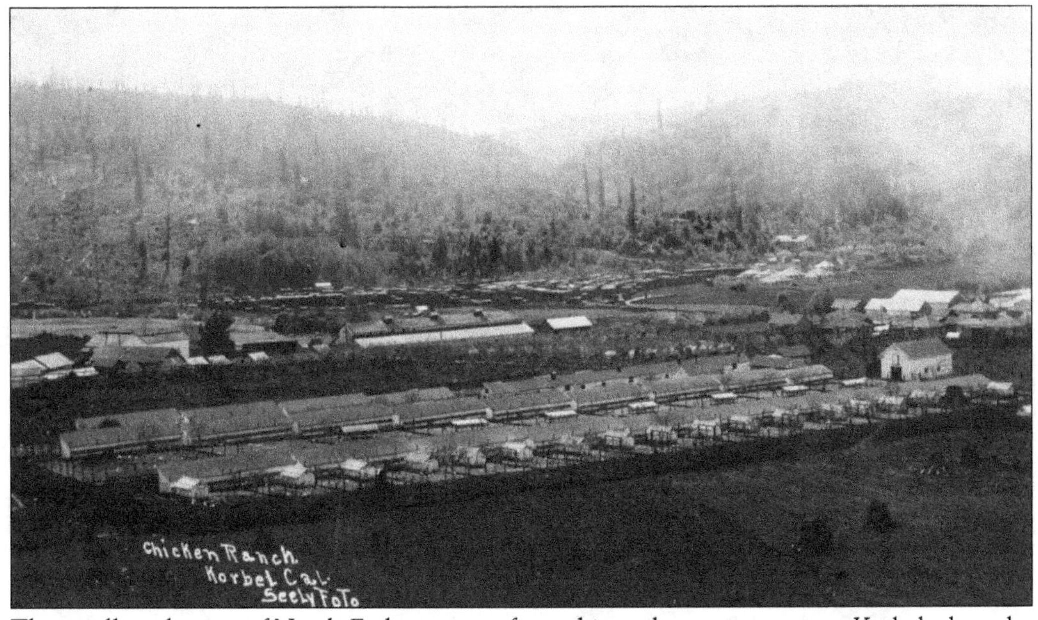

The small settlement of North Fork was transformed into the company town Korbel when the Korbel brothers from Bohemia built their mill there in 1883. In 1905, Korbel's population was 500. Shown in the foreground of this early-20th-century photograph is Korbel's "chicken ranch," just one element of the complex infrastructure required to support workers at the mill. (HSU.)

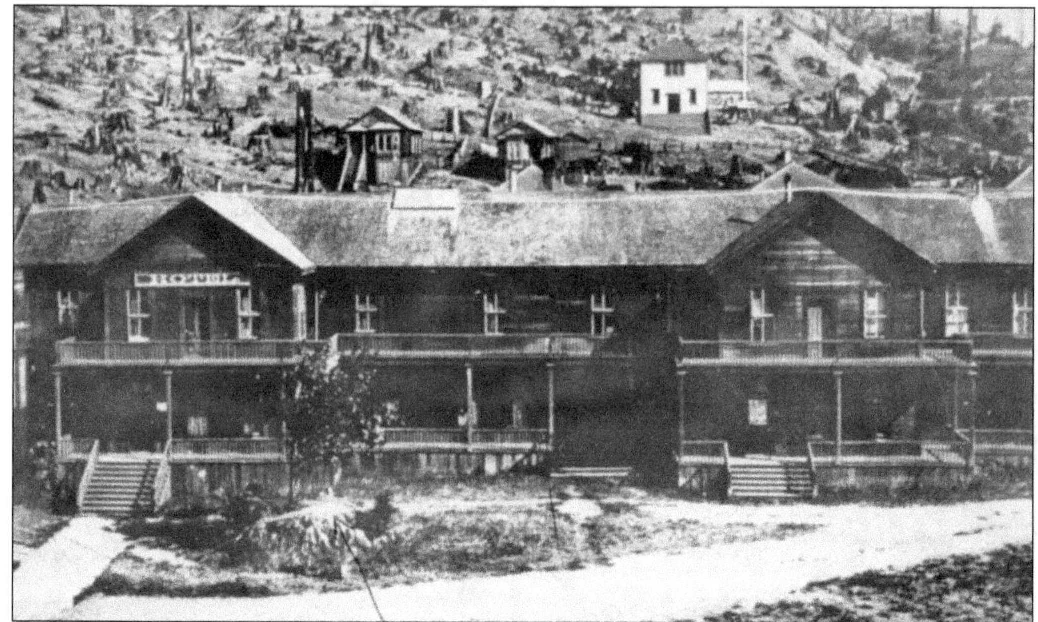

After two years as Forestville, TPL Co.'s growing mill town was renamed Scotia in 1888. Legend says that the choice of name was between Brunswick, honoring New Brunswick, and Scotia, honoring Nova Scotia. These two Canadian provinces were the homelands for numerous Humboldt workers. Scotia supposedly won on a coin toss. Shown is TPL Co.'s first hotel around 1890, when its advertised amenities included "a fine mineral spring and an inclosed [*sic*] swimming bath."

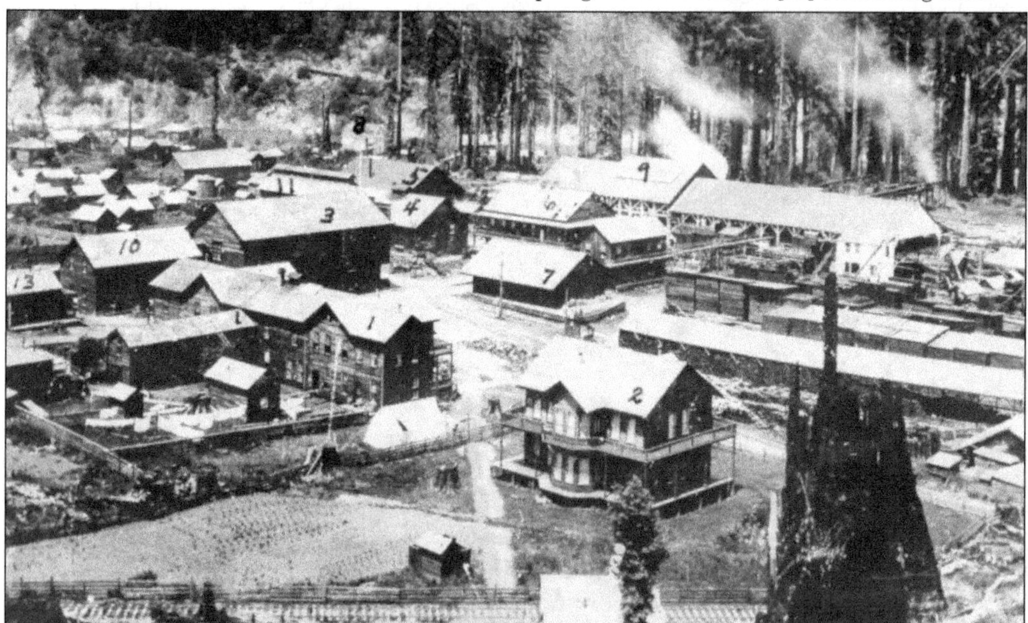

Scotia-area historian Fred Elliot labeled with numbers the features of this Scotia photograph, taken around 1895: 1. hotel, 2. Curtis home, 3. town hall, 4. cookhouse, 5. machine shop, 6. store, 7. warehouse, 8. Epps home (later hospital), 9. Mill A, 10. saloon, 11. engine house, 12. pond, and 13. butcher shop. In 1895, Scotia also included an office, creamery, two stables, dairy barn, shingle mill, dry kiln, 48 dwellings, and a one-room schoolhouse built in 1888.

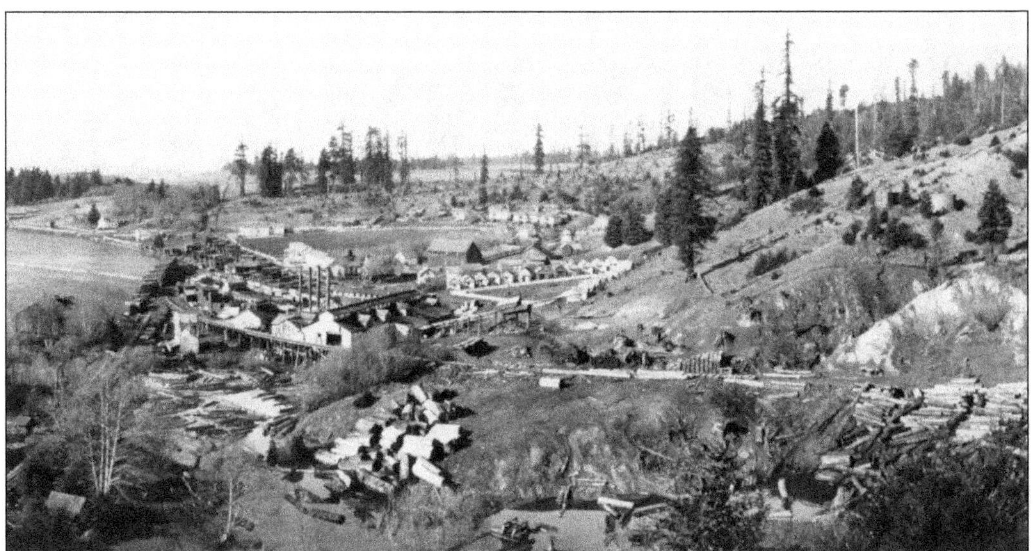

The Eel River Valley Lumber Co.'s town of Newburg, named for owner E.J. Dodge's New York hometown, was founded in 1888. The *Humboldt Beacon* wrote of Newburg in 1912: "Employment is given to some 200 men . . . cabins are provided for all of the single men and a considerable number of modern dwellings . . . for the comfort and convenience of those of its employees who have families."

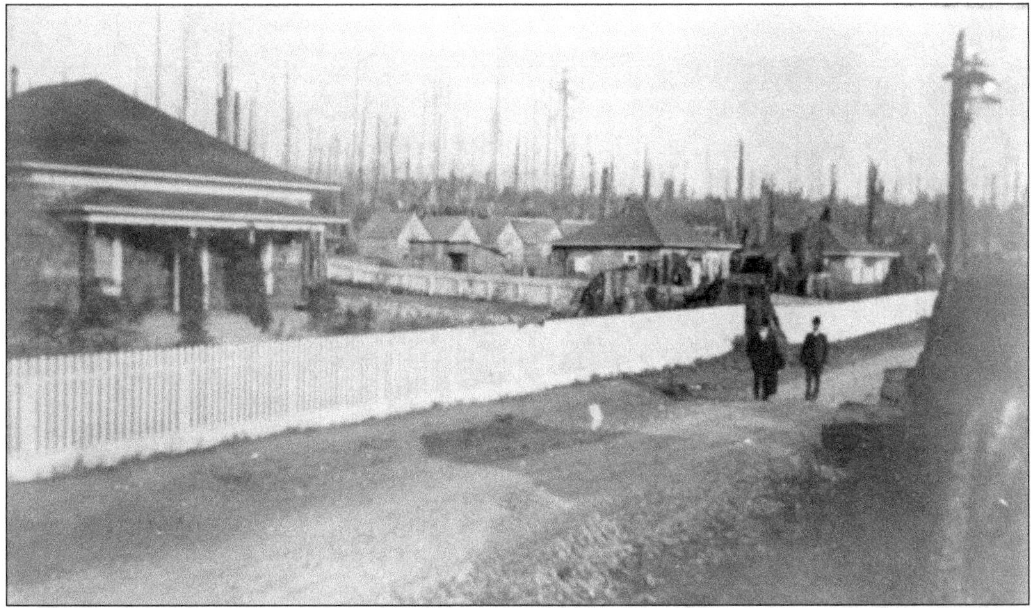

Luffenholtz, named for the German immigrant who briefly owned a Trinidad-area mill in the 1850s, was a company town for Vance Redwood Lumber Company. In 1905, it had a population of 390. It was described in the county business directory as "one of the largest lumbering camps in Humboldt." The town was destroyed by fire three year later. Fires were a constant threat to mills and the communities around them. (HCHS.)

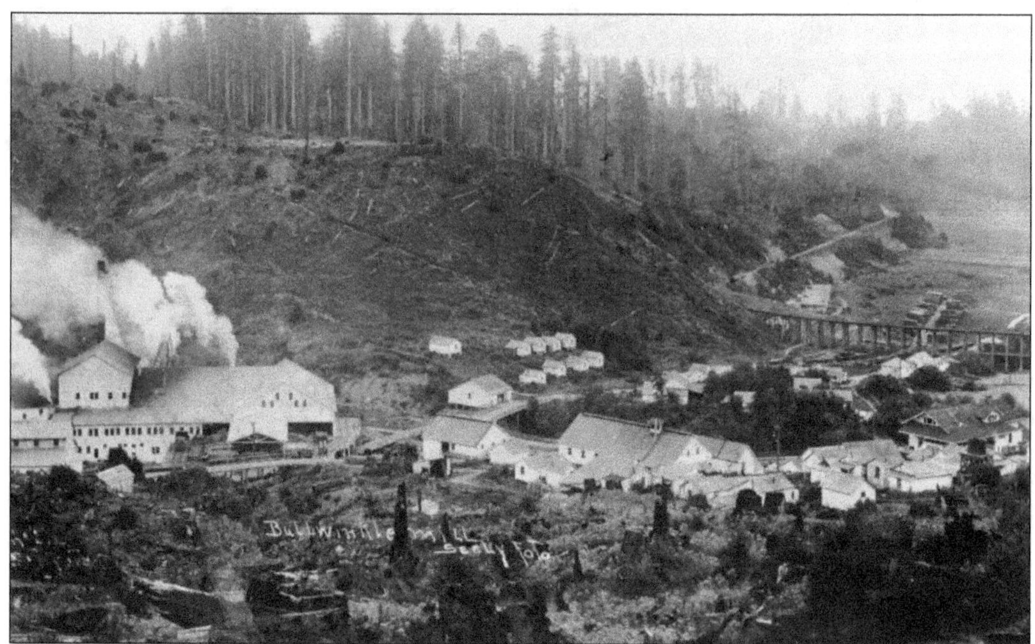

Bullwinkle was named for another German immigrant, Conrad Bullwinkel, who came to Humboldt in 1855. Part of his homestead became the Little River Lumber Company's town in 1909. Shown here in the background at right are the railroad and stacks of lumber. At center are workers' cabins and more sizeable houses. The cookhouse is among the buildings in the foreground, and a bungalow, probably the house of a company official, is near the front right corner. (HSU.)

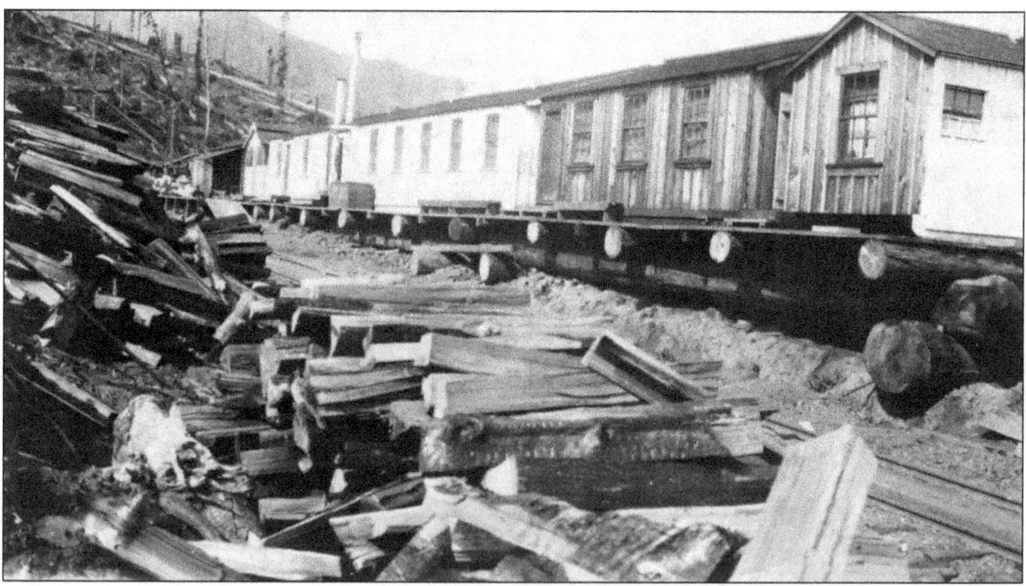

When trees in one area were depleted, a lumber company would move its logging show to an area of uncut timber. Woods camp buildings themselves often moved to each new show. Neil Price, reminiscing on Falk's early-20th-century woods operations, remembered that the camp cookhouse was repeatedly "dismantled and moved as the camp was moved to new locations." (HSU.)

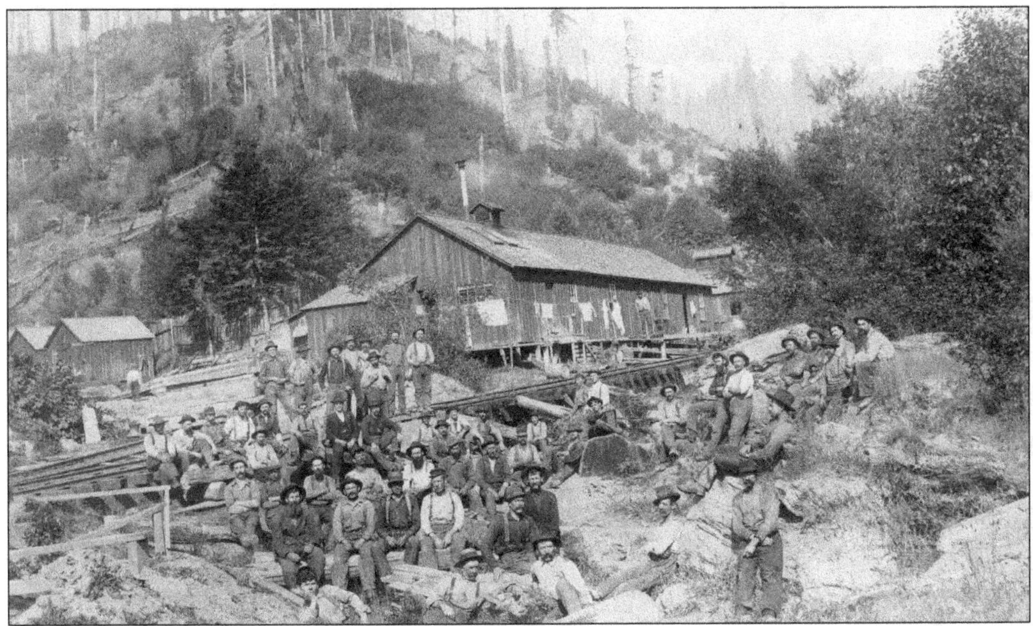

Shown here is Pinkerton's Freshwater camp in 1896. *Redwood and Lumbering in California Forests* (1888) described the typical woods camp: "A dozen shanties twelve feet square, in which the men sleep in bunks . . . the cookhouse fifty or sixty feet in length, and thirty feet in width, wide enough to accommodate the sitting of two tables lengthwise . . . the repair shop . . . [and] the long barn in which the oxen are fed." (HCHS.)

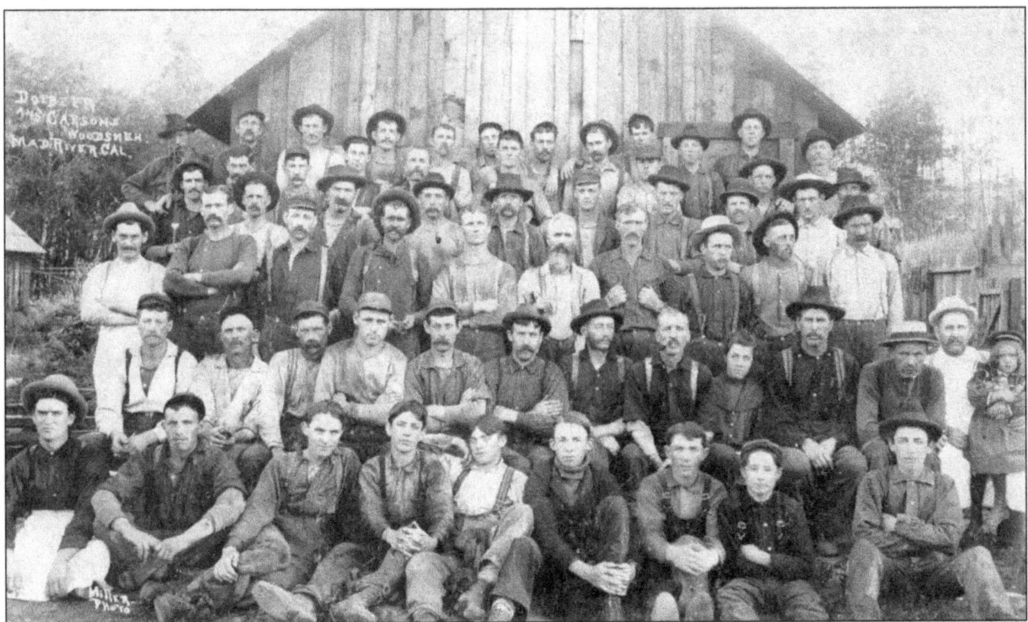

The Dolbeer & Carson Company's Mad River woods crew around 1899 includes cook Uriah Christie with his daughter and her doll at right. *Redwood and Lumbering in California Forests* called the camp cook "the oracle of the camp, occupying about the same social position as does the Justice of the Peace in a mining district. He is invariably appealed to by his boarders to settle disputes, whether concerning questions of law, love or labor." (HCHS.)

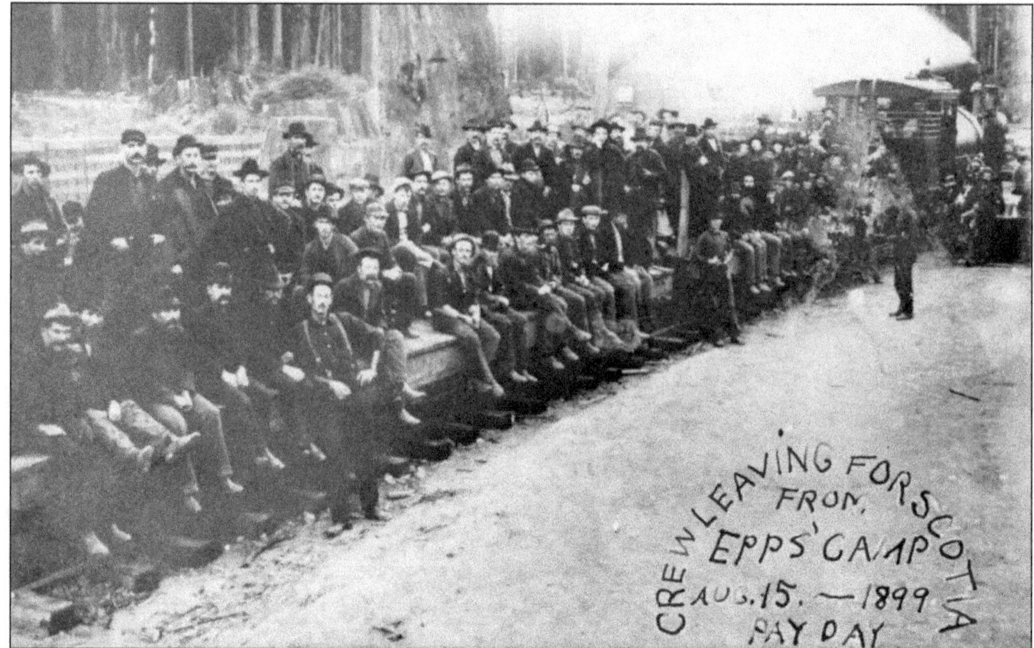

Humboldt's lumber company workers labored six-day weeks, 12 hours a day, and were paid once a month. In September 1890, William Carson, genuinely concerned for his workers and also hoping to forestall the growth of labor activism, announced that he would reduce his men's workday from 12 hours to 10, without cutting pay. The Excelsior, Vance, Occidental, Glendale, Newburg, Korbel, and TPL Co. Mills soon followed Carson's example.

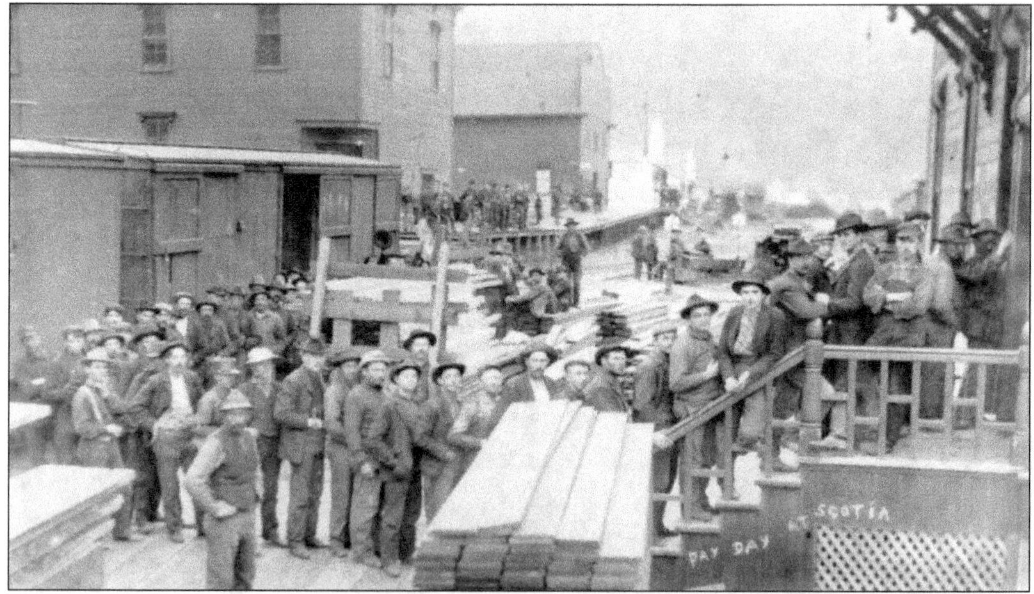

The *Blue Lake Advocate* reported in August 1905 that Humboldt's woodsmen's union received a charter from the American Federation of Unions: "Until the Humboldt woodsmen conceived the idea of establishing a national union for the woodsmen, no such organization existed. . . . The woodsmen of this section are an intelligent and independent body of men, who appreciate the value of being organized even though they did not declare a strike every month."

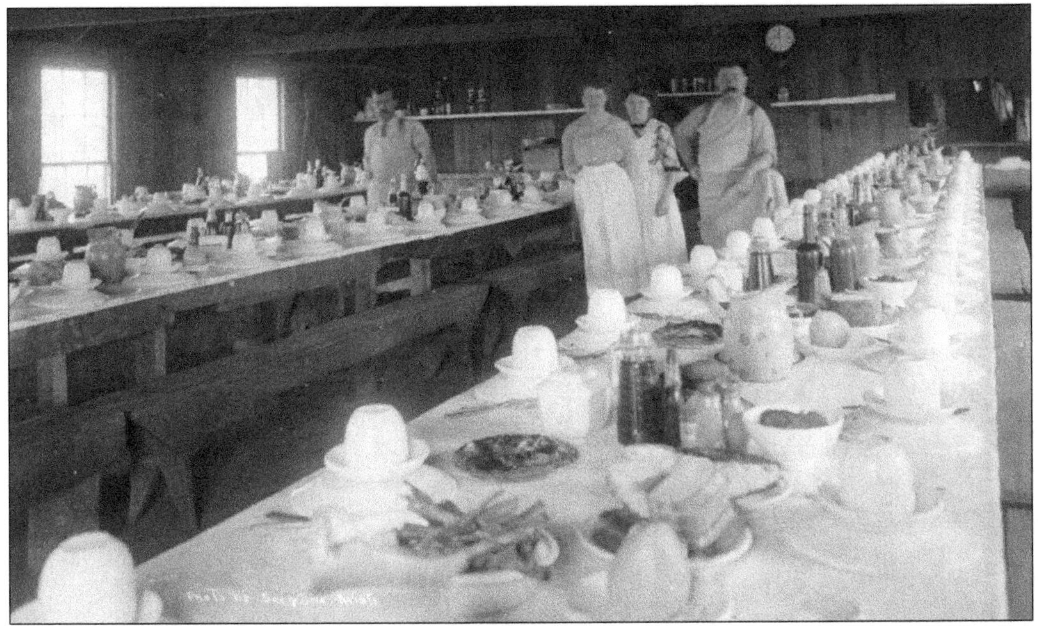

An unidentified cookhouse crew was photographed minutes before the noon onslaught of hungry men. The adage "an army marches on its stomach" held equally true for woodsmen and mill men. The *Humboldt Times* reported an early Humboldt workers' strike in 1881 at Vance's Eureka mill: "At breakfast a large majority of the men refused to work unless properly cooked food was given them and the mill had to be closed." (Clarke.)

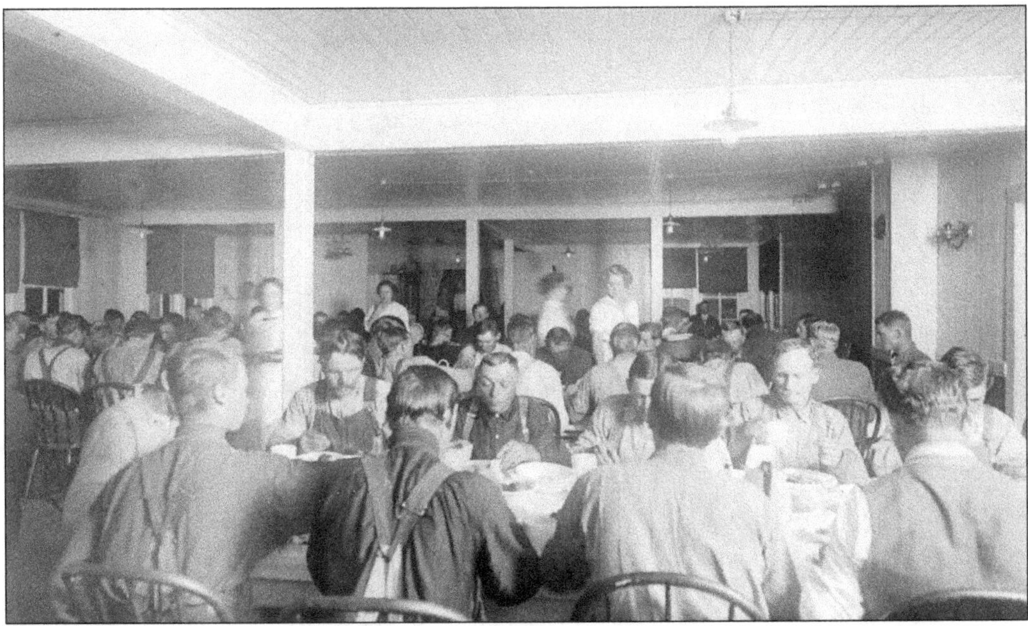

Mill and woods workers required large amounts of food. A cookhouse breakfast might include oatmeal, cooked fruit, various meats, eggs, fried potatoes, and biscuits. Dinner, the noon meal, featured meats (fish on Fridays), potatoes, fresh vegetables in season, various salads, fruit, and dessert. Finally, supper again included meats, potatoes, salads, vegetables, fruit, and fresh bread. Soup was served at both dinner and supper. (HCHS.)

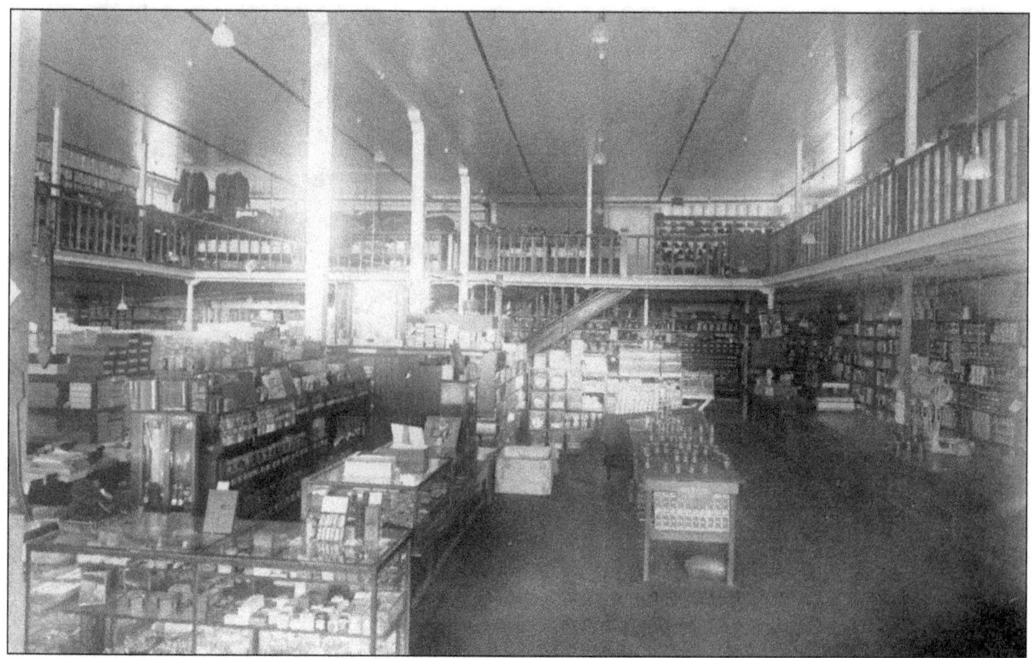

This photograph is tentatively identified as depicting Hammond's company store at Samoa. In 1897, the California Assembly passed a bill requiring companies to pay their workers in cash rather than credit at the company store. Lumber industry historian Brett Melendy wrote: "some companies still insisted that their employees trade at the company stores. In times of depression, it was worth the laborer's job for him to trade elsewhere." (HCHS.)

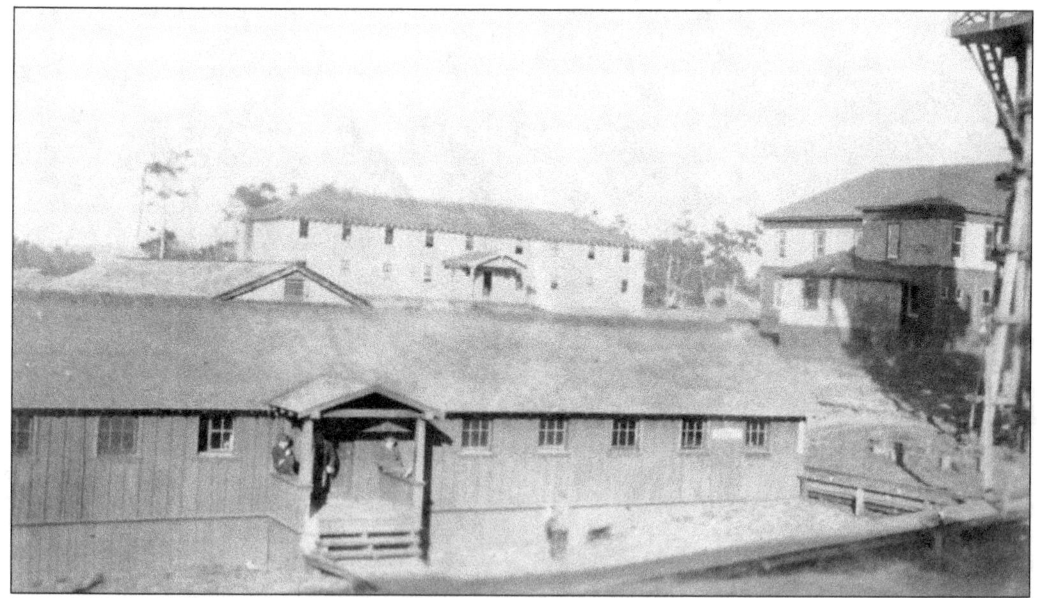

Shown here is an employee bunkhouse at Samoa. Historian Greg Gordon notes that, when Andrew Hammond purchased Samoa in 1900, he "oversaw the construction of nearly a hundred houses, a new bunkhouse and cookhouse capable of seating the entire workforce, and a general store." Hammond's goal was "to create a captive workforce entirely dependent upon the company—not just for jobs but also housing, food, education, recreation, and a social network." (HCHS.)

Six

Faces of the Lumber Industry

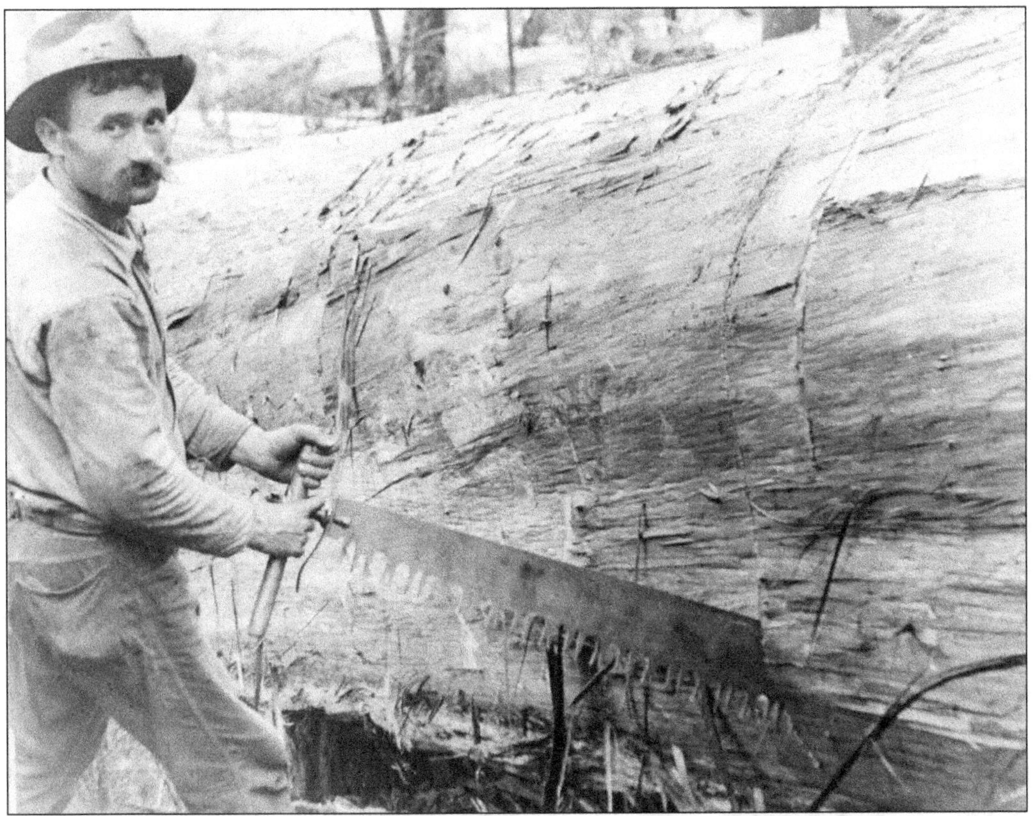

In 1854, the *Alta California* newspaper described Humboldt's "steam that belches forth from . . . numerous mills, together with the sound of the hammer and the woodsman's axe." According to *California as It Is*, "There is generally a good demand for labor in Humboldt County. . . . The kind of labor wanted is that possible to strong, able-bodied men. The mills and logging woods are not places for weaklings." (HCHS.)

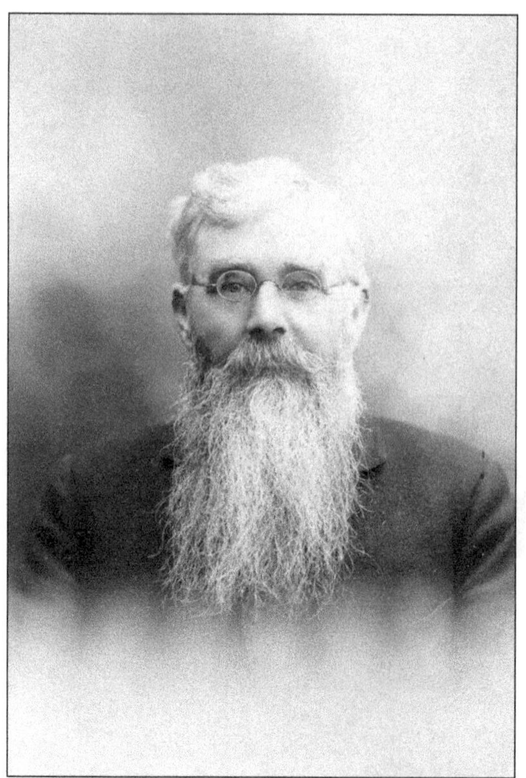

David Evans, twice Eureka mayor and inventor of "Evans' third saw," was born in Wales in 1838. Biographer Barbara Saul observes that he left home at the age of 12 "to escape the life of a coal miner and seeking adventure." After sailing and gold mining, he settled in Eureka in 1861, getting a job hauling sawdust at the Bay Mill. He rose through the ranks, becoming one of the mill's owners 10 years later. (HCHS.)

The widely varying appearances of these TPL Co. men at Scotia suggest their probable job titles. The man at left could be a millwright, and the man at far right, a sawyer. The worker shown second from right may be a mill superintendent. The man second from left might give his occupation as "lumberman." A woodsman worked in the woods; a lumberman owned the company. (Greg Rumney.)

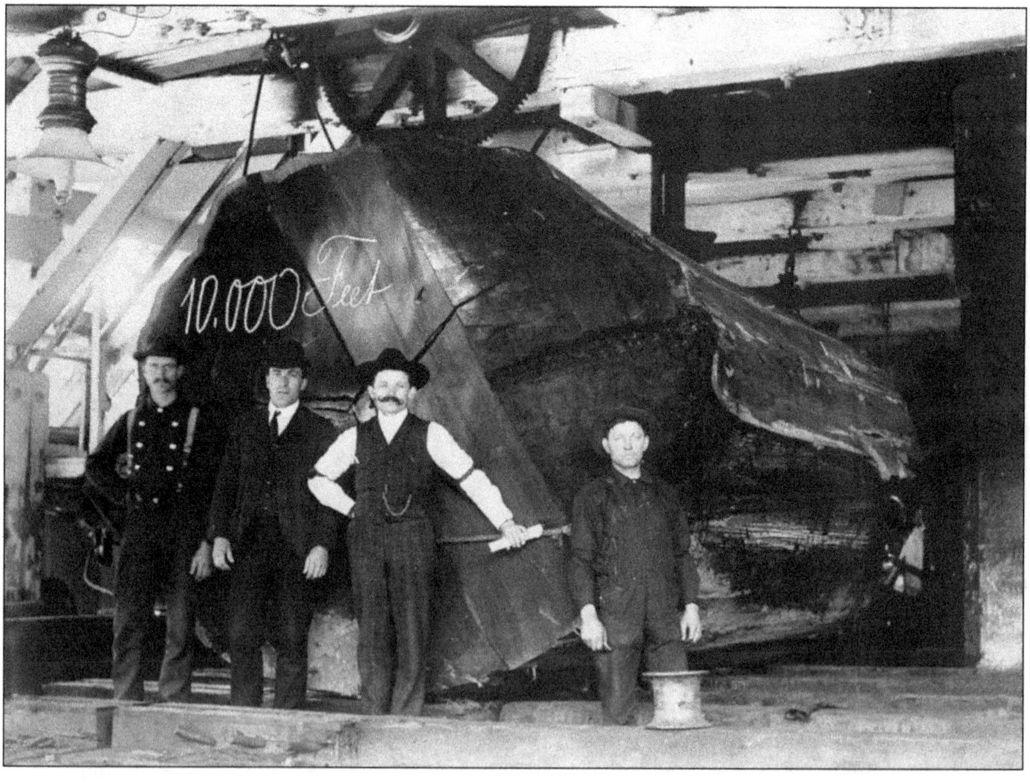

Photographer Augustus William Ericson (seated in front of log) left Sweden for America in 1868 at the age of 18. He worked as a laborer building Trinidad-area logging railroads. Ericson became bookkeeper for the Trinidad Mill Company and later was an Arcata telegrapher and storekeeper. He took up photography around 1885 and gained widespread acclaim when 200 of his Humboldt County photographs were exhibited at the 1893 World's Columbian Exposition in Chicago.

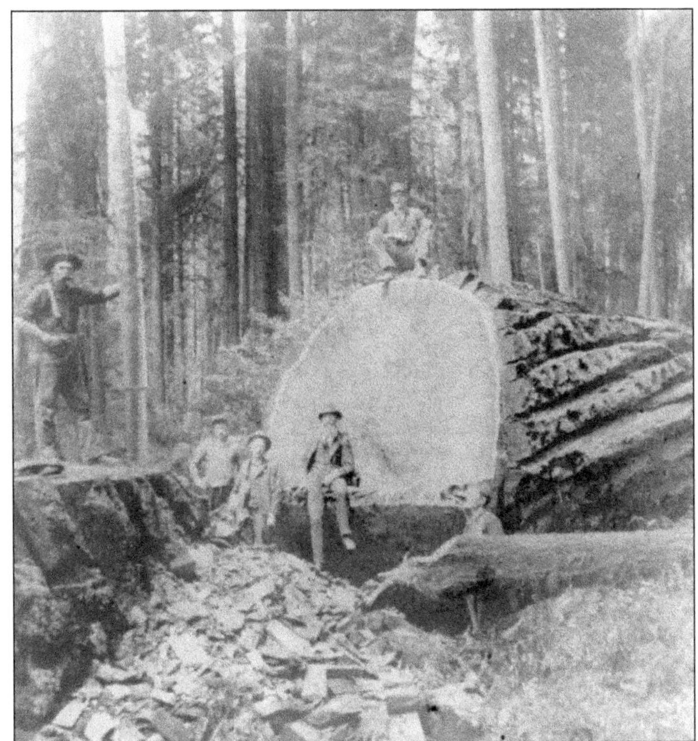

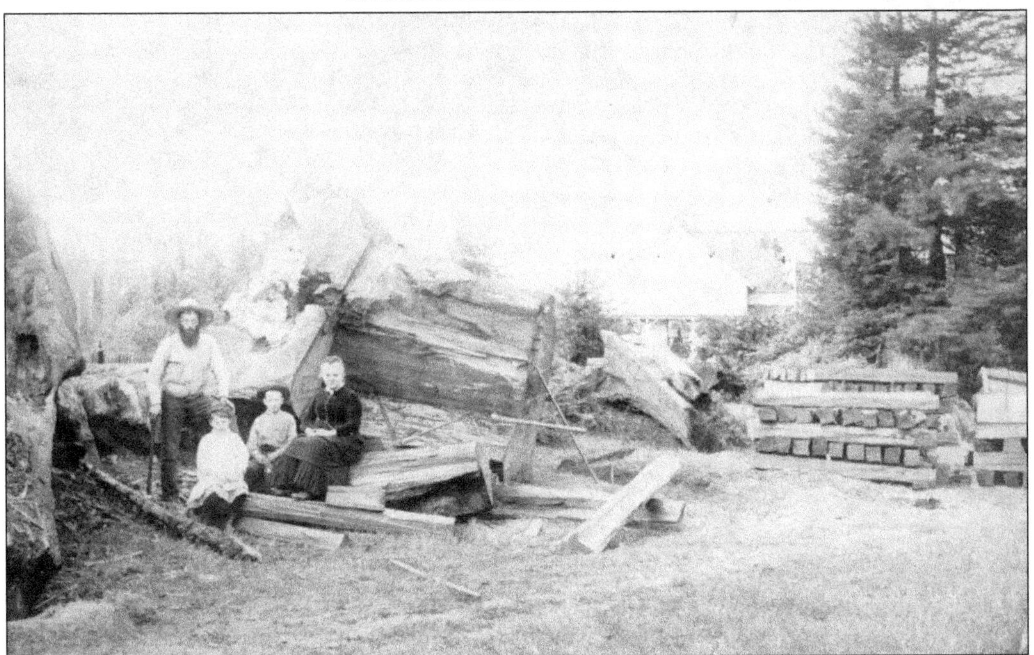

Hume and Sophia Fry, with children Donald and Winifred, came to Arcata from England in 1885 during the scandal over Scottish investors buying up Humboldt timberlands. Arcatans initially suspected that Hume Fry was a disguised British lord attempting a landgrab. Instead, Hume farmed and eventually manufactured shingles. He was locally famous for the observatory he built atop a redwood stump. (HSU.)

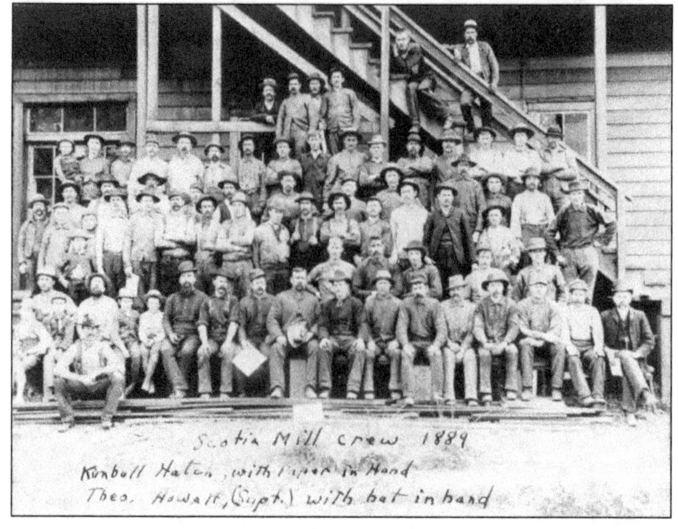

Scotia's mill crew around 1889 included Maine-born saw-filer Kimball Hatch, holding a paper in the front row. To Hatch's left, hat in hand, is Nova Scotian mill superintendent Theodore Howatt. The three Howatt brothers owned a Gunther Island shingle mill in the 1870s. In 1883, the Eureka Chamber of Commerce reported that their mill had recently "passed into the hands of J.G. Loveren." Theodore Howatt was later county auditor.

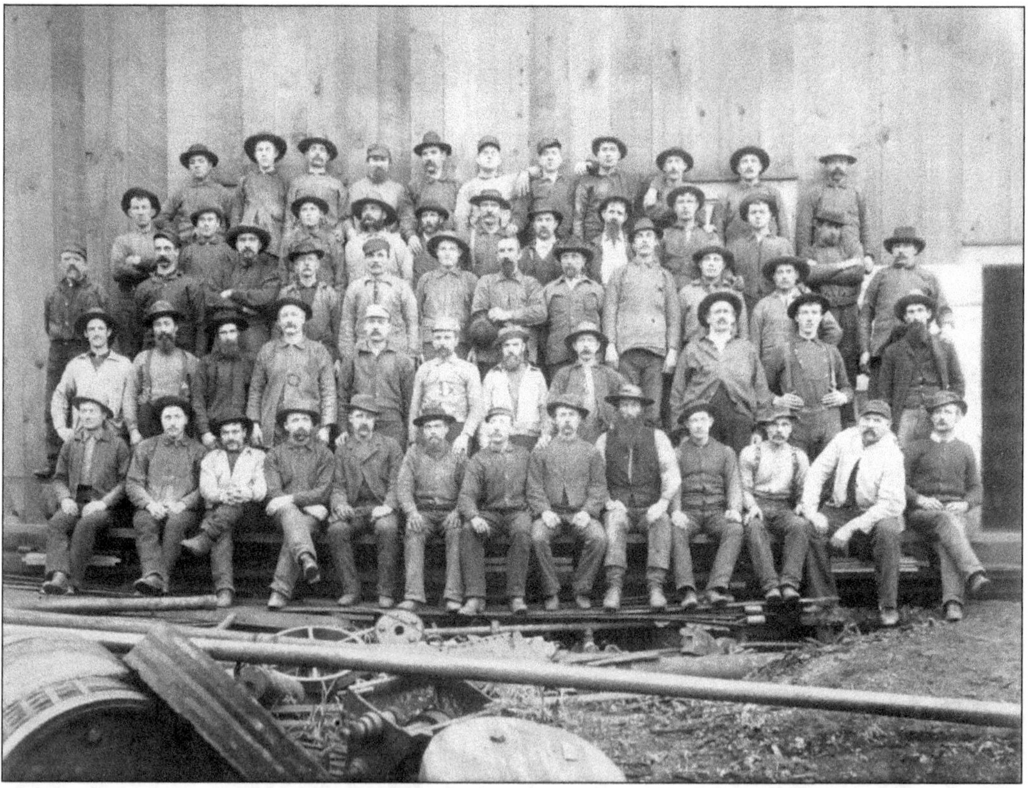

Identified among these Dolbeer & Carson Company millworkers are Louis Rice (third row, fifth from right), Ansel Brown (second row, fourth from left), and Atchison Baldwin Hill (second row, sixth from left). Planer man Rice arrived in the United States from Denmark in 1870, and machinist Brown came from Canada in 1885. Hill came from New Brunswick, Canada, in 1884, working his way up from mill laborer to sawyer. (HCHS.)

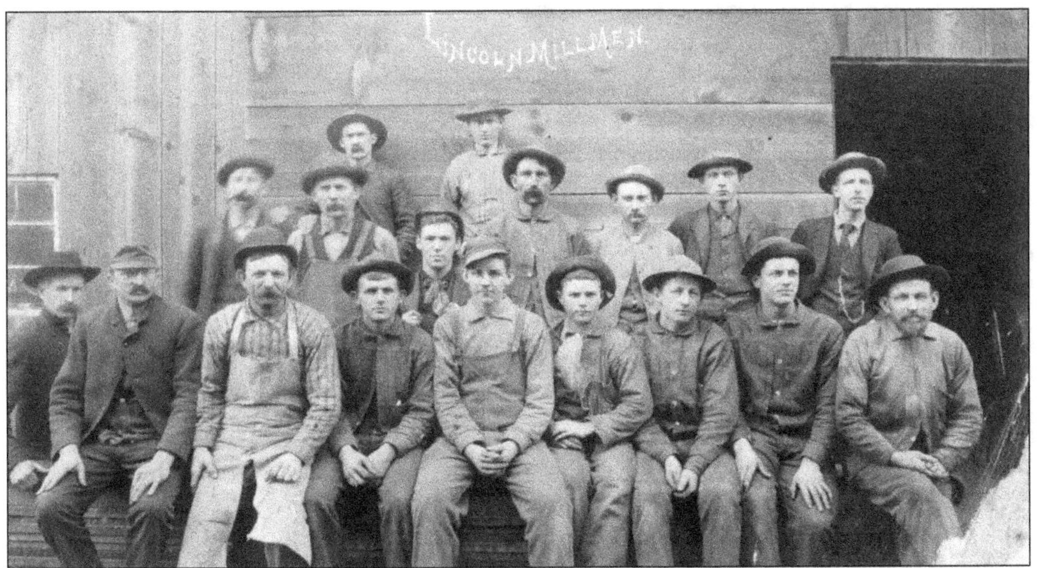

Injury and death were everyday threats. On August 13, 1888, the *Humboldt Standard* reported two mill accidents. At Springville's molding and sash factory, Charles Lawrence had a hand "badly mangled by the jig saw." At Newburg, Michael Banning was crushed to death when a log jumped the track on the log chute. The next day, Oster Howland's death at the Elk River mill was reported in an article headlined "Another Fatal Accident." (Clarke.)

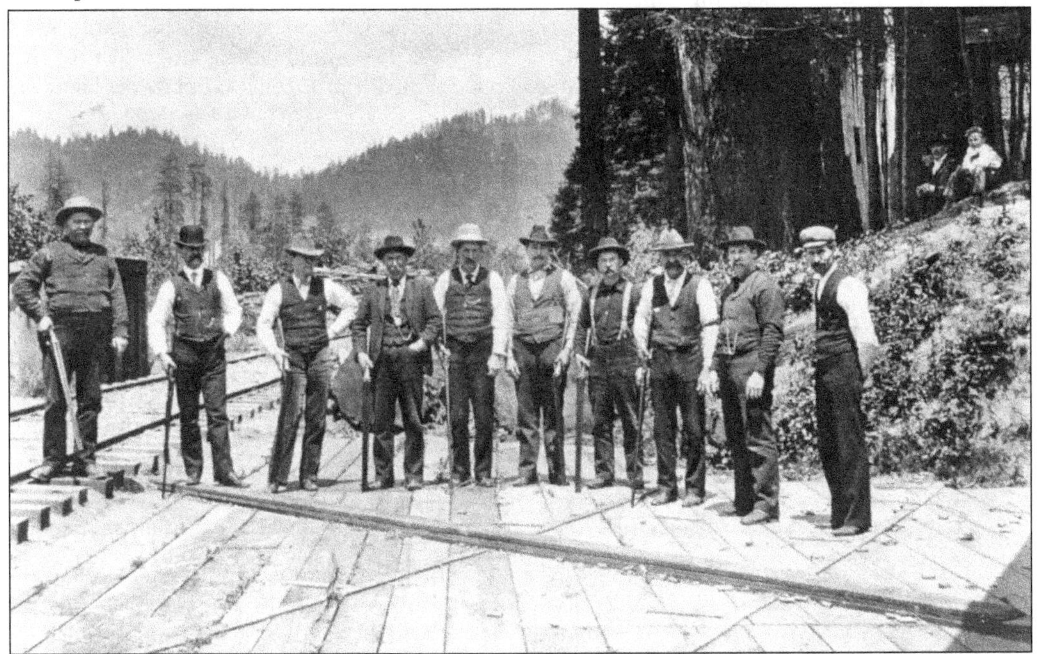

Scotia Gun Club members pose around 1900. They are, from left to right, general superintendent G.C. Douglas, butcher George Perrott, timekeeper/cashier M.L. Gillogly, electrician Dick Gribble, stockman Charles Whitney, sawyer William Pond, unidentified, bartender Ed Brock, sawyer William Forsyth, and filer George Miller. TPL Co. historian Ben Shannon Allen wrote in 1949 that the club's membership showed "several grades in economic status, but no social differences . . . that could be labeled fairly as class distinctions."

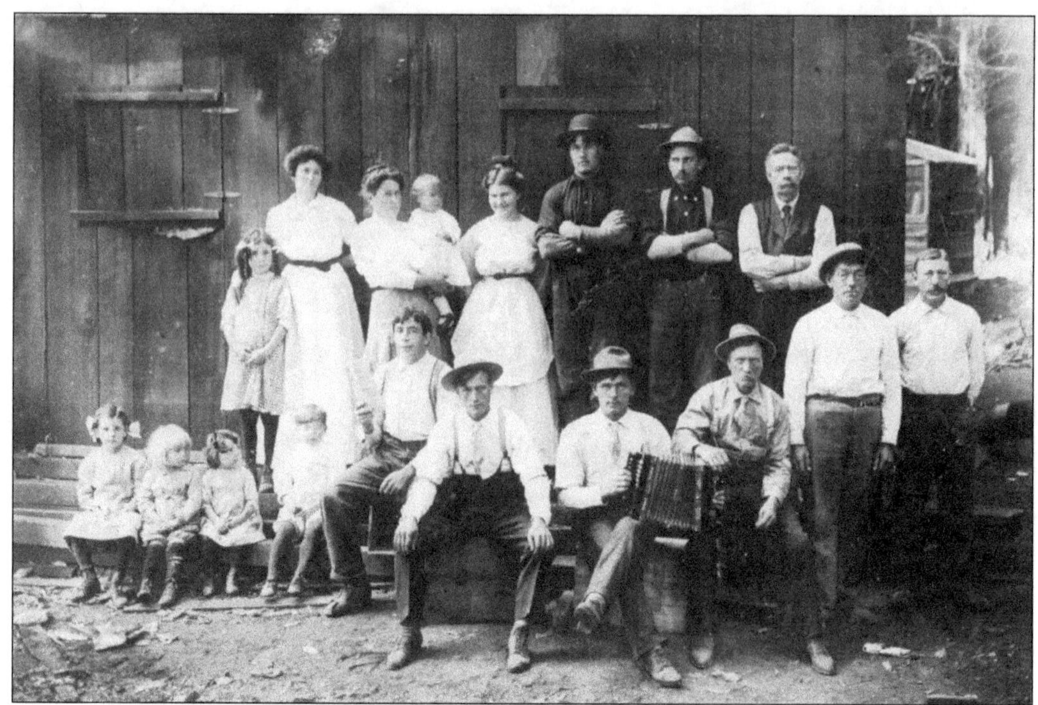

The grinning young woman standing fourth from left in the back row is believed to be Dora Effa Lewis. In Humboldt County's voter registration records from 1912, the year after California's women gained the right to vote, she is listed in Shively as a 31-year-old Democratic waitress, and her husband, John, as a 33-year-old Socialist cook. Dora died in a 1916 automobile accident on the steep road grade near Luffenholtz. (HCHS.)

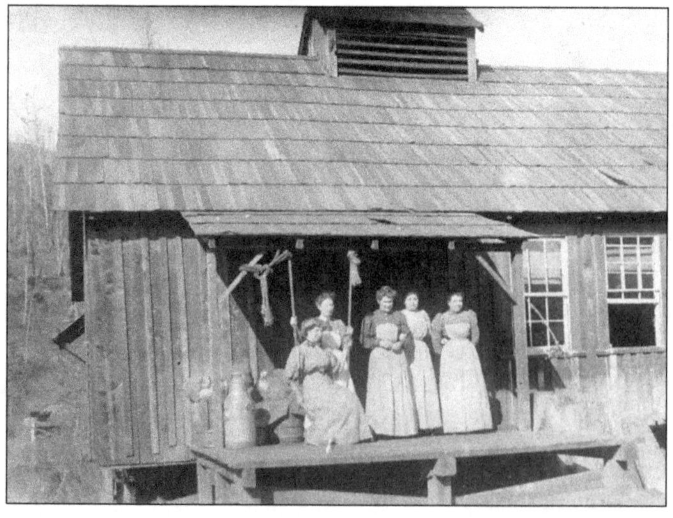

Second from left at Korbel Camp No. 7 in 1906 is Annie Adams Pinkerton. Also shown, although not identified by location, is her sister Eleanor Adams Parks. They were children when their family emigrated from Canada in 1875. Their father found work in Humboldt's woods. Widowed in 1905, Annie presumably joined the cookhouse crew to support her daughter. Mildred Rodgers (seated) came from Canada in 1905 at age 17. (HCHS.)

These Falk woods camp cookhouse workers are, from left to right, Bernice Barnes, Maggie Biord, and Maggie's sister Suzi Glass. The children are, from left to right, Ruby Barnes, Suzi Glass's daughter, and James Biord. Maggie Biord was one of the few Humboldt women to build a successful career as a cookhouse head cook, rather than working as assistant cook or waitress. The Falk camp was dubbed Camp Maggie in her honor. (HSU.)

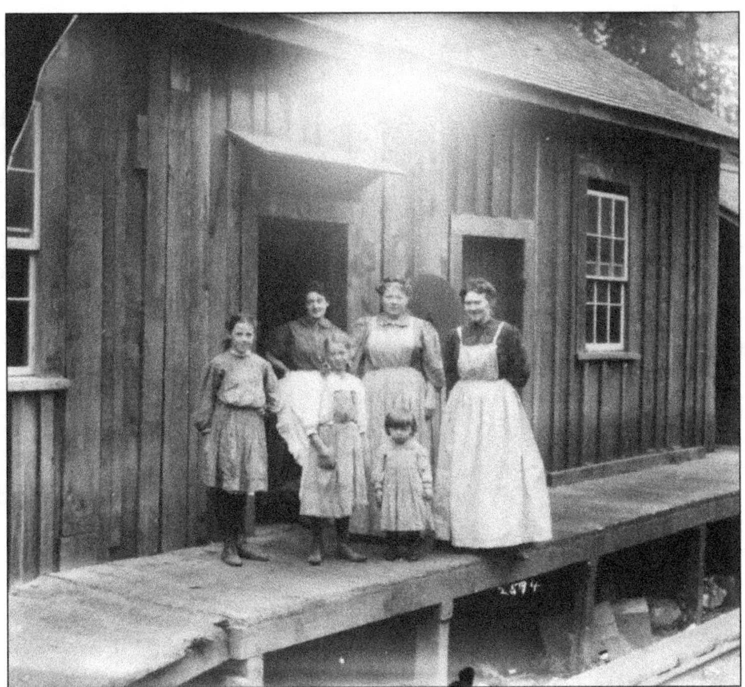

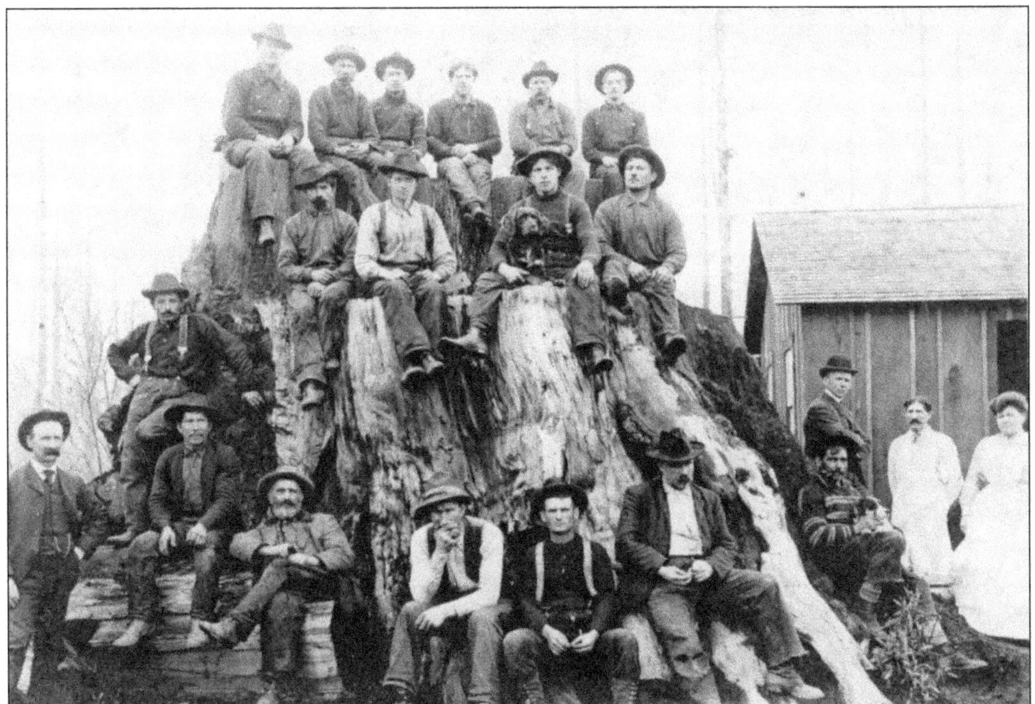

This photograph of a Glendale crew is annotated "E. Brodie with dog." Edmund Francis Brodie was born at Dow's Prairie near McKinleyville in 1879. His father, from Newcastle-Upon-Tyne in northern England, was a logger. In 1900, Ed was a shingle sawyer in Eureka. He was foreman of the Blue Lake shingle mill by 1905 and later alternated between mill foreman and saw-filer at other mills.

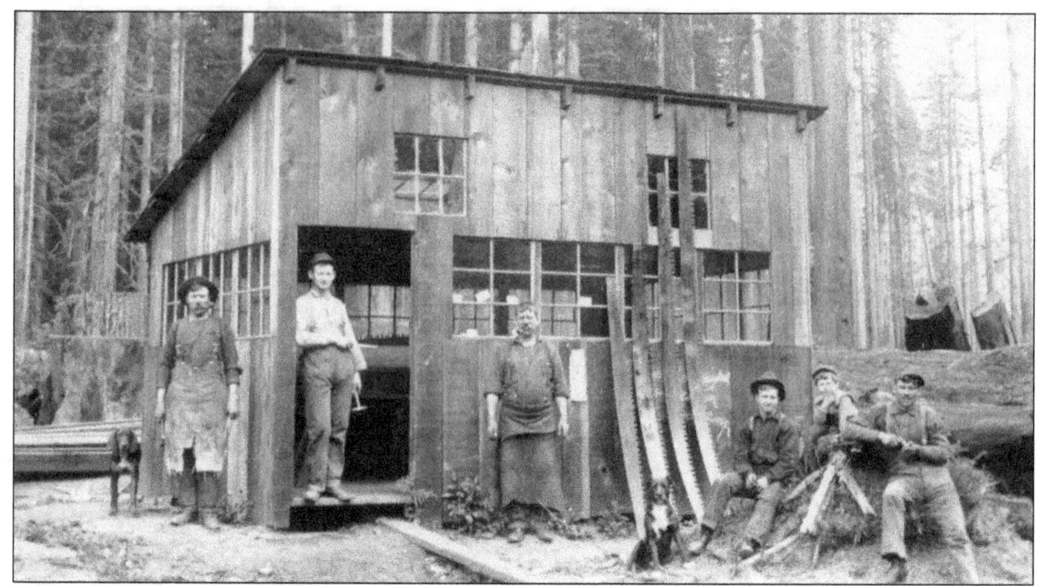

A crew of saw-filers are shown in the Vance/Hammond woods. Filer was a prestigious job in woods and mills. *California as It Is* reported that Humboldt saw-filers earned wages ranging from $85 to $100 per month, compared with $65 to $75 for choppers in the woods and $30 to $60 for "common hands in the yard." (HCHS.)

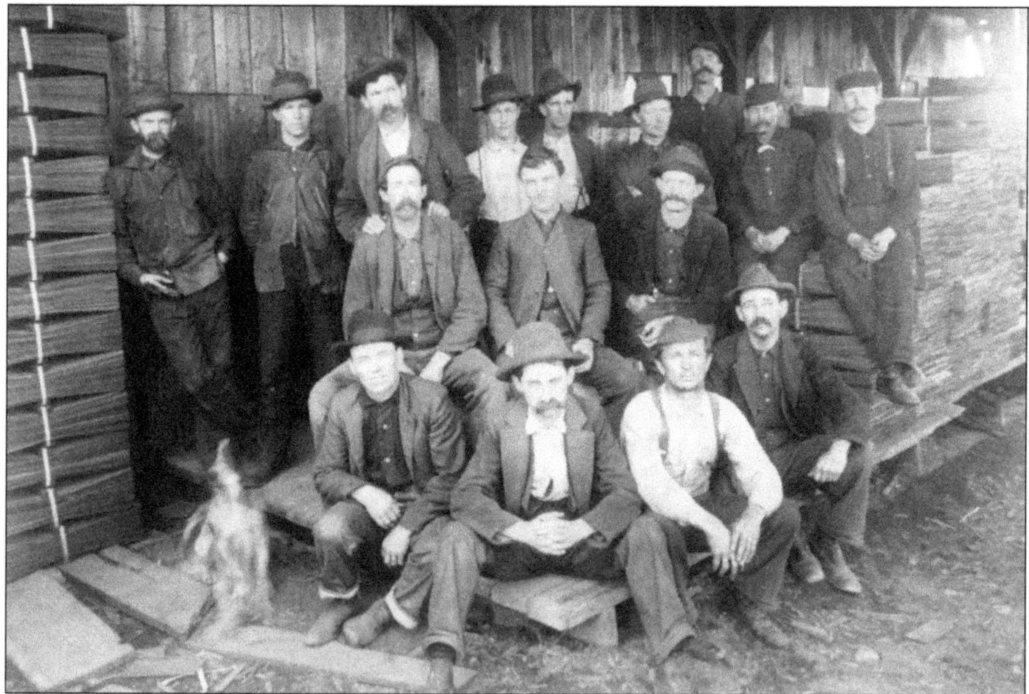

In the front row of these Swortzel & Williams shingle mill men are, from left to right, Jim Byron, Dallas Duff, Gratton Little, and Virgil Duff. Little, born in Maine in 1866, was 10 years old when his family came to Springville (renamed Fortuna). Elected a Fortuna city councilman in 1910, he moved to Eureka in 1914, becoming receiver at the US Land Office. Little later owned a Eureka candy store.

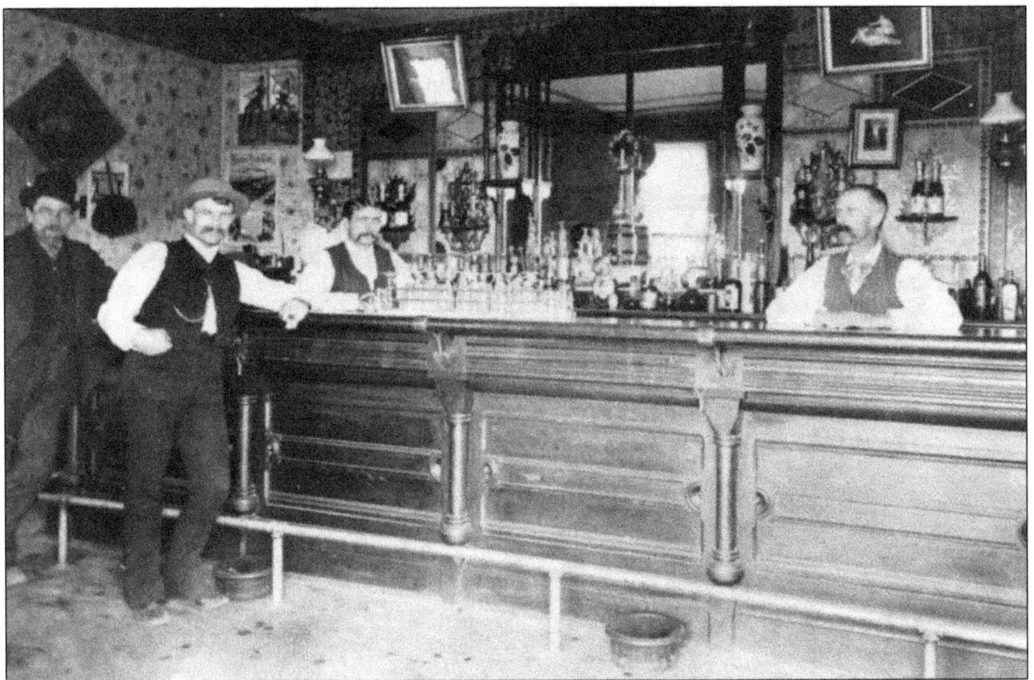

Walter Ingham (right) is behind the bar of his appropriately named Logger Saloon in Blue Lake. Lon Acorn (second from left) stands in front of the bar. Ingham had a leg amputated, probably due to a woods or mill accident. He found a new career as a saloon owner. Similarly, Jim Lane, bartender of the Scotia company saloon, was a TPL Co. locomotive engineer until a disabling accident. (HSU.)

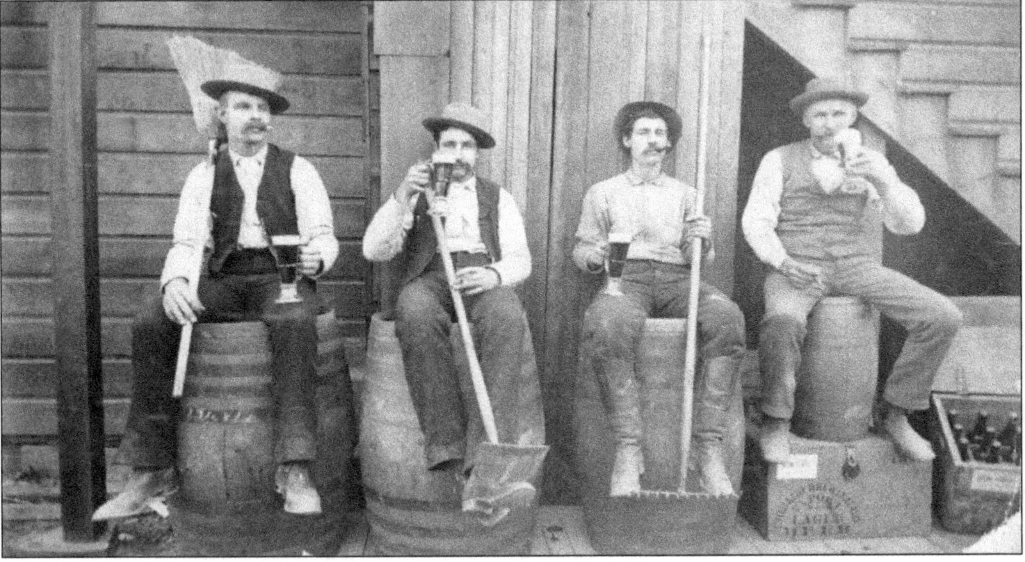

Blue Lake shingle mill man Lon Acorn is seen again, at left, enjoying his beer with, from left to right, George Smith, George Garner, and Knyphausen Geer. The typical woodsmen and mill men were known for enthusiastic drinking, particularly just after payday. Scotia bartender Jim Lane encouraged self-control among his customers by evicting everyone and closing the saloon until the next day whenever he judged a man was excessively drunk. (HSU.)

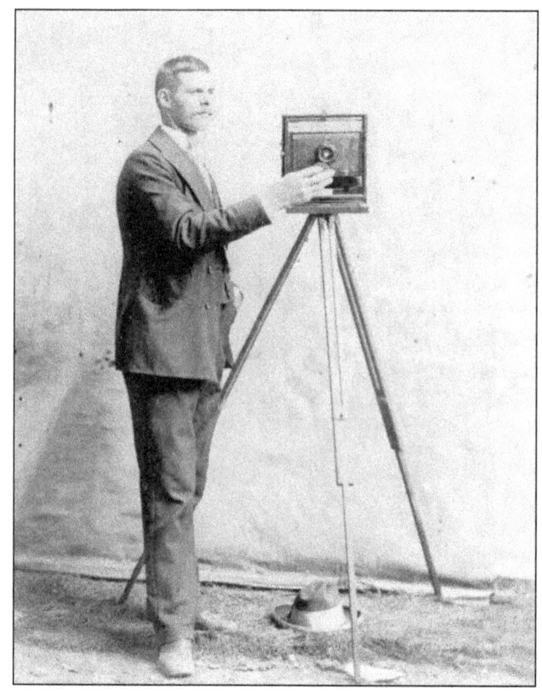

William Henry Stephenson and his twin brother, Jesse Hiram, were born in Mendocino County in 1876. In Mendocino and Humboldt, the Stephensons were primarily farmers, also working as lumber-industry teamsters. William is listed as a teamster in the 1898 Humboldt voter registration records. As seen here, he was also a photographer.

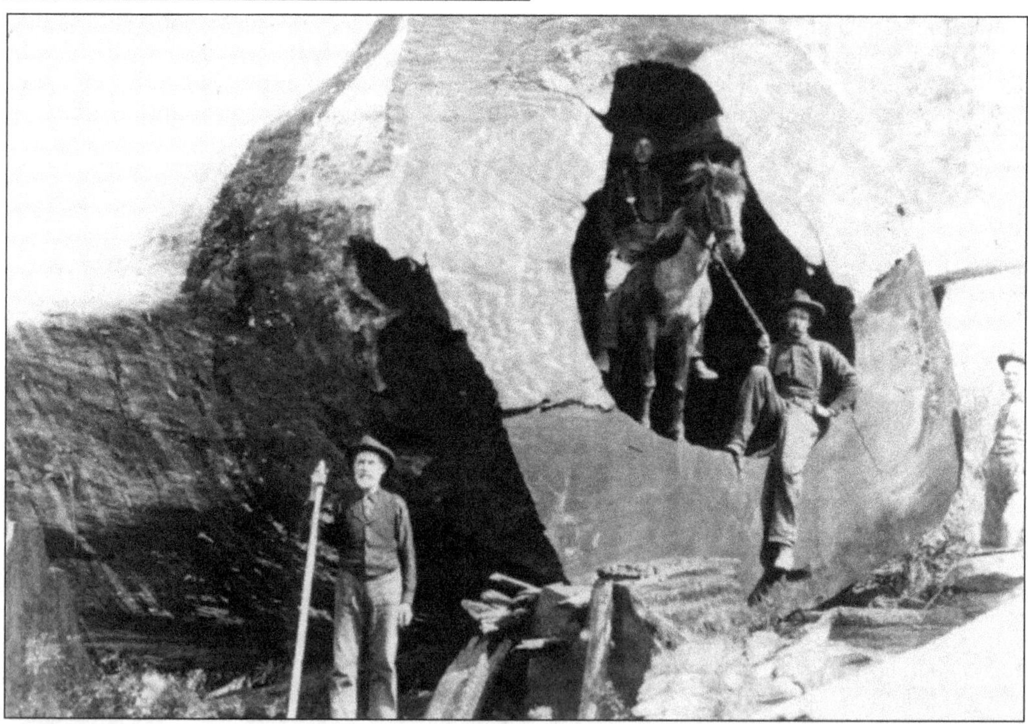

William Stephenson photographed this well-known image for McKay & Co. at Ryan's Slough in 1904. Shown are, from left to right, William and Jesse's father, George Stephenson, Jesse Stephenson on horseback, teamster William St. Clair holding the reins, and an unknown man. According to Stephenson family recollections, "It took some sizeable time to get [the] horse in the log. It had to be led up a ramp with a man's coat on its head."

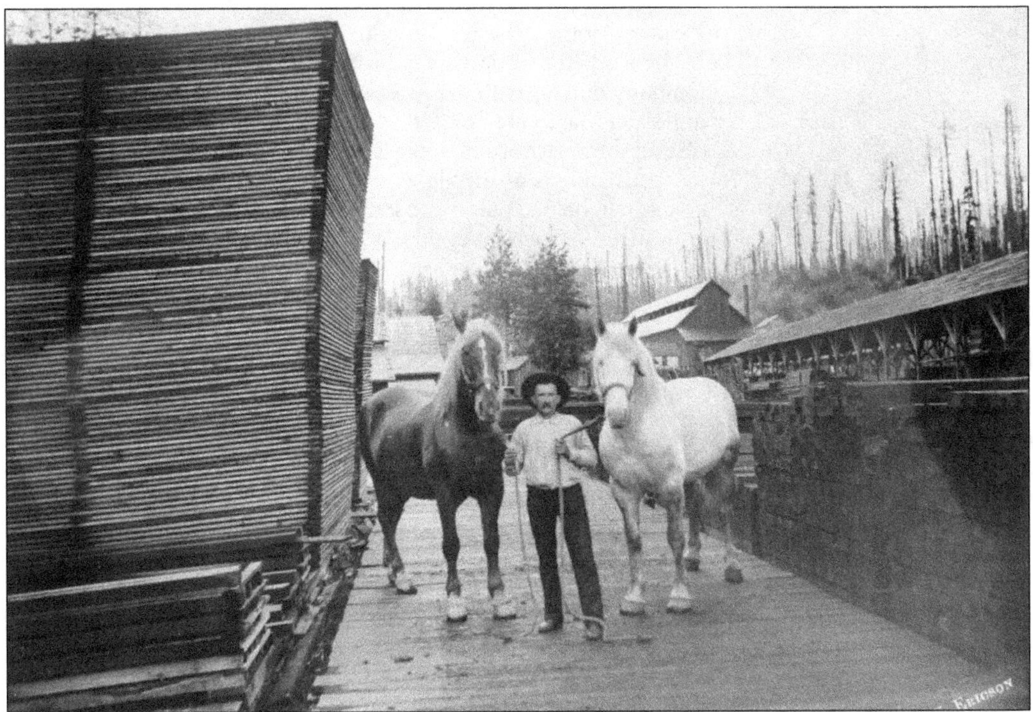

Carl Wilhelm Duse, head teamster at Glendale, was born in Gothenburg, Sweden. He came to America in 1885 around age 30, leaving his wife, Anna, and three young children behind. Anna and the children joined him five years later. Carl was naturalized as a US citizen in 1894 and immediately registered to vote. Around 1907, he retired as a teamster and took up poultry farming. (HSU.)

Karl Johan Strömnäs, or Charlie Strom, as he became known in America, was a Swedish Finn. A Humboldt woodsman from about 1905 to 1915, he met his future wife, Amanda Smeds, when she worked at Hammond's cookhouse. Younger relatives recall Charlie as so strong from his labor in the woods that his normal handshake was still a crushing grip when he was nearly 90. (Dave Smeds.)

Frank Spesert joined the US Navy in 1898 at age 17. Mustered out in 1906, he worked as a donkey engineer for the Metropolitan Lumber Company during each dry season. During the winter rains, Frank and sister Mary Jane Spesert Rowley operated a photography studio. Several Spesert Studio images appear in this book. Their brother Ned, listed as a shingle-weaver at Pepperwood in 1912's voter register, helped out in the studio and later became a professional dance instructor. (HSU.)

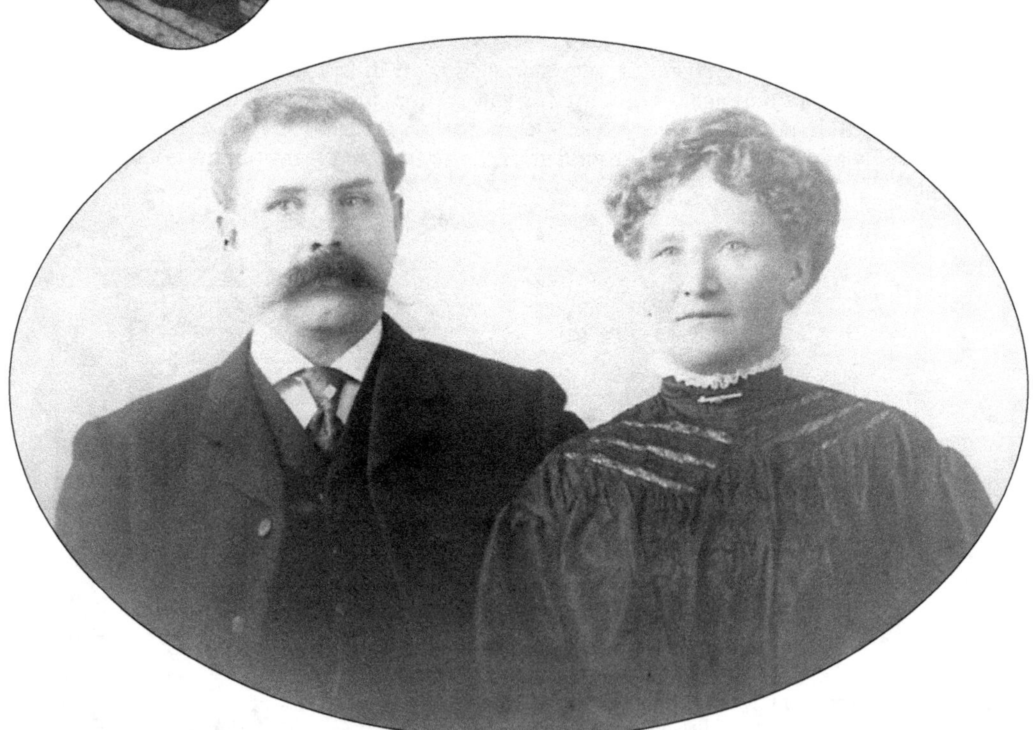

Per and Wilhelmina Nelson left Sweden with their six-year-old son in 1891. Per became head trimmer man and, eventually, millwright at Newburg. An inventor, he held several patents, including one for a combination bread box/bread slicer. Per died in a fall from neighbor George Byard's hayloft while helping put up hay in 1917. The Newberg mill shut for the day so that Per's fellow mill men could attend his funeral. (David Heinle and Carol Lang.)

Nova Scotian woodsman Wylie John Gordon was photographed working for F.W. Beckwith near Carlotta around 1910, having recently gone through two major upheavals. He and his wife, Della, divorced, and in 1906, their son Gustavas died around age 17. At the time of the 1940 census, Wylie, aged 80, lived with a niece's family in Madera County. He listed his occupation as "lumberjack—process lumber industry."

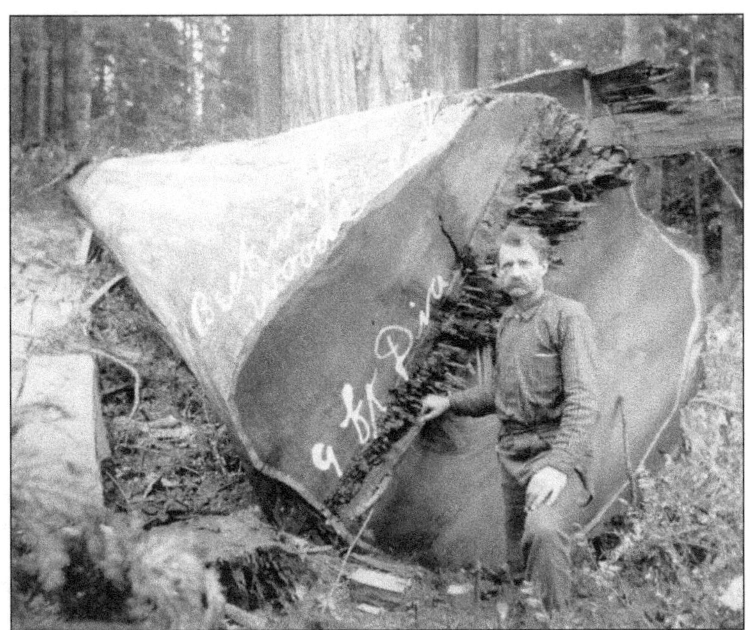

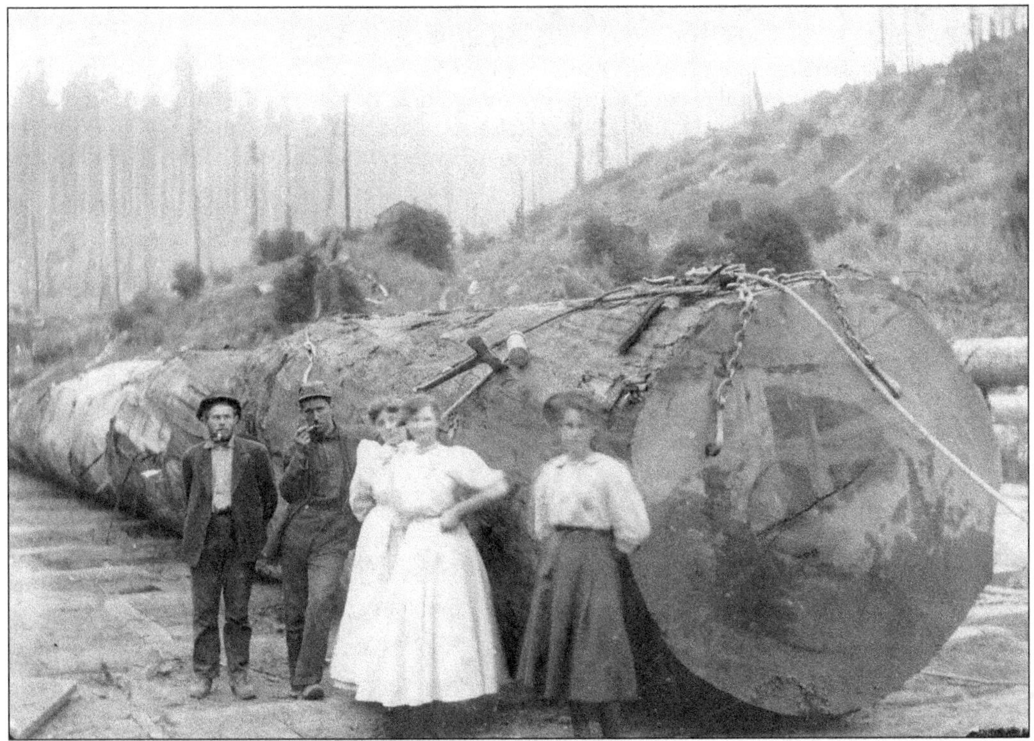

Emil Frank (left) was photographed at Laribee around 1910. He was the ninth of ten children. His parents, Heinrich and Barbara, were Germans from Russia. The family journeyed from Russia to New York, then to South Dakota, and finally to Mendocino County, where Barbara Frank died at age 40. As a young man, Emil left the family profession of farming to become a woodsman, building a career as a donkey engineer. (HCHS.)

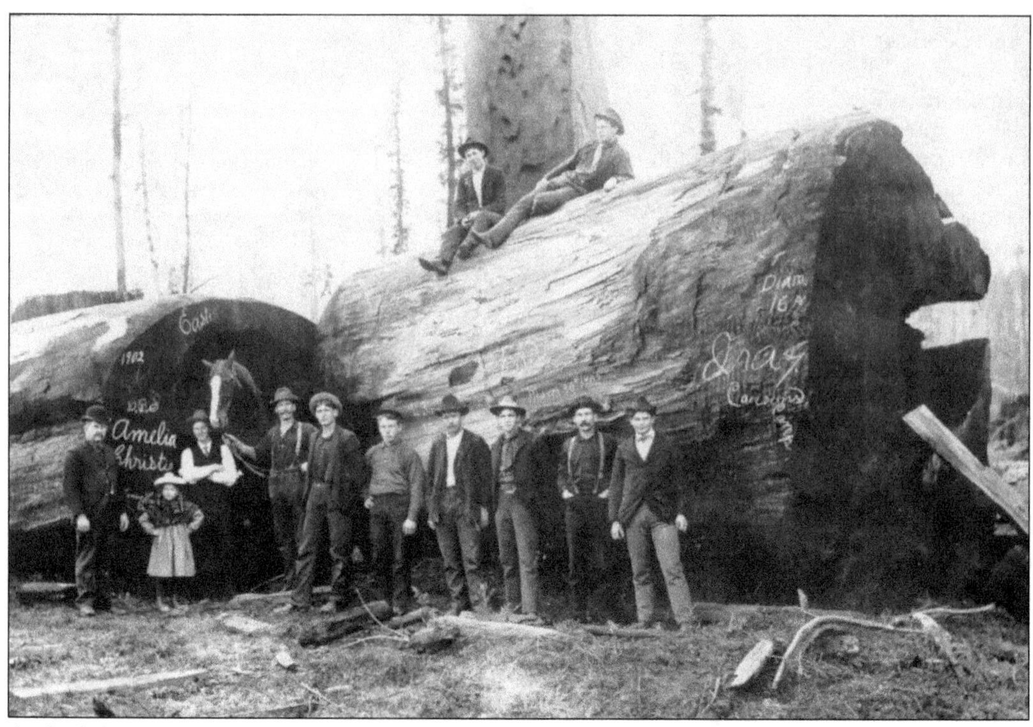

At far left in Carson's camp on Easter, March 30, 1902, is Uriah Willard Christie with daughter Amelia. Christie was a popular cookhouse chef for Dolbeer & Carson and later at Korbel. For several years, he managed Eureka's Grand Hotel at Second and C Streets. In 1905, the *Blue Lake Advance* called Christie "a thorough hotel man, known from one end of the county to the other." (HSU.)

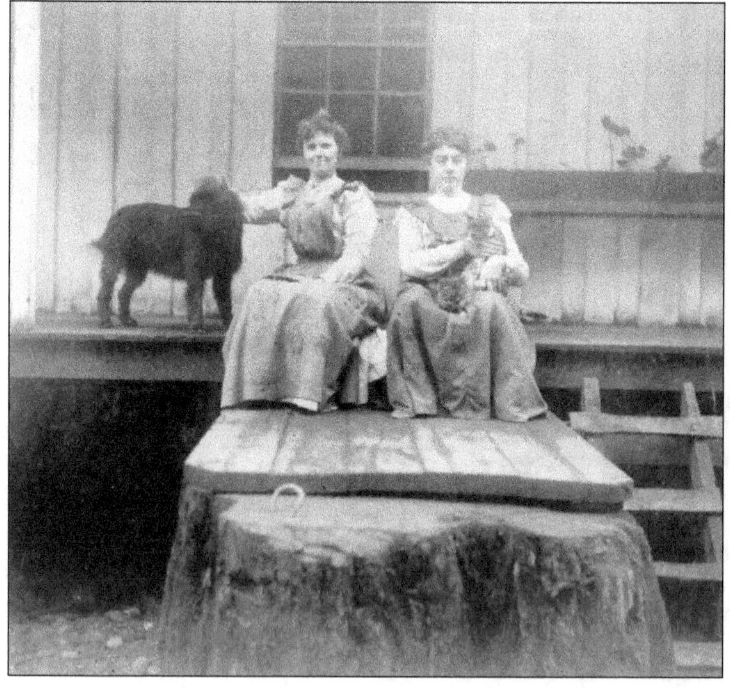

Pictured at Beckwith's shingle mill cookhouse around 1903 are head cook Ella Millsap (left) and assistant Lottie Langdon. Like Falk's Maggie Biord (see page 115), Ella Millsap headed a cookhouse crew rather than working for a male cook. Both Ella and Lottie appear to have retired from cookhouse work when they married, Ella in 1905 and Lottie in 1907. The 1912 voter register lists Ella as a Republican housewife and her husband, Jesse Payton, as a Republican woodsman.

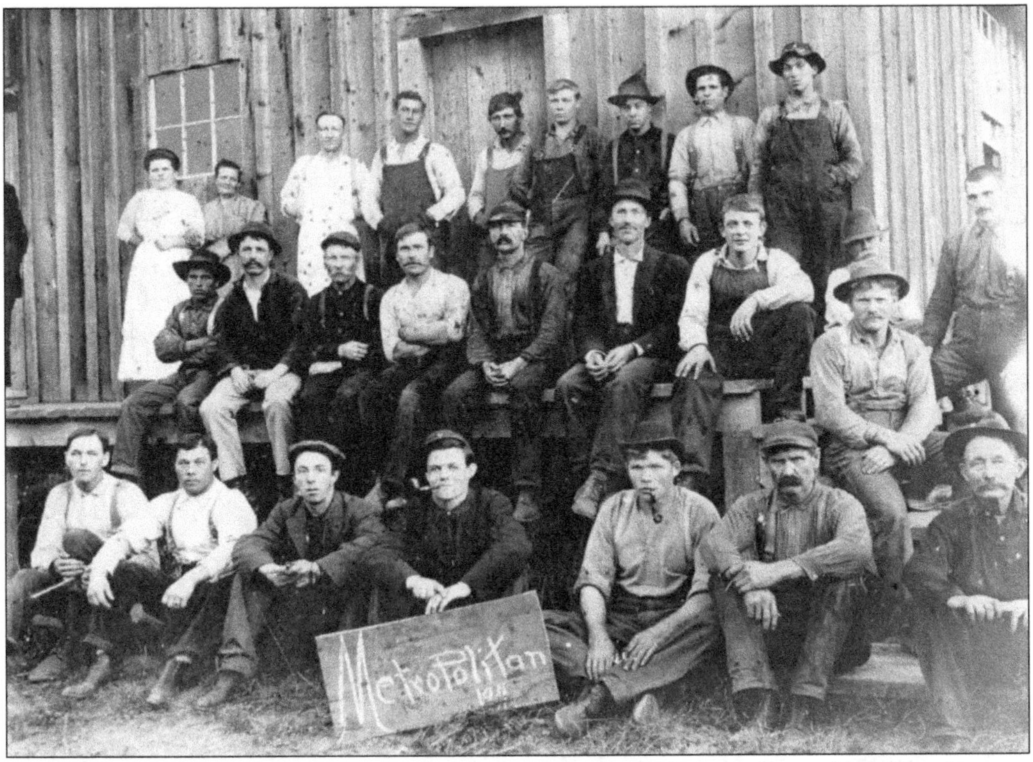

The younger woman at left may be Bertha James, a 25-year-old Republican cook registered to vote at Metropolitan in 1912. That year, 15 Metropolitan mill and woods workers registered to vote, including two woodsmen registering as Socialists. The mill owner, a mill man, and a shingle-weaver declined to state party preference. Republicans were the assistant mill superintendent, one mill man, the millwright, the yard foreman, a lumber surveyor, two saw-filers, a shingle-weaver, and a machinist.

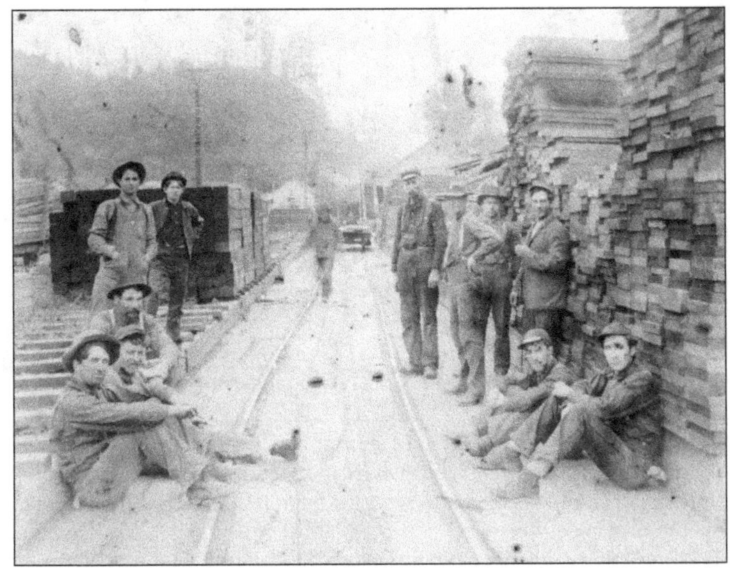

Metropolitan Lumber Co. workers are shown in their mill yard around 1910, six years after the mill opened. Working in the woods and at mills was a way of life for generations of Humboldt men, but the risks inherent to these jobs were also constant. A photograph of the Metropolitan mill in the Humboldt County Historical Society collection bears the grim notation, "This is the mill where Uncle Ben was killed."

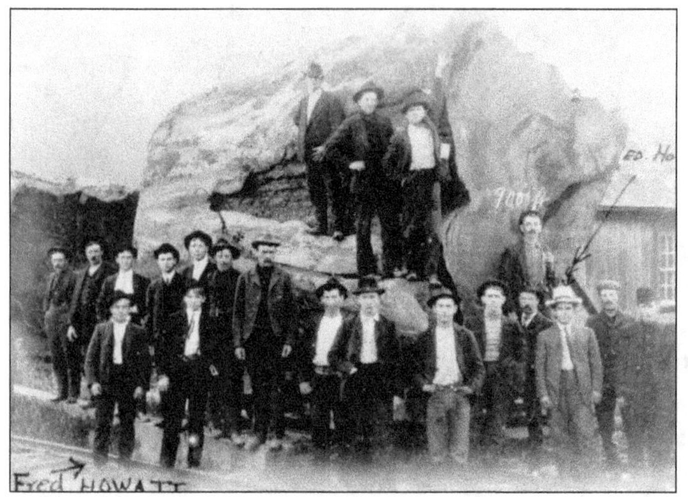

Cousins Fred and Ed Howatt are identified in this early-20th-century TPL Co. photograph. Their fathers, Arthur and Theodore, were two of the three Howatt brothers who came to Humboldt from Nova Scotia in 1871 and ran a Gunther Island shingle mill. Several photographs in this book are from Ed Howatt's collection, donated to the Fortuna Depot Museum by third-generation Humboldter Arthur Stephenson Howatt.

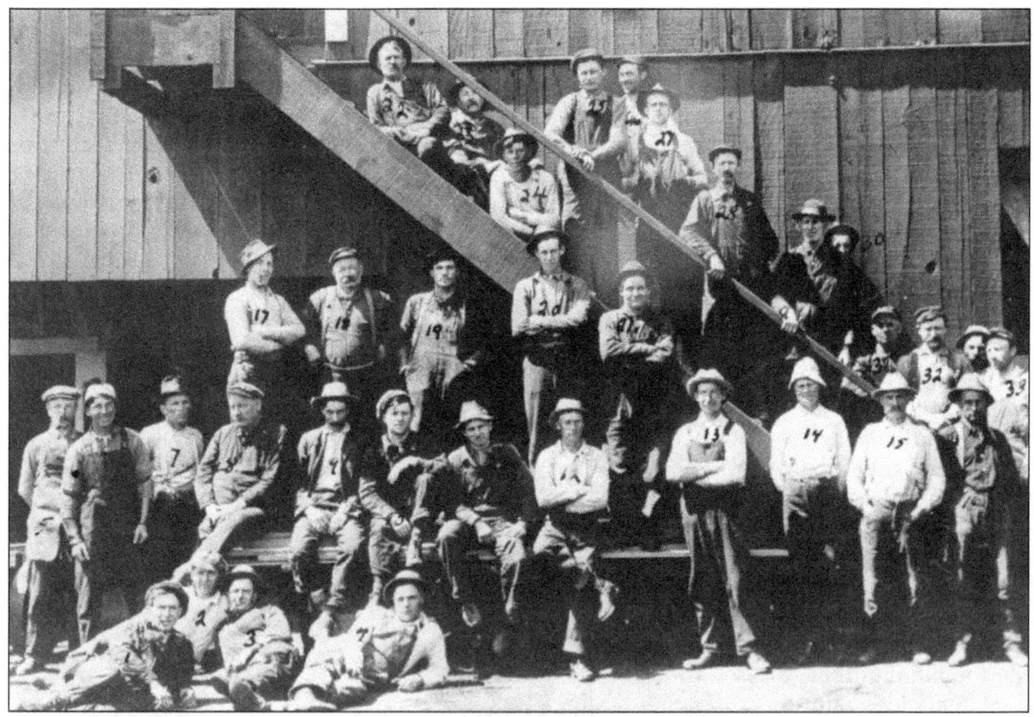

Holmes-Eureka mill workers are shown in 1912. The 1912 voter register gives glimpses into some of their lives. Saw-filer Walter Kinney (second row, fourth from left) declined to state party preference. In the second row, seventh from left, is Republican filer George Hartman. Elias Hewitt (seated at top of the stairs) was a Socialist mill man. Christian Heinbach (fourth from right on the stairs) was a Democratic engineer.

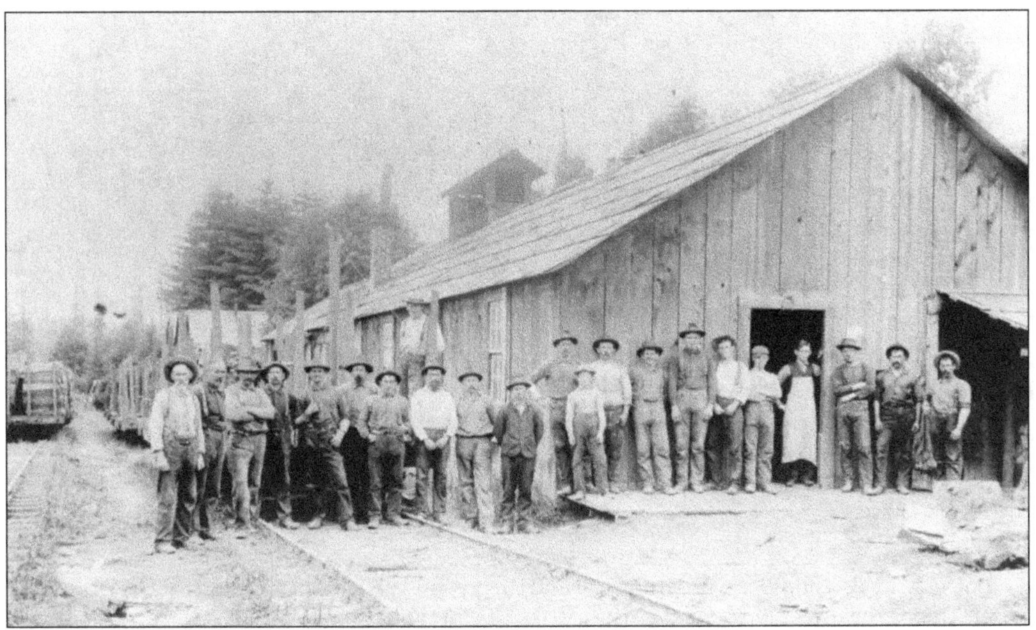

William Porter Guthrie (sixth from right) is seen at an unidentified cookhouse. Porter's wide-ranging career included service as a sergeant in the US Army in the Philippines around 1910. He worked peeling tanbark, as a bookkeeper, a salesman, and at a Department of Forestry fire-lookout station. As a judge in Fortuna in the 1950s, he sided with loggers in a controversy over weight limits on logging trucks.

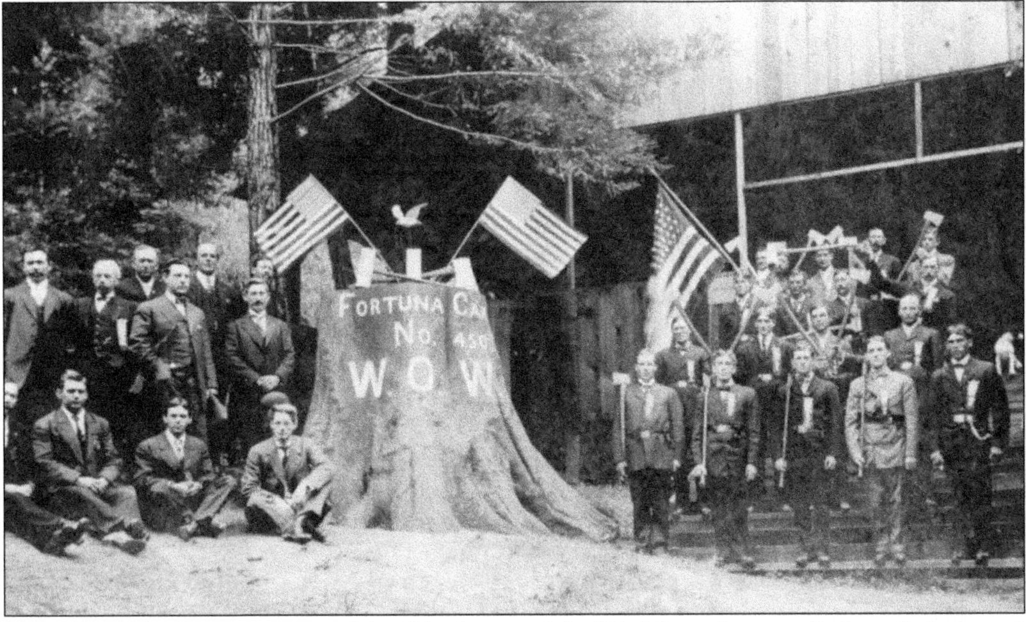

Members of the Fortuna camp of the Woodsmen of the World are shown at Rohner Park around 1907. This fraternal organization, founded in 1890, provided affordable life and health insurance for members. Henry Natwick, seen second from left in the third row right of the stump, was millwright at Newburg, president of the Fortuna Building & Loan Association, and father of the first triplets born in Humboldt County.

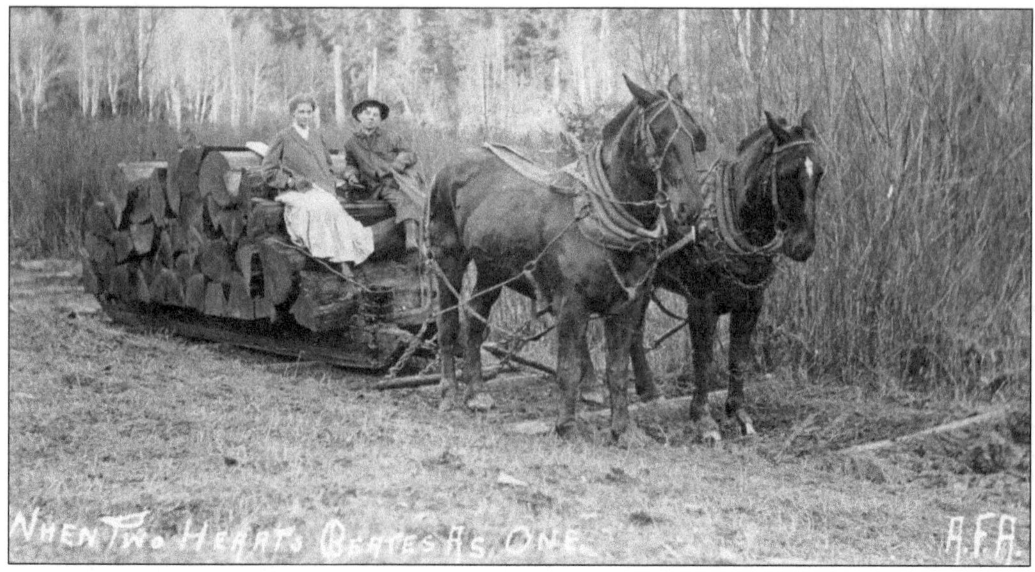

As indicated by this photograph's whimsical and slightly misspelled title, "When two hearts beates as one," many romances blossomed in the setting of Humboldt's lumber industry. A June 7, 1902, newspaper article reported that two weddings were expected soon at Carson's Camp No. 4 and suggested the young couples get "spliced standing on the stump . . . of the big redwood tree that is to be felled on the 24th." (HSU.)

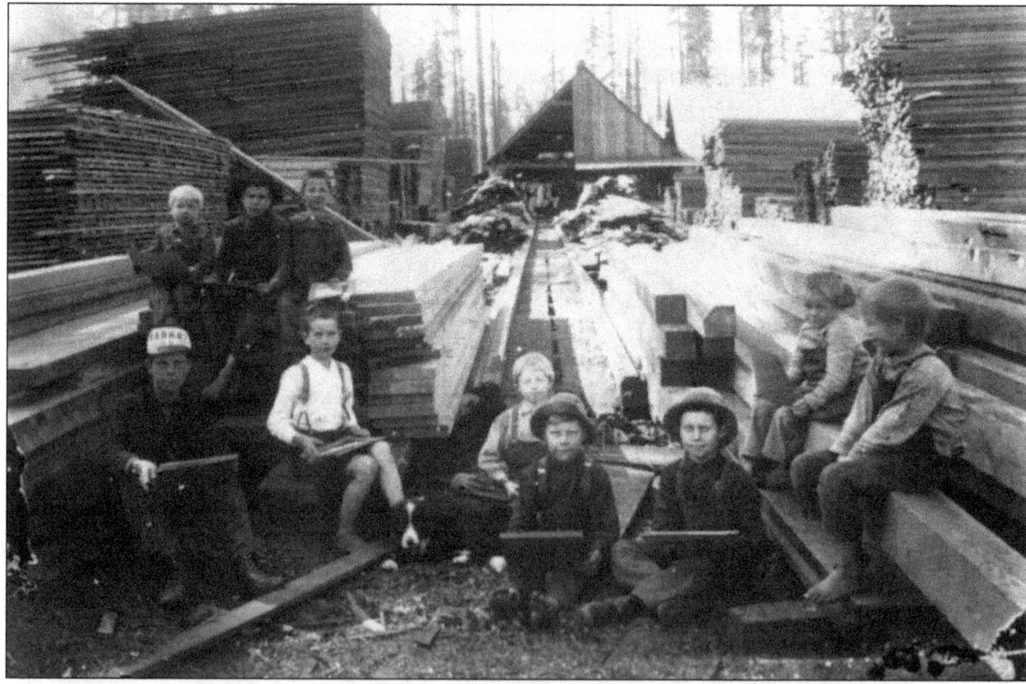

For generations of Humboldters, like these boys photographed in an early-20th-century mill yard, the lumber industry promised stability and security. Many of their fathers and grandfathers worked in the woods and mills, and most of these boys probably followed in their forebears' footsteps. Despite the risks of accidents and economic downturns, the generations that followed knew they had a future harvesting the "red gold" of Humboldt County. (HSU.)

About the Fortuna Depot Museum

On October 9, 1974, Fortuna's 85-year-old train station was moved across town to a new home in Rohner Park. Built by Carson and Vance's Eel River & Eureka Railroad and later a stop on the Northwestern Pacific route from San Francisco to Humboldt, the depot was scheduled to be demolished by the NWP. Fortuna citizens convinced the city council to purchase the building and refurbish it as a local history museum. With its roof removed in order to fit under the town's power lines, the depot was raised from its foundations and loaded on a flatbed trailer. Through the work of city staff, local businesses, and many volunteers, Fortuna's venerable train station made its way down Main Street.

There followed a year and a half of renovations and the assembling of the nucleus of a museum collection through donations by area residents. The Fortuna Depot Museum had its grand opening on July 4, 1976, as Fortuna's Bicentennial City project celebrating the nation's 200th birthday.

The train station was a center of community life, and the depot museum holds a special place in the hearts of Fortuna's people. Its mission is to preserve, share, and interpret the history of Fortuna and the Eel River Valley. The museum's reference room is a resource for historical and genealogical research, and its photograph collection has thus far formed the basis of three Images of America and Images of Rail publications. A highlight of the museum collection is Northwestern Pacific caboose No. 11, built in 1909 and donated to the museum in 2006. The greatest artifact in the collection is the depot building itself, showcasing Victorian construction and woodworking techniques and using the "red gold" of Humboldt's redwoods.

www.ingramcontent.com/pod-product-compliance
Lightning Source LLC
LaVergne TN
LVHW081549100826
845153LV00004B/342
9781531698126